The pandemic sent many of us into depths of depression and isolation we had not previously suffered. *Playful Pedagogy in the Pandemic* offers a thoughtful reflection on the many curious and creative outlets using play, whether in virtual classrooms or out in the wild, to process the stress of these uncertain times. No doubt, these same play practices will serve us post-pandemic as well.

Mark C. Marino, Professor of Writing and Director of the Humanities and Critical Code Studies Lab, University of Southern California, USA

Playful Pedagogy in the Pandemic is a sharp and savvy examination of the promises and pitfalls of games-based learning in a world transformed by COVID-19. Past blunders and current perils are laid bare in this thoughtful chronicling of educational technologies in transition, but at its core is a hopeful vision for future learning that puts play and co-creation at the forefront.

Robb Lindgren, Associate Professor of Curriculum and Instruction and Director of Technology Innovations in Educational Research and Design, University of Illinois at Urbana-Champaign, USA

Playful Pedagogy in the Pandemic

Educational technology adoption is more widespread than ever in the wake of COVID-19, as corporations have commodified student engagement in makeshift packages marketed as gamification. This book seeks to create a space for playful learning in higher education, asserting the need for a pedagogy of care and engagement as well as collaboration with students to help us reimagine education outside of prescriptive educational technology.

Virtual learning has turned the course management system into the classroom, and business platforms for streaming video have become awkward substitutions for lecture and discussion. Gaming, once heralded as a potential tool for rethinking our relationship with educational technology, is now inextricably linked in our collective understanding to challenges of misogyny, white supremacy, and the circulation of misinformation. The initial promise of games-based learning seems to linger only as gamification, a form of structuring that creates mechanisms and incentives but limits opportunity for play. As higher education teeters on the brink of unprecedented crisis, this book proclaims the urgent need to find a space for playful learning and to find new inspiration in the platforms and interventions of personal gaming, and in turn restructure the corporatized, surveilling classroom of a gamified world.

Through an in-depth analysis of the challenges and opportunities presented by pandemic pedagogy, this book reveals the conditions that led to the widespread failure of adoption of games-based learning and offers a model of hope for a future driven by new tools and platforms for personal, experimental game-making as intellectual inquiry.

Emily K. Johnson is Assistant Professor of English at the University of Central Florida, USA. She conducts research focusing on user experience (UX), user-centered design, educational technology, learning games, playful/gameful learning, simulations and learning, self-regulated learning, learner motivation, and self-efficacy. She designs and researches educational games in virtual reality, augmented reality, mobile, PC/Mac, and non-traditional platforms. A former middle school teacher, Johnson has published work on games-based learning in journals, including *Computers & Education*; *Journal of Universal Computer Science*; and *Journal of Science Education and Technology*.

Anastasia Salter is Associate Professor of English and Director of Graduate Programs at the University of Central Florida, USA, where they also coordinate the innovative interdisciplinary Texts and Technology doctoral program. Their research draws upon humanities methods alongside computational discourse and subjects. They have authored several books, including *Twining: Critical and Creative Approaches to Hypertext Narratives* (with Stuart Moulthrop, Amherst College Press, 2021), *Portrait of the Auteur as Fanboy* (with Mel Stanfill, University of Mississippi Press, 2020), and *Adventure Games: Playing the Outsider* (with Aaron Reed and John Murray, Bloomsbury, 2020). Salter previously wrote for ProfHacker, a blog on technology and pedagogy formerly hosted by the *Chronicle of Higher Education*, and has taught workshops around the world on approaches to experimental, personal games in the classroom.

The COVID-19 Pandemic Series

This series examines the impact of the COVID-19 pandemic on individuals, communities, countries, and the larger global society from a social scientific perspective. It represents a timely and critical advance in knowledge related to what many believe to be the greatest threat to global ways of being in more than a century. It is imperative that academics take their rightful place alongside medical professionals as the world attempts to figure out how to deal with the current global pandemic, and how society might move forward in the future. This series represents a response to that imperative.

Series Editor: *J. Michael Ryan*

Titles in this Series:

Experiences of Health Workers in the COVID-19 Pandemic
In Their Own Words
Edited by Marie Bismark, Karen Willis, Sophie Lewis and Natasha Smallwood

Creative Resilience and COVID-19
Figuring the Everyday in a Pandemic
Edited by Irene Gammel and Jason Wang

COVID-19 and Childhood Inequality
Edited by Nazneen Khan

The Color of COVID-19
The Racial Inequality of Marginalized Communities
Edited by Sharon A. Navarro and Samantha L. Hernandez

COVID-19, Communication and Culture
Beyond the Global Workplace
Edited by Fiona Rossette-Crake and Elvis Buckwalter

Social and Political Representations of the COVID-19 Crisis
Daniel Feierstein

Playful Pedagogy in the Pandemic
Pivoting to Game-based Learning
Emily K. Johnson and Anastasia Salter

Playful Pedagogy in the Pandemic
Pivoting to Game-Based Learning

Emily K. Johnson and Anastasia Salter

LONDON AND NEW YORK

First published 2023
by Routledge
4 Park Square, Milton Park, Abingdon, Oxon OX14 4RN

and by Routledge
605 Third Avenue, New York, NY 10158

Routledge is an imprint of the Taylor & Francis Group, an Informa business

© 2023 Emily K. Johnson and Anastasia Salter

The right of Emily K. Johnson and Anastasia Salter to be identified as author of this work has been asserted by them in accordance with sections 77 and 78 of the Copyright, Designs and Patents Act 1988.

All rights reserved. No part of this book may be reprinted or reproduced or utilised in any form or by any electronic, mechanical, or other means, now known or hereafter invented, including photocopying and recording, or in any information storage or retrieval system, without permission in writing from the publishers.

Trademark notice: Product or corporate names may be trademarks or registered trademarks, and are used only for identification and explanation without intent to infringe.

British Library Cataloguing-in-Publication Data
A catalogue record for this book is available from the British Library

Library of Congress Cataloging-in-Publication Data
A catalog record has been requested for this book

ISBN: 978-1-032-25126-4 (hbk)
ISBN: 978-1-032-25127-1 (pbk)
ISBN: 978-1-003-28169-6 (ebk)

DOI: 10.4324/9781003281696

Typeset in Times New Roman
by Deanta Global Publishing Services, Chennai, India

This book is dedicated to all educators who persevere day in and day out doing the best they can for their students. We see you.

Contents

List of illustrations   x
Foreword   xi
Preface: Positioning our play   xii

   Introduction: Play for serious times   1

1   The problem of gamification   22

2   These aren't the games you're looking for   42

3   Searching for meaningful pandemic play   63

4   Confronting the perils of play   85

5   Designing playfully for a distant future   106

   Conclusion: The fatigue is real   127

Index   147

Illustrations

Figures

3.1	Shared play on a "virtual table top"	68
3.2	An example of co-creative play in Jackbox	69
C.1	A masked encounter in *It Comes in Waves*	128

Tables

3.1	Use statistics on Tabletop Simulator	67
5.1	Framework for meaningful play in education	107

Foreword

When the world went online in early 2020, at least the parts lucky enough to be able to do so, nobody could have imagined the changes that were in store. Students were suddenly learning from home, but also from Starbucks parking lots, libraries, and hotel lobbies, anywhere they could find to be able to connect to the Internet. Many workers also shifted online, while "essential workers," and those whose jobs could not be done digitally, faced increased health risks by having to continue facing people, too many of them often maskless, in face-to-face situations. Still others simply lost their jobs, access to education, and many of the fundamental aspects of social life necessary to maintain positive mental health.

In the midst of these serious disruptions to our lives and livelihoods, one aspect of human existence that has been largely overlooked is that of play and the ways in which play and games might offer solutions, or at least mediations, to some of the more pressing challenges of pandemic consequences. By expertly drawing on both historical challenges to games-based learning and ongoing successes in implementing playful forms of learning, Emily and Anastasia offer us critical insights into the ways in which we might be able to address not only ongoing issues of technology fatigue but also the increasing use of gamification for corporate profit and surveillance. This book is a much needed reminder that we must not ignore the pedagogical opportunities of play and games, nor must we allow such opportunities to be used to further the increasing intrusion of corporate actors into our personal lives. As the authors so skillfully advocate, we must seize on the opportunities and insights from these pandemic times and continue to think about the ways in which we might be able to reimagine the relationship between education and play.

The pandemic has presented us many opportunities to critically reflect on education, especially on the ways in which teaching and learning happen. In this brilliantly written book, Emily and Anastasia have added another point of critical reflection, only this time one more playful. After years of Zoom fatigue, battling technology, and watching myself lecture to a series of tiny boxes, their analysis of the value of play and games is a most welcome reflection.

J. Michael Ryan
Series Editor, *The COVID-19 Pandemic Series*
February 2022

Preface: Positioning our play

While this book seeks to intervene broadly, we would like to open with an acknowledgment that it is personal. Begun in 2020, under the shadow of collective uncertainty and school closures and "pivots" in the United States; and primarily completed in 2021, while navigating the challenges of Florida's limited pandemic response; this book by necessity reflects some of the anxieties, frustrations, and hopes of our position.

We also note our personal contexts at the time of writing. We both are white, privileged faculty at a large, public, Hispanic-serving institution (HSI) in the southeastern United States: the University of Central Florida. This project is necessarily informed by this position as educators working in a large university in the United States, navigating the challenges of pivots while struggling with highly politicized pandemic responses in the state of Florida, which would quickly become a battleground for policy and medical care. As a graduate program director working to negotiate controversial and challenging policy implementations throughout these years, Anastasia Salter was continually confronted with trying to find new strategies for care at a time when care became lacking. Their own approach to education,—from games to deadlines and grading,—changed fundamentally during the "pivots" and their fallout. This book is in part a negotiation of what lessons might carry forward, and where we can learn from these struggles.

It is also informed by personal experience with pandemic education from another lens: from March 2020 to May 2021, Emily Johnson worked from home, teaching courses, holding Zoom office hours, and attending virtual conferences all while monitoring her two young children's virtual schooling, as her husband was deemed an "essential worker" and commuted to work each day. Their youngest child experienced fully virtual live-streamed Kindergarten from the local public school via Google classrooms, and the oldest similarly live-streamed second grade. The children followed the same daily schedule as their face-to-face peers, which meant that each child had different breaks, lunch times, and ending times (Kindergarten was released an hour early for end-of-day recess, with occasional "surprise rewards" like extra, unannounced earlier releases). Emily looked on (when she could) and witnessed these incredible teachers overcoming unbelievable obstacles to meaningfully engage each student in the class content each day. The school ended this livestream instructional option in May 2021, and beginning in Fall 2021, both children attended their mask-optional face-to-face school and were able to be vaccinated in late December 2021.

This was a difficult time to write, made more difficult by the fact that even as we are wrapping up this book in the transition into 2022, new questions are arising about the future of education, and indeed about the future of the pandemic. The political attacks on science and blatant refusals of some to take basic precautions and make minimal efforts to prevent the spread of a deadly airborne virus highlight the necessity of education. These difficult days have strengthened the feeling of responsibility we have to our work, and it has made palpable the need to combat all types of ignorance through our teaching and research.

We acknowledge that our own concerns continue, and our experience of the pandemic's impact on education is thus different from our colleagues around the world in areas and institutions with dramatically different responses. We hope that there is value in the insights we can offer from that positioning, as we look toward uncertainty as the norm globally. We do not believe that there is a meaningful post-pandemic so much as an ongoing series of shifting expectations and crises we must prepare to navigate collectively.

Writing a book without the usual support structures of in-person conference feedback, networking, and conversations on-site has proven even more challenging than we imagined, but we are incredibly grateful to colleagues across the globe who have shared their experiences and connected with us at conferences and through our research communities, including the Electronic Literature Organization, Association of Internet Researchers, Foundations of Digital Games, Society for Cinema and Media Studies, Modern Language Association, North American Simulation and Gaming Association, and many others. We are grateful to the members of pandemic-informed faculty support groups on Twitter, Facebook, and Discord, and note that our concerns about the futures of online education expressed throughout are mediated by some of the value we've seen from those same communities.

We would like to thank the COVID-19 Pandemic Series editor, J. Michael Ryan, for his enthusiasm about this proposal even as it evolved to reflect the pandemic conditions changing around us; the editorial team at Routledge; our families; our faculty group-chat; our game nights companions (including Alice "Bomb Trader" Burnett, Jennifer and Zach Gamiel, Heather Brundage, Bridget Blodgett, and many more), players, and co-conspirators; our colleagues in English and in the Texts and Technology program; and the amazing students who worked with us through some of the most challenging semesters of instruction we have ever experienced. Anastasia would particularly like to thank the members of the English faculty writing group formally dedicated to Medieval Studies for their welcome and feedback (including Tison Pugh, Anna Jones, Bill Fogarty, James Campbell, Stephen Hopkins, and Mel Stanfill). And always, thanks to our mentors (Stuart Moulthrop, Rudy McDaniel, Matthew Kirschenbaum, and many others).

Introduction
Play for serious times

Before the pivot

In 2004, James Paul Gee offered a provocation to humanist educators to consider the video game: his book, *What Video Games Have to Teach Us about Learning and Literacy*, emphasized the potential of games in the K-12 classroom but has been seen as a call to action across education (Gee, 2004). The year 2004 was a very different time for games: the Nintendo GameCube, PlayStation 2, and the original Xbox were competing for the attention of the console gamer. The first in an interminable series of military propaganda shooters, *Call of Duty*, was released, as well as real-time strategy PC game *Warcraft III*. Through this lens, and admittedly relying on hindsight, Gee picked a surprising moment to press for the revolutionary power of games for learning. Commercial educational titles, or edutainment, had emerged primarily targeted to the home market: outside of *Oregon Trail*, most have been relatively forgotten, perhaps in large part because they fell into the category of what Brenda Laurel derides as "chocolate-covered broccoli" (Laurel et al., 2001). While they inspired imitators, their success was limited.

These early experiences of educational gaming are embedded in the memories of many of today's educators, and carry with them nostalgia and warning: *Oregon Trail*, for instance, notoriously embedded an empire-building mindset, inviting the player to participate uncritically in colonization (Mukherjee, 2017). As gaming systems improved, the representational range was not necessarily keeping up. Alternatives to the PC software or expensive console hardware world were emerging but limited. Mobile gaming (exemplified by the slimmed down, single-purpose Game Boy Advance) was in its infancy, and casual games were in their early stages thanks to Flash and popular portals such as Newgrounds (Salter & Murray, 2014). While Flash gave us a glimpse of a more distributed future of game-making, it was decidedly in its infancy—and the games that rose to the top did not point to its useful future in educational contexts. The history of Newgrounds, for instance, highlights characteristic games of the moment were still in the early stages of documentation. Exemplars on Newgrounds at the time included Shawn Tanner's horror-survival game *Escape from Elm Street* (Tanner, 2003) and the *Gunny Bunny* shooting game (Net Terminator, 2003). While the

DOI: 10.4324/9781003281696-1

site was certainly reaching young audiences thanks to viral animation like *Potter Puppet Pals!* (Trapezoid, 2003), it was more likely to be blocked than embraced in the average classroom. Flash's appeal to educators was primarily in the making: as one of the most versatile and accessible engines, it would fuel new interest in game-making with students, which foreshadowed important trends in game-based pedagogy today.

Perhaps in part thanks to the limits of digital offerings, physical games would continue to play a major role in educational games despite Gee's call to recognize the potential of the video game. An emphasis on physical games early on, drawing on the traditions of educational simulations and historical wargames, would work to create a more inclusive space for educational play. Versions of these game systems are ongoing: *Reacting to the Past* stands out as an exemplar of an educator-driven movement toward feasible classroom games, anchored in historical scenarios and role-based learning (Carnes, 2014). Digital games fared less well: while conferences and communities of educators and researchers such as Games, Learning + Society (now the Connected Learning Summit) and Meaningful Play have arisen dedicated to the pursuit of better educational games, the meaningful integration of play continues to have major barriers for most classrooms. Existing instead in a supplemental role, most educational games are opt-in or specialized learning, while the average classroom game continues to resemble the Jeopardy and augmented worksheet approaches—the emblematic games of Laurel's derision.

Even as course management systems began to promise new platforms for play, so-called "meaningful play" seems even more out of reach for the average educator (Salen & Zimmerman, 2003). Instead, a now-notorious iteration on the edutainment model rose in prominence: gamification, or the use of game-like mechanics to infuse play into experiences that are not inherently playful. Frequently, these mechanics draw on the easiest systems to imitate: badges, rewards, victories, points, and progression. Ian Bogost appropriately called out this strategy of gamification as "bullshit" in his 2011 address, noting:

> I've suggested the term "exploitationware" as a more accurate name for gamification's true purpose, for those of us still interested in truth. Exploitationware captures gamifiers' real intentions: a grifter's game, pursued to capitalize on a cultural moment, through services about which they have questionable expertise, to bring about results meant to last only long enough to pad their bank accounts before the next bullshit trend comes along.
>
> (Bogost, 2011)

Gamification capitalized, quite literally, on a moment when games were "in": the visibility of games and gaming as public activities, enjoyed by broad audiences, would only grow even as every other vendor (from credit card companies to gyms) found a space for achievements and other gamified elements in their mobile apps and other ecosystems. Nearly ten years later, gamification would be so ubiquitous as to not require naming: badges are everywhere, rewards are built into the ecosystems of gyms and home machines such as Peloton, and platforms no longer need to call out the features that shape our engagement and record our participation.

Are we learning, then? Not necessarily: but outside these ecosystems, increased potential for game-based learning waits, powered by the same platforms and technologies that have lowered the barrier to entry to making. However, to see them truly realized, we need a more complete reimagining of higher education, and our relationship to "content" and play.

Pandemic play

Let us skip ahead another decade, to 2021. This is not a playful time.

In the wake of COVID-19, a massive shift in working and teaching conditions across higher education has brought with it more emphasis on screen time for all of us: in the United States, the impact was particularly painful, and strained an ecosystem ill-suited to digital learning as we will recount in part in this work. With it, we have adopted platforms of corporate communication for hasty reimaginings of the classroom: before 2020, Zoom was a footnote, a Skype competitor with low market adoption. Before 2020, fully online programs were typically demarcated from hybrid and classroom-centered programs. But as "safer at home" mandates spread across the globe, the landscape shifted, often overnight: some faculty were given as little as a day's warning before overhauling their semester's coursework in the "pivot" to distance learning.

Some games have emerged as essential to this shared moment: *Animal Crossing: New Horizon*, released near the start of widespread lockdowns, became one of the top-selling games of the year (Gilbert, 2020). *Among Us*, a web-based social game featuring betrayal, similarly rose to iconic status. Both games became visibly recognized for more than their escapist potential, offering spaces for political discourse, and featuring in memes during the 2020 election (Stanfill et al., 2021). Other games rose to fill the social voids of distanced gatherings: the Jackbox games collections rose to a bestselling status on Steam, featuring familiar mechanics framed in animated and distantly social compatible interfaces (Favis, 2020). Virtual Tabletop Simulator and other tools for recreating game night (with some questionable legalities and copyright violations) became central to sustaining community (Grebey, 2020). With these tools came a revival of interest in games such as *Dungeons & Dragons*, which took off on Discord channels and with the help of *D&D Beyond* and other dedicated virtual platforms for campaign and character management. Distance brought players together virtually for frequently awkward social encounters, and gaming became one tool for interrupting the endlessness of video and distracting from the challenges of the so-called "new normal."

Meanwhile, education soldiered on, with many educators making their initial course revisions with, at most, mere days of warning (Gardner, 2020). These abruptly online classes frequently removed active learning components, with faculty hastening to create lecture videos and quizzes to replace planned in-person content. Spring 2020 was a nightmare of student complaints and faculty facing a daunting learning curve, assisted by understaffed and overwhelmed learning centers on campus. Distance education staff used to supporting only a small percentage of faculty were abruptly transitioned to supporting everyone, while faculty who had resisted teaching online found themselves confronted with the daunting interfaces of learning management systems for the first time. As Lee Skallerup Bessette noted in May, the challenges for staff mounted as summer approached:

> We have been working in crisis mode without a break for the last eight weeks, and there is no relief in sight as we prepare (or, rather, as we prepare to prepare faculty) for courses to be online, hybrid, or hyflex (hybrid-flexible) for fall. Summer plans have, understandably, been canceled, but so too has any summer reprieve we may have hoped for.
>
> (Bessette, 2020)

As Bessette's words foreshadowed, Fall 2020 was only slightly better, particularly for faculty in the United States and other areas strongly impacted by pandemic spread: after summers of arguing, anticipating, and dealing with external pressures to recreate "normalcy," campuses opened with various degrees of mixed modality and a faculty now thoroughly accustomed to meeting on Zoom (Hartocollis, 2020). The delay in decisions about reopening conspired with invented, high-pressure modes such as "blendflex" to place instructors in the unenviable position of trying to prepare for all scenarios at once. Even as faculty and staff navigated these challenges, students and their parents raised questions about the cost value of education, leading to endless editorials questioning the very value of higher education—and attacks categorizing higher education as the world's most expensive streaming service (*The World's Most Expensive Streaming Service*, 2020).

The shift to 2021 brought with it a new type of troubling play: the QAnon alternate reality game took a public, violent turn in the United States (Godfrey, 2021). Already associated with a type of shared fantasy construction, QAnon became abruptly visible alongside better-known white supremacist organizations, bringing an unexpected element of fan expression to the insurrection. The markers of fandom and play were unmistakable in the January 6th attacks on the US Capitol, prompting Suzanne Scott to coin the term "fascism bound" to describe the type of costumed performance that accompanied the selfie-taking, posturing, and brandishing of both weaponry and symbolism of white supremacy. As the realities of misinformation and conspiracy-as-play continue to mount alongside a pandemic, play is even more contested, and consequential. QAnon is but one small manifestation of an ongoing link between online platforms, including games themselves, and the spread of misinformation and hate globally: the pandemic reliance upon these platforms has if anything accelerated both our awareness of these challenges and their potential for widespread impact.

How can we recapture play at a time when play is more political than ever? Is play even the answer at a time when game companies are under increased scrutiny for discriminatory practices and toxic environments? And how can play be harnessed for learning as instructors across the world are facing budget cuts, burnout, and exhaustion in the face of a screen-based or "hybrid" institution? For answers, we must turn to those who have found ways to sustain play even through these difficulties. For instance, University of Chicago's Patrick Jagoda and team built alternate reality games to navigate the pandemic, and to build community in the face of a distanced fall (Jagoda et al., 2020). By placing their emphasis on storytelling and social collaboration, the team demonstrated what is possible when we look to games for guidance and sustained both the team of designers and teams of distanced participants in collaboration toward shared goals. It certainly stands as a landmark moment of effort and creativity in the face of unexpected challenge, evoking the best of Jane McGonigal's concept of "gameful" play as a response to adversity and potential tool for handling personal and social difficulty (McGonigal, 2011). However, the path to following their example looks more perilous than ever from our position looking ahead to a potential post-pandemic, but still highly strained, future for higher education. Reality might be broken, as Jane McGonigal said, but is it fixable?

Corporate education, or education in a time of Zoom fatigue

The tools we have tried to sustain education virtually so far are certainly far from gameful, and have worked against collective confidence and community, providing more fuel for calls to reopen through their inadequacy. Prior to the global pandemic, the predominant free videoconferencing tool used in higher education was Skype along with the corporate premium Skype for Business. These tools allowed for video conferences, text chat, and phone access, and were popular in the public sphere for their app availability on android as well as iOS. Skype for Business is capable of facilitating meetings of up to 250 people. Pre-pandemic, Skype was used to facilitate virtual participation for the handful of faculty who could not attend various meetings in person as well as the occasional one-on-one student meeting when needed, and it was reliable enough. However, the limitations of the platform were immediately apparent to all users, and its more social competitor Google Hangouts offered only slightly more reliability. The video meeting was a necessary evil: relied upon for groups unable to convene at a distance, but far from a day-to-day practice for most.

Once the pandemic hit, Skype was suddenly dropped for Zoom, a platform that marketed itself fiercely as the solution for moving one's entire life into a single terminal in one's home. This videoconferencing tool also has free and premium versions, and on the surface does not appear much different from the platforms it abruptly displaced. The free version limits the user to 40 minute calls and up to 100 people per meeting, which proved ideal for luring in the new crowds exploring the terrain of virtual happy hour. The paid plan allows 30 hour calls and up to 300 people, with the option to pay an additional annual fee to allow meetings of up to 1,000 people—and immediately marketed that scale as the best possible solution for large classes, conferences, and other gatherings abruptly displaced from large lecture halls and convention centers. The sudden popularity of Zoom took even the company by surprise (Yuan, 2020). Early on in the pandemic, the company had to upgrade its security by defaulting new meetings to include passwords and waiting rooms. The company had never considered the possibility that people would type in random meeting codes to join and disrupt someone else's meeting (Khalili, 2020). This practice of Zoom-bombing became such an issue that it was declared a federal offense in the United States in April of 2020 (Andone, 2020). There were even several Zoom-bombing discord servers, where potential Zoom-bombers could go for tips and meeting codes.

Zoom-bombing is just the latest in another type of dangerous and disruptive play common on the web: trolling. As the title of Whitney Phillips's book on the subject reminds us, trolling is frequently "why we can't have nice things" (W. Phillips, 2015). Trolling is frequently associated with "lulz," or the search for humor out of the pain of others. Creating outrage, fury, and misery is the primary goal. Zoom-bombing proved quickly to be a particularly challenging force in trolling because it was so frequently released on the unprepared: unlike the users of moderated Internet platforms like Twitter and Facebook, who through exposure inevitably become used to reporting tools or curating their networks to avoid attack, Zoom-bombing often hit inexperienced moderators such as educators already struggling with the challenges of rapid pedagogical conversion. And, as it kept many of the historically racist and misogynist traditions of trolling, such bombing was frequently successful in disrupting and disturbing participants.

Zoom-bombing is not the only problem with suddenly ubiquitous virtual meetings. Many students and faculty suffered from "Zoom fatigue," negative physical effects from spending hours participating in virtual meetings (Wiederhold, 2020). The need to demonstrate attention—by nodding, making eye contact, and smiling—is heightened when we can see live images of ourselves. In face-to-face meetings, people typically take notes, look around the room or out the window, and multitask on their laptops. In video calls, the close-up of each meeting participant makes it more difficult to do much other than attention-performative actions. Other experts describe our natural reliance on non-verbal cues to determine the full meaning of what is being spoken in face-to-face settings, noting that many of these body language cues are diminished (by a small camera frame) or erased completely when cameras are off (Sklar, 2020). The listener needs to focus more intently on the speaker's words, and, at the same time, the speaker has little to no feedback from their audience. When a student's camera is turned off, the teacher does not know if they are grasping the concepts being discussed or even if they are still in the room. This puts yet another layer of stress on faculty teaching virtually.

The phrase "Zoom fatigue" has become synonymous with the feeling of being overwhelmed by pandemic strategies for replacing the live with the nearly live. While Zoom existed prior to 2020, it was a little-utilized platform without widespread corporate adoption, and certainly wasn't targeting the educational technology market. By the end of March 2020, the term Zoom fatigue had definitions at Urbandictionary.com, with the highest-rated one humorously outlining the odd situation where millions of people suddenly found themselves: "Sore buttocks and slight throbbing of head from staring at everyone in their pajamas while participating in meeting after meeting in your dining room due to social distancing due to COVID-19" (Conferencewifeofmany, 2020). The jarring juxtaposition of real business and school meetings taking place in people's homes and bedrooms erased all boundaries between work and home life, leaving educators overdependent over solutions chosen for convenience, not educational efficacy.

Pandemic pedagogy, not online education

This time of corporate education has challenged the very notion of what education is—and what it could and should be. Fully online courses were initially viewed through a tech-utopian lens, with a widespread belief that technology could bring education to everybody: an heir to public television, it assumes an equity of access that physical instruction arguably lacks. Institutions, however, quickly realized that online courses could increase enrollment far beyond the capacity of any on-campus lecture hall. Faculty and the public just as quickly realized that, beneath the claims of increasing access to education, universities were looking at online courses as cash cows.

Despite all of this, the reality of enrollment in fully online coursework suggests that the primary reason that students were choosing this modality was their schedules. The primarily asynchronous nature of online courses (with many of them set up as at-your-own-pace timelines) allowed these classes to assume the role of the previous generations' night classes. The credits and degrees could be earned after the standard eight-hour workday, with the increased convenience of not requiring travel, or, requiring travel only to a library or other places providing public access to computers and Internet. For these students, online learning was chosen not out of preference to in-person classes, but out of necessity because traditional coursework was not available to them due to schedule, location, or both.

One of the major issues with the pivot to all-online, beyond the unreasonably short amount of time in which classes were converted to fully online, was the attempt to fully replace in-person activities with online ones. Online classes have been offered for over three decades, and educators have learned quite a bit about effective technologically mediated instruction. It requires intentional design and typically emphasizes asynchronous interaction. A majority of students who enroll in online courses tend to do so because they have a non-traditional schedule, so coursework needs to be assigned accordingly, so that it can be completed in a flexible time frame. The traditional student is likely unprepared for the shift in expectations—the traditional faculty member, even more so, particularly as online courses are typically built well in advance to allow for methodical scaffolding and content organization.

When schools shut in the spring of 2020 around the world, however, there was little time nor volition to attempt such intentional design. In US institutions, many faculty who had never taught online (some of whom had never used teleconferencing methods at all) before the pandemic were required to do so with minimal training or support. Abruptly, everyone was installing new technology, providing their own home office space, and working without the auspices of campus information technology support. Many faculty prefer to lecture to their students, so that is what they attempted to do, synchronously with Zoom. The desire to recapture the familiar, and minimize the shift in modality, was understandable—but the students and faculty both suffered for it, as the realities of teleconference exhaustion against the backdrop of collective anxiety and isolation mounted. Even faculty seeking to implement more intentional design would find themselves daunted by continual challenges: short or non-existent lead time; confused and overstressed students; and understaffed distance learning and faculty support centers suddenly supporting more faculty than ever before.

The challenges mounted. Students lacked reliable Internet connections and quiet places to attend live virtual class meetings off campus. Faculty proceeded through the remainder of the semester with unreasonable expectations for student attendance, online etiquette, and quality of coursework—or, particularly in the case of underresourced adjuncts and caretakers, found themselves in similar constraints as their students. Adjuncts taught from closets; student and faculty parents logged on their own children into Zoom classes while trying to attend their own; and the worst possible model for virtual education would for many students become their first, lasting impression of the format. Institutions told the public that virtual learning was equal to in-person learning, and there were faculty who believed these claims and therefore made no syllabus adjustments.

In a provocative essay, "Teaching into the Void," Donatella Della Ratta delineates a number of issues with blended teaching, including the relentless self-gaze participants face, the privilege required of students to even have their cameras turned on during class, and the resulting oppression from requiring camera on attendance (Ratta, 2021). These issues exacerbate instructors' fears that they are not being heard or understood by their students, as teaching remotely prevents them from seeing students' physical body language in a classroom setting which provides constant feedback. Additionally, remote teaching places faculty in the role of a 24/7 call center operator or food delivery service. Even before the pandemic, students had come to expect near-immediate replies to emails, regardless of the day or time they sent them. The pandemic exacerbated this, whether it was the loss of the sense of time from lockdowns or the inability to escape the classroom, given that the remote classroom existed wherever virtual learning was conducted.

Students were outraged at the additional distance learning fees their universities charged to compensate for the increased workload on IT departments and the revenue losses of room, board, and other campus services (Pohle, 2020). Feeling grifted out of a "true" university experience, students and their parents petitioned for decreasing the tuition costs, despite the exorbitant amount of extra work and resources these courses require. Outside of the university, students and faculty faced public unrest over mask mandates, police reform, politics, and more. The combination of this multitude of stressors tested the mental health of every individual over the course of 2020. The idea of Zoom fatigue soon became synonymous with a more general exhaustion from living in this time.

Alternative platform visions

As we continue to fight this fatigue, the struggle against the corporatization of education becomes more difficult. The ideals of learning for knowledge's sake have always butted heads with the need to fund education systems. The sudden capability to aggressively and constantly monitor students and faculty is likely irresistible to administration teams longing for "data" that they can use to justify budget and position cuts, especially as the economic effects of the pandemic are only beginning to be felt. Tools like Gather.town offer alternative visions for what Zoom could be, but those visions are haunted by the past of educational technology. The shadow of *Second Life* hangs over efforts at locative education, and the abandoned online campuses of institutions that invested heavily in their online islands are a harsh reminder to anyone who becomes too invested in recreating their campus virtually. Lack of shared platforms and intentional guidance hampers many, meaning that educators who seek to innovate beyond the learning management system might unintentionally find themselves exhausting their students with platform fatigue.

The replication of "real" life into *Second Life* (down to the campus buildings) should hint to its lack of success. If nothing innovative is happening—no matter how innovative the platform is or seems to be—the preexisting instructional ecosystem will surely be seen as sufficient (and more lucrative for the university). Once the "novelty effect," to borrow Richard Clark's term from the early use of media for learning (Clark, 1983), wears off on a technology, the educational activities taking place there can be more honestly inspected, and, in the case of *Second Life*, found wanting.

While Zoom fatigue was on the rise, another video platform took off during the pandemic, and became a contested model that points to a brighter future for the form. TikTok, launched in 2016, is a video sharing platform that has become infamous for its viral challenges: dance numbers and other performances circulate with continual remixing and reimagining. Inevitably given the launch date, the platform has become inextricably linked to Trump's administration in the United States, a circumstance amplified by the use of the platform as a site of parody, and the corresponding attacks by Trump on its prominence.

Later in this work, we will look to TikTok for inspiration as a site of creative pandemic play: at its best, TikTok creative work is reminiscent of an Oulipian, avant-garde game, building upon constraint-driven art and collective experimentation. Moments such as the Woodchuck revolution, where users drew upon existing TikTok formats, or filters, and envisioned an uprising against the Woodchuck overlords all set to the tune of "How much wood could a woodchuck chuck?" in a dystopian, autotuned chorus, demonstrate the collective creativity the platform harnesses. Likewise, TikTok has been host to several breakthrough artists and acts, such as Trump impersonator Sarah Cooper—her viral lipsyncs of Trump speeches led to a full Netflix special—and *Ratatouille: The Musical*, which emerged from an artist's collective of out-of-work theater folks motivated in part by their pandemic isolation to imagine a new type of collaborative video.

TikTok's enabling of additive creativity is particularly addictive, offering a vision of compelling video content that provides a flow of emergent juxtapositions: this experience of immersion went mainstream with the "Sea Shanty" craze of early 2021 (Piscioniere, 2021). The "Sea Shanty" trend (which went viral enough to attract coverage from late night host Stephen Colbert) is an exemplar that allows groups of strangers to sing together, building harmony (or not) through continually expanding choruses. In a time when the chorus is one of the most inherently risky gatherings (infamously, a choral recital early in the pandemic led to significant numbers of cases and deaths), TikTok enables collective making that was otherwise difficult under the new normal. In contrast to Zoom's fatigue and amplification of disconnectedness, TikTok suggests a possibility for intimacy.

In stark contrast to the numbing experience of Zoom, TikTok harnesses the playful experience of flow, exemplifying what emergent, connected media can best provide—while curation is possible, the need to curate is minimal. The focus is typically on the individual or pair, although TikTok's additive properties enable groups to form. Those groups do not suffer from the same *Brady Bunch*-evoking configuration of the Zoom gallery, and instead offer the opportunity for a better sense of foreground and background, allowing new voices to take center stage as the creativity spirals. These offer the important reminder that technology alone is not the source of the pandemic pedagogy challenges: rather, the ways we employ technology in the classroom, and the passivity that models such as Zoom suggest for most participants, recreate the broadcast of the lecture rather than the creative play of game or TikTok.

Surveillance and pandemic panopticons

However, TikTok's publicness brings with its surface play deeper reminders of the challenges of platform control and the realities of surveillance, both within educational technology and in digital culture more broadly. While Zoom fatigue is exhausting, a more sinister turn in educational technology serves as an important reminder that, left unchecked, the worst is yet to come. Several software platforms have taken off with services of "remote proctoring," which amount to exam surveillance relying upon a combination of human and automated monitoring techniques intended to address cheating. The stories rising from this Foucaultian technology have been unsurprisingly harrowing: a law student was unable to take his bar exam without a lengthy back and forth with customer service due to its failure to recognize his face (Tribune News Service, 2020). More widely, students point to the "creepiness" of monitoring services, particularly when a person is employed to essentially peer into their homes and watch their exam process live (Chin, 2020a).

This is not new—universities were already tracking their students' every move through smart phone applications (Harwell, 2019) and learning management system analytics have always encouraged instructors to surveil participation—however, it is, like so many things, amplified by the pandemic's speed. The pandemic brought an abrupt increase in business for proctoring companies with little time for reflection: "Proctorio's chief executive, Mike Olsen, said his steady business grew 900 percent after campuses began closing, as the 235,000 exams his company proctored last April grew this April to 2.5 million" (Hubler, 2020). Meanwhile, live services such as ProctorU increased their staff—even as fears (and realities) of layoffs started to hit institutions of higher education across the globe. A privacy group filing a complaint has noted the data collection practices as particularly troubling:

> Respondents' collection of sensitive personal information, including biometric data, is unjustified, excessive, and harmful to students who have no meaningful opportunity to opt out of such systems ... Forcibly collecting personal information from test-takers, including sensitive biometric data, is inherently invasive.
>
> (Chin, 2020b)

Perhaps the most alarming aspect of these types of surveillance tools is the resemblance they bear to some practices of gamification, which can feel similarly invasive, and often rely upon automated metrics to determine engagement. Student metrics and gamification badges alike are touted as motivational tools—allowing students (and their instructors) to see for themselves their successes (and failures) as learners. However, the implementation often fails to engage, instead redirecting student energy from learning the proposed subject, encouraging them to jump through hoops of metrics rather than exploring and learning about the subject the course purports to cover.

Edtech companies aiming to own the future of presumed post-pandemic higher education are trying to meld Zoom with aspects of gamification and Proctorio. For instance, Engageli promises to "keep tabs on how much students are participating" while adding active learning features (Busta, 2020). The emphasis on what the start-up terms "data-driven engagement" is framed as recreating the classroom, but employs the techniques of automation:

> One of the affordances of in-person classroom group work is that, in addition to visiting tables and listening in, an educator can scan the room to see which tables look like they might need some attention. If half the students at a table are looking down at their phones rather than talking to each other, the instructor can walk over to that table and bring everyone's attention back to the work. Engageli attempts to replicate that experience with engagement analytics. Algorithms running on the student video can detect situations where students might be drifting.
>
> (Feldstein, 2020)

The reframing of engagement through this lens of algorithmic monitoring offers a grim future for gamification not too far afield from the one proposed in the "Fifteen Million Merits" episode of *Black Mirror* (2011), in which workers earn points through every action, and are required to spend them to escape marketing and "level up" in privileges and opportunities. The system has been starkly compared to the real social gamification of "ratings" at work in China (Vincent, 2017), and while this is certainly an oversimplification, it is not so far removed from the institutionalization of badges and achievements. A decade later, some elements of the original episode, like the warnings that appear on-screen when the user attempts to block out content, are perhaps even quaint.

Coping through play

One way people have tried to cope with the multiple challenges of 2020 has been through play. Even attempts to subvert the surveillance state of university software can be seen as play—for instance, trends such as the use of Zoom virtual backgrounds to create the illusion of presence through a pre-filmed self (Berry, 2020). Shira Chess particularly draws our attention to the importance of making time for play as a feminist act, and encourages all of us to consider the ways in which play is a privilege, a reminder that is even more timely as mothers have borne the brunt of pandemic job loss and disruptions (Kashen et al., 2020). The inequities of the pandemic make play feel out of reach for many, and even less likely in the Zoom classroom. However, as the QAnon riots remind us, not all of this play is feminist, and the call to play is heavy with these associations.

Imaginative play is frequently restricted: in who plays, and whose imagination is valued. In Bill Watterson's lasting vision of meaningful play, Calvin and Hobbes, titular protagonist Calvin is continually living in his own reality with his companionable philosopher stuffed tiger-turned-real. His counterpart and foil, Susie Derkins, continually brings "reality" back through her presence. Notably, Calvin's play is frequently destructive to others, and out of control: the sport of *Calvinball* with its ever-changing ruleset can perhaps serve as a prescient metaphor for this type of play, which seeks to exclude the outsider. (A variant of the game, *True American*, presented on episodes of *New Girl* makes this explicit, emphasizing the power of play to exclude.)

Though initially intended for serious business meetings, Zoom does allow for some playful behavior. For example, one student went viral for changing their name display to "Reconnecting ..." With the student's video and microphone turned off, it appeared as though they were having Internet connection issues, and the teacher would not be able to call on that student to participate in a discussion. Another playful feature of Zoom is the ability to set up virtual backgrounds, filters, and still images that display when the participant's video is turned off. Thousands of people experimented with virtual backgrounds and the ability to appear in any location, real or fiction: outer space, the beach, or a tidy office. The motion backgrounds allowed for additional humor: students quickly realized they could create a looping video of themselves paying attention to class, then step out of frame without others noticing. Others took this a step further and created virtual backgrounds of themselves walking in on the meeting—and acting surprised to see themselves in a virtual meeting. T-shirt companies even jumped in on the fun, advertising shirts and mugs with phrases like "You're on mute," insignia for "Zoom University," and allusions to the musical *Hamilton*: "the Zoom where it happens." Faculty even added syllabus policies such as "All pets must be introduced once seen on camera," to lighten the mood. Yet the realities of surveillance (and frequently of recording) overshadow the playfulness, especially as Zoom is further integrated with the monitoring mechanisms of the content management system.

It is no exaggeration to say that the year 2020 has been a serious one, full of uncertainty and fear. Despite it all, play has bubbled to the surface again and again. This is not a playful time, and yet we continue to play in small and large ways. Play helps us take on unfamiliar roles to learn, explore, and understand new things. The promise of serious games (and gamification) was to lessen the consequences of failure and to allow learners to practice in a safe sandbox to prepare for assessments or life. Too many well-meaning educators tried to force games into the curriculum without success. Assigned tasks in school rarely capture much fun. Looking more closely at the ways people have managed to infuse play into the grim reality of the past year, the key to unlocking the educational potential of games may be more about attitude surrounding them than the actual structure of the learning game. A playful *perspective* could help students (and faculty) let go of the fear of failure, to embrace it and grow from the experience.

Ratta (2021) suggests that we embrace the awkward aspects of virtual teaching and learning using a playful perspective:

> Why not make a space for potential flourishing out from our own self-acknowledged impotence and collective discomfort? How about we just make the best, make maximum awkwardness, make shameless *fun*, of this one massive "awkward moment" that we're living in? (emphasis original)

Moving from the serious, surveillance-state, business tools described above to a more playful, inclusive, empathetic tone for our courses may be exactly what faculty and students alike need in the years of pandemic recovery we are about to face. Looking ahead, the types of games available to play continues to grow exponentially. Even more exciting is the increasing availability of user-friendly, open-source authoring tools such as Twine and Ren'Py (as well as the calls for user-friendly authoring tools for games and XR experiences) (Murray & Johnson, 2021).

We are finally at the edge of being able to truly leverage games for learning. We just have to remember that games aren't stand-alone solutions for other problems. Our perspectives and attitudes can take us a good part of the journey toward a playful learning environment. The role-playing game *Reacting to the Past* (Carnes, 2014) works so well because it focuses on specific subjects that are already conducive to role-playing games: historical events full of conflict on par with trashy novels. The history itself is often already fascinatingly scandalous, so adding the wrapper of a role-playing game to the content is easy and effective. However, other subjects and content do not lend themselves so obviously to such enjoyment, and teachers feel lost and uninspired by the existing games at their disposal, whether or not they are billed as educational. A common problem educational games seem to consistently face is that of content: engaging games are interdisciplinary. Viewing educational games as alternatives to worksheets or field trips, educators have sought games that fit only in the narrow parameters of their field, course, or even a single unit of a course, with little success.

The perfect game (or game design) that can replace an informed teacher and purposeful course design simply does not and cannot exist. The culture of education still has not shifted sufficiently enough to allow games to take a meaningful place in a course or grade. Education advocates have been protesting the siloing of instruction for decades, and yet it persists, pervades, and prevents the rich learning experiences that could be taking place through games.

Constructivist learning theory has been advocated for more than 40 years and yet it is still difficult to find activities where students take the primary responsibility for their learning through exploration in most K–20 classrooms. The drastic revisions required to achieve this conception of student-centered education require far more than the addition of learning games, but the two go hand in hand. When so-called accountability measures are structured to limit the breadth and depth of what is learned in any given classroom or course—altering the end goal of learners and educators to the passing of a multiple-guess assessment rather than fostering curiosity or love of learning—games have little value or place in instruction.

Games for learning have much to learn from the failures of the past as well as those of other technologically mediated educational tools like *Second Life*. The shift to fully online learning was done hastily and out of necessity, but the claim that educators aren't adept with technology is no longer valid (if it ever was). Instruction is being mediated through technology more than anyone could have ever predicted (or hoped)—the time to embrace playful learning is here.

For too long, educational technology has been viewed as something "cute" for teachers to experiment with—but only after the "real" learning for the semester had concluded and standardized assessments had been taken. These activities were typically one-offs, extra little lessons or units with shiny new gadgets that could briefly capture student attention and motivation. The novelty effect (Clark, 1983) was almost relied upon for favorable results in pretest–posttest study designs with student participants. This decades-old effect was used to counter every effort or study that used a new technology, and many educators who were uninterested in adopting technology in their classrooms were able to avoid doing so by pointing to this novelty effect.

The suddenly online phenomena caught everyone off guard, but it resulted in the use of educational technology for the right reasons: as a tool that can be used to teach students. Rather than focusing on student motivation or novelty, educators far and wide turned their attention toward mitigating these effects in order to continue teaching their curriculum—modified or not as required by different situations and pressures. The result has taken educational technology one step in the right direction. We are not teaching around technology for one isolated unit and then returning to "normal" lecture and worksheets. We are using the technology to teach, but the remaining step lies before us: the step from corporate education to truly engaged online learning, from Zoom fatigue to TikTok creative collaboration, from QAnon to informative, co-creative play experience.

Chapter overview

Game-based learning, or the use and development of games for pedagogical usage, has been on the rise across both higher education and K-12 environments as part of widespread adoption of educational technology. However, much of this implementation, upon examination, fails to engage: popular solutions often rely upon the framework of "gamification," or the use of superficial mechanics of games such as points, achievements, and competition without narrative, interaction, and agency (Bogost, 2011). Our educational technology capabilities are more advanced and widespread in their usage than ever—yet the opportunities for meaningful play in the classroom continue to be limited. In this work, we set out to examine these inherent contractions of our current moment in educational technology and pedagogical design, and seek answers and opportunities for its future. Namely, we set out to address:

1. Given the widespread challenges demonstrated by pandemic education around the world, and the demonstrable failure of the collective online experiment (particularly in the United States), how can educational games be salvaged?
2. As games and learning experimentation has devolved into gamification, is there still value in game-based learning? How can it be harnessed given the larger challenges of gaming culture?

Notably, this presumes that the pandemic educational experiment will be deemed a failure, which from our perspective is self-evident if not fully assessed in terms of learning outcomes: instead, we would point to Zoom fatigue, collective disengagement, and the general exhaustion of students, faculty, and staff even as institutions around the world face cuts and funding challenges moving forward. The awkward efforts to adapt corporate educational technology to the purposes of the classroom might prove in hindsight to demotivate further adoption rather than motivate it: students exhausted by the over-assignment of "engagement" exercises will likely bring new wariness to their future online courses. Faculty frustrated by poor student evaluations and the intense work of conversion will bring that fatigue to future attempts at technology integration. And, perhaps most troubling of all, the structures of gamification are only growing in their resemblance to the structures of surveillance increasingly embedded in corporatized education.

These concerns are only amplified by the realities of digital game culture, which have been well-studied in recent monographs pointing to efforts to resist overwhelming cultures of toxicity. Megan Condis has pointed to the embattlement of *Gaming Masculinity*, and the violence with which the traditional gamer identity is enforced (Condis, 2018); Kishonna Gray points us to the challenges of *Intersectional Tech*, and the significant work done by black gamers to craft space in the face of intense hostility and racism (Gray, 2020); and Amanda Phillips reminds us that resistance to *Gamer Trouble* continues in the face of intense conflict (A. Phillips, 2020). The shadow of GamerGate still looms over the field, and the realities of game designer demographics are not much improved from the early state of the industry, particularly when we look at mainstream games.

Yet—in spite of this—we love games. We make, and teach, games as a space for learning, for conversation, for interactive experiences that push us to reflect, co-create, and improve. We advocate for rethinking the discourse of games as spaces of learning, for looking toward the margins of play rather than the mainstream for the inspiration to revisit playful education. In a landscape of polished course management systems, we advocate for unpolished, experimental, and weird games. The discourse of personal games (Anthropy, 2012) exists alongside what Juul has termed *Handmade Pixels*: games that forefront the personal and center "authenticity" (Juul, 2019).

In this work, we will position the crisis, and look beyond it, drawing on both historical challenges in game-based learning and current successes to reimagine the role games might play in remedying the damage of both educational technology fatigue and widespread, shallow, gamification. Unlike much of the previous work in this area, we acknowledge from the outset that the challenges of inclusive technology must be foregrounded if game-based learning is to provide a meaningful intervention. Through bringing a critical lens informed by intersectional feminist theory, we advocate for reform influenced by current awareness of both representational and labor challenges in the games industry, arguing that the games we embrace must model the inclusive pedagogy we seek at all levels of their development.

In Chapter 1, we dive further into Bogost's claim of gamification as "bullshit," considering both the resistance to and widespread adoption of this illusion of play (Bogost, 2011). Inescapably, the term continues to rise in popular usage, and the positioning of gamification as a "feature" to be incorporated through educational technology threatens to popularize it further. Bogost's critique drew much-needed attention to the lack of game-ness of most of these solutions, a problem that has only been amplified by the COVID-19 reliance on readily accessible tech, promising to turn worksheets into play: Blackboard offers "achievements"; Canvas a system of "Choose Your Own Adventure" content and "Canvabadges"; and startups aiming to displace Zoom such as Engageli promise engagement through polls and quizzes. These familiar, tired, patterns are at risk of becoming the standard for playful learning, well-targeted toward exhausted, overwhelmed educators trying to navigate new systems and challenges. However, their tacked-on mechanics offer little in the way of meaningful play, and the continual turn to the tech start-up industry to "solve" the problems of education is filled with cautionary tales.

Turning from this marketing-driven, rhetorically empty, promise of gamification, to games more broadly, Chapter 2 critiques the current state of the "educational" game, positioning play as we entered into the pandemic classroom. The history of games-driven engagement in the classroom is filled with attempts to reclaim studio titles, often amplifying the very narratives of settler representation and colonial discourse embedded in their mechanics. However, these same challenges heighten our awareness of the importance of games such as *Minecraft* that enable constructive and creative play. At the same time, those titles present their own obstacles to meaningful learning, particularly as they suffer from challenges of inclusion, moderation, and corporate platform restrictions (which we will explore further in Chapter 4).

In our search for meaningful pandemic play, Chapter 3 shifts focus to the successes of three engaging patterns of play at a distance stand out as potential models for the future: the suspicion-driven multiplayer of *Among Us*; the revamped competitive structures of Jackbox games; and the collaborative platforms powering distant *Dungeons & Dragons*. By examining the design choices, affordances, and play mechanisms of these games, we can see not only the potential structures for the future gameful classroom but also harsh lessons on why the Zoom classroom of today has proven unwieldy and disengaged. We position these current models alongside historical patterns, hearkening back to the lessons of MUDs and MOOs, *Second Life*, and MOOCs, to consider an essential question: why is our digital pedagogy stalled in a time of apparent platform innovation, and how can we adopt the lessons of meaningful pandemic play?

Looking across platforms where innovation is prevalent, we note some of the perils: in Chapter 4, we address the reality that the risks of play are unevenly distributed. Previous studies have noted the tendency of toxic technocultures to reproduce and amplify racism and misogyny (Massanari, 2017), and gaming cultures in particular have become infamous for trolling, harassment, and outright abuse of prominent women and people of color (Chess & Shaw, 2015). The regimentation of gaming as dominated by this cultural discourse, and the influence of game-like structures in the popular discourse through conspiracies and politicized streaming inevitably accompanies gaming's entry into the classroom. Can play in the classroom transcend this history of discrimination in gaming? Can informed teaching help prevent this in the future? As we look ahead to technologies that seek to amplify existing online education mediation, such as the looming metaverse, what lessons can games bring to the table?

Certainly, we see hope for those changes: in Chapter 5, we put forth a proposal for design patterns that forefront a "messy," personal, and co-created approach to play, drawing on examples of pandemic successes which point toward a future driven by co-creative gaming. We look to exemplars from around the world, drawing on emerging practices ranging from the alternate reality games of Patrick Jagoda's campus team to the improvisational exercises of "Netprov" to the results of pandemic-inspired game jams and distant exercises in critical making. Often, these examples don't look like mainstream games at all – we see the most promise in treating students as co-designers of their experience, and engaging in creative play together, with room for failure and experimentation. Through analyzing these cross-platform successes, we construct a framework for a meaningful pedagogy of play.

If it seems as though we are reinventing the wheel, it is because we are. Games designed for entertainment by for-profit companies have mastered the ability to teach players a myriad of skills (Gee, 2004, 2008). Educators can and must do better, but the demand to innovate through play comes alongside a myriad of contradictions, many of which have driven learning toward models of assessment and surveillance. In the chapter "Conclusion," we embrace those challenges and look inward: why are we stuck in cycles of educational technology that promise disruption, but deliver monotony? Is there space for meaningful play in the neoliberal university? We find hope outside the technical: in communities of ungrading; in pedagogy that rewards failure; in pedagogy that embraces play rather than incentives and punishments, and in the co-creative play that exemplifies the best innovations of pandemic pedagogy. This is not a playful time, but we need play now more than ever.

References

Andone, D. (2020, April 2). *FBI warns video calls are getting hijacked. It's called 'Zoombombing'—CNN.* CNN. https://www.cnn.com/2020/04/02/us/fbi-warning-zoombombing-trnd/index.html.

Anthropy, A. (2012). *Rise of the videogame zinesters: How freaks, normals, amateurs, artists, dreamers, drop-outs, queers, housewives, and people like you are taking back an art form.* Seven Stories Press.

Berry, S. (2020, April 7). How you can fake being on a Zoom video call. *Videomaker.* https://www.videomaker.com/news/how-you-can-fake-being-on-a-video-call-on-zoom/.

Bessette, L. S. (2020, May 19). *Affective labor and COVID-19: The second wave.* https://er.educause.edu/blogs/2020/5/affective-labor-and-covid-19-the-second-wave.

Bogost, I. (2011, August 8). *Gamification is bullshit.* Bogost.Com. http://bogost.com/writing/blog/gamification_is_bullshit/.

Busta, H. (2020, October 27). *These companies are redesigning "Zoom University."* Higher Ed Dive. https://www.highereddive.com/news/these-companies-are-redesigning-zoom-university/587876/.

Carnes, M. C. (2014). *Minds on fire: How role-immersion games transform college.* Harvard University Press.

Chess, S., & Shaw, A. (2015). A conspiracy of fishes, or, how we learned to stop worrying about #GamerGate and embrace hegemonic masculinity. *Journal of Broadcasting and Electronic Media, 59*(1), 208–220. https://doi.org/10.1080/08838151.2014.999917.

Chin, M. (2020a, April 29). *Exam anxiety: How remote test-proctoring is creeping students out.* The Verge. https://www.theverge.com/2020/4/29/21232777/examity-remote-test-proctoring-online-class-education.

Chin, M. (2020b, December 9). *Privacy group files complaint against five online test-proctoring services.* The Verge. https://www.theverge.com/2020/12/9/22166023/epic-proctorio-examity-privacy-online-testing-school-lawsuit-proctoring.

Clark, R. E. (1983). Reconsidering research on learning from media. *Review of Educational Research, 53*(4), 445–459. https://doi.org/10.3102/00346543053004445.

Condis, M. (2018). *Gaming masculinity: Trolls, fake geeks, and the gendered battle for online culture.* University of Iowa Press.

Conferencewifeofmany. (2020, March 26). *Urban dictionary: Zoom fatigue*. Urban Dictionary. https://www.urbandictionary.com/define.php?term=Zoom%20Fatigue.

Favis, E. (2020, August 14). Playing remotely: The massive success of Jackbox Games during the pandemic. *Washington Post*. https://www.washingtonpost.com/video-games/2020/08/14/playing-remotely-massive-success-jackbox-games-during-pandemic/.

Feldstein, M. (2020, October 24). *Engageli: First look at a zoom educational alternative*. E-Literate. https://eliterate.us/engageli-first-look-at-a-zoom-educational-alternative/.

Gardner, L. (2020, March 20). *Covid-19 has forced higher ed to pivot to online learning. Here are 7 takeaways so far*. Chronicle of Higher Education. https://www.chronicle.com/article/covid-19-has-forced-higher-ed-to-pivot-to-online-learning-here-are-7-takeaways-so-far/.

Gee, J. P. (2004). *What video games have to teach us about learning and literacy*. Palgrave Macmillan.

Gee, J. P. (2008). Cats and portals: Video games, learning, and play. *American Journal of Play*, *1*(2), 229–245.

Gilbert, B. (2020, May 7). *The new "Animal Crossing" is setting sales records for the switch—Business Insider*. Business Insider. https://www.businessinsider.com/animal-crossing-new-horizons-launch-sales-nintendo-switch-2020-5.

Godfrey, E. (2021, January 9). It was supposed to be so much worse. *The Atlantic*. https://www.theatlantic.com/politics/archive/2021/01/trump-rioters-wanted-more-violence-worse/617614/.

Gray, K. L. (2020). *Intersectional tech: Black users in digital gaming*. LSU Press.

Grebey, J. (2020, March 25). *Dungeons & Dragons players turn to virtual tabletops in record numbers due to coronavirus*. SYFY WIRE. https://www.syfy.com/syfywire/dungeons-dragons-roll20-fantasy-grounds-virtual-tabletop-online-coronavirus.

Hartocollis, A. (2020, May 19). Fever checks and quarantine dorms: The fall college experience? *The New York Times*. https://www.nytimes.com/2020/05/19/us/college-fall-2020-coronavirus.html.

Harwell, D. (2019, December 24). Colleges are turning students' phones into surveillance machines, tracking the locations of hundreds of thousands. *Washington Post*. https://www.washingtonpost.com/technology/2019/12/24/colleges-are-turning-students-phones-into-surveillance-machines-tracking-locations-hundreds-thousands/.

Hubler, S. (2020, May 10). Keeping online testing honest? Or an Orwellian overreach? *The New York Times*. https://www.nytimes.com/2020/05/10/us/online-testing-cheating-universities-coronavirus.html.

Jagoda, P., Coleman, H., Downie, M., Sparrow, A., & Schilt, K. (2020). A labyrinth: Designing and playing a collaborative game during COVID-19. *Electronic Literature Organization Conference, 2020*. https://stars.library.ucf.edu/elo2020/live/roundtables/2.

Juul, J. (2019). *Handmade pixels: Independent video games and the quest for authenticity*. MIT Press.

Kashen, J., Glynn, S. J., & Novello, A. (2020, October 30). *How COVID-19 sent women's workforce progress backward*. Center for American Progress. https://www.americanprogress.org/issues/women/reports/2020/10/30/492582/covid-19-sent-womens-workforce-progress-backward/.

Khalili, J. (2020, May 19). Zoom app hijackers disrupting calls with pornographic and hateful imagery. *TechRadar*. https://www.techradar.com/news/zoom-app-hijackers-disrupting-calls-with-pornographic-and-hateful-imagery

Laurel, B., Crisp, D. G., & Lunenfeld, P. (2001). *Utopian entrepreneur*. MIT Press.

Massanari, A. (2017). #Gamergate and the Fappening: How Reddit's algorithm, governance, and culture support toxic technocultures. *New Media and Society, 19*(3), 329–346. https://doi.org/10.1177/1461444815608807.

McGonigal, J. (2011). *Reality is broken: Why games make us better and how they can change the world*. Penguin.

Mukherjee, S. (2017). Videogames and post colonialism: An introduction. In S. Mukherjee (Ed.), *Videogames and postcolonialism: Empire plays back* (pp. 1–28). Springer International Publishing. https://doi.org/10.1007/978-3-319-54822-7_1.

Murray, J. T., & Johnson, E. K. (2021). XR content authoring challenges: The creator-developer divide. In J. A. Fisher (Ed.), *Augmented and mixed reality for communities* (1st ed., pp. 249–268). CRC Press. https://doi.org/10.1201/9781003052838-16.

Net Terminator. (2003, September 4). *::Gunny bunny::* Newgrounds.Com. https://www.newgrounds.com/portal/view/120798.

Phillips, A. (2020). *Gamer trouble: Feminist confrontations in digital culture*. New York University Press.

Phillips, W. (2015). *This is why we can't have nice things: Mapping the relationship between online trolling and mainstream culture*. MIT Press.

Piscioniere, K. (2021, January 14). Sea shanty TikTok is on fire. *Slate Magazine*. https://slate.com/culture/2021/01/sea-shanty-tiktok-wellerman-trend-explained.html.

Pohle, A. (2020, August 28). The coronavirus pandemic is making college students question the price of their education. *Wall Street Journal*. https://www.wsj.com/articles/the-coronavirus-pandemic-is-making-college-students-question-the-price-of-their-education-11598619781.

Ratta, D. D. (2021, January 6). Teaching into the void. *INC Longform. Network Cultures*. https://networkcultures.org/longform/2021/01/06/teaching-into-the-void/.

Salen, K., & Zimmerman, E. (2003). *Rules of play: Game design fundamentals*. The MIT Press.

Salter, A., & Murray, J. (2014). *Flash: Building the interactive web*. MIT Press.

Sklar, J. (2020, April 24). *'Zoom fatigue' is taxing the brain. Here's why that happens*. Science. https://www.nationalgeographic.com/science/2020/04/coronavirus-zoom-fatigue-is-taxing-the-brain-here-is-why-that-happens/.

Stanfill, M., Salter, A., & Sullivan, A. (2021, August). Orange is Sus: Among us and political play. In *The 16th international conference on the foundations of digital games (FDG) 2021* (pp. 1–9).

Tanner, S. (2003, February 6). *Escape from elm street*. Newgrounds.Com. https://www.newgrounds.com/portal/view/81945.

'The world's most expensive streaming service.' (2020, September 2). Intelligencer. https://nymag.com/intelligencer/2020/09/kara-swisher-and-scott-galloway-on-the-state-of-higher-ed.html.

Trapezoid. (2003, September 27). *Potter puppet pals!* Newgrounds.Com. https://www.newgrounds.com/portal/view/125471.

Tribune News Service. (2020, November 11). *"Unfair surveillance"? Online exam software sparks global student revolt*. Tribuneindia News Service. https://www.tribuneindia.com/news/jobs-careers/unfair-surveillance-online-exam-software-sparks-global-student-revolt-169347.

Vincent, A. (2017, December 15). Black mirror is coming true in China, where your "rating" affects your home, transport and social circle. *The Telegraph*. https://www.telegraph.co.uk/on-demand/2017/12/15/black-mirror-coming-true-china-rating-affects-home-transport/.

Wiederhold, B. K. (2020). Connecting through technology during the coronavirus disease 2019 pandemic: Avoiding "zoom fatigue." *Cyberpsychology, Behavior, and Social Networking, 23*(7), 437–438. https://doi.org/10.1089/cyber.2020.29188.bkw.

Yuan, E. S. (2020, May 4). Navigating a new chapter for zoom. *Zoom Blog.* https://blog.zoom.us/navigating-a-new-chapter-for-zoom/

1 The problem of gamification

Playing in lockdown

The global nightmare that was COVID-19 caught many countries off guard and unprepared. The US president had just cut funding to the Centers for Disease Control and disbanded its global contagious disease response department; leaders of Italy and Brazil joined the United States and others in denouncing the virus as anything more concerning than the seasonal flu. Meanwhile, countries like Taiwan and New Zealand more readily took centralized measures to prevent infection, using strict precautionary guidelines with contact tracing and lockdown orders, respectively, to protect public health, with both countries initially closing their borders entirely. Eventually, however, most countries did enact some sort of "lockdown," or stay-at-home mandate. In this time of mass confusion, fear, and misinformation, people across the globe discovered or rediscovered hobbies and pastimes that could be done within whatever safety guidelines were in place in their areas, many of which were games.

The sudden restriction of our physical movements—and for many, the unexpected pause in required work tasks and travel—brought with it opportunities to explore new leisure activities. People found virtual ways to connect socially and entertain themselves through platforms like Zoom and TikTok. Playful videos emerged of sea shanties, dance moves, and practical jokes as people looked for moments of joy within otherwise bleak circumstances. It could be argued that many of these activities were attempts by people to "gamify" their lockdowns. The Internet was awash with videos depicting travel-restricted residents playing games they invented, from cross-balcony tennis games to sock puppets pretending to eat passing vehicles complete with classic video game sound effects (Bruk, 2020), to curling using a Swiffer and a Roomba (Wanshel, 2020), and beyond. We turned to games to preserve our sanity and satisfy emotional and social needs.

In valiant attempts to prevent students from falling behind academically, educators worldwide found ways to engage students intellectually, with many online classrooms and assignments serving as a glimpse of "normal" for learners of all ages who found themselves in precarious and confusing situations many had never fathomed possible. Those looking to Maslow's hierarchy of needs understood that the rigor of academic tasks would have to take a backseat to the emotional

DOI: 10.4324/9781003281696-2

needs of their students, even as others launched into debates almost immediately about what educational progress might be lost (Mcleod, 2020). While the public outside of online schooling seemed to have formed opposing sides for or against one measure or another, teachers struggled with a whole host of new challenges to their professions. In many areas, students were still expected to perform well on high-stakes standardized tests while teachers struggled with unfamiliar technology, a new layer of behavioral regulations, uninvited windows into students' personal home spaces, and for primary and secondary students especially, easy access for criticism from parents.

With concerns of spreading the virus in high-capacity courses and close-proximity dormitories, university students were, sooner or later, kicked off campus. Those who had relied on libraries, computer labs, and common areas at their schools for high-speed Internet connections had difficulty attending virtual class sessions and submitting assignments. Many students returned home to chaotic environments with distracting siblings also attempting to stream their education, logging into classes from closets, balconies, and their own beds. Any sense of privacy they may have enjoyed on campus was quickly eroded, as they were now juggling shared space and differing priorities across multiple age groups. Instructors, attempting to simulate in-person lectures and replicate more familiar routines, often required students to attend synchronous virtual classes at the times scheduled when students enrolled without fathoming the possibility that they would find themselves in these precarious living arrangements. Frequently, such practices were mandated as part of maintaining a sense of routine in the face of widespread disruption. Uncomfortable lecturing into a void of black rectangles, and ignorant of the invasion of privacy, lack of reliable Internet, and general sense of discomfort their students faced being on live video in potentially embarrassing living situations, many educators mandated that students attend these classes with their cameras on.

Coupled with these situations that were physically and logistically challenging during the pandemic were the incredibly difficult emotional situations students were handed. Many returned home to high-risk elderly family members who required their assistance, parents who were essential workers and needed the adult children to provide childcare for their younger siblings, not to mention students who fell into the higher risk categories themselves due to preexisting health conditions. Caretakers were particularly impacted, and as we write these words, those challenges have not ended: in a duoethenographic examination of motherhood during the pandemic, it was emphasized that "the gendered expectancy of mothers to adhere to their designated feminine-coded duties of care has impacted their ability to remain productive and active in the workforce" (Almanssori & Hillier, 2020, p. 175). Teachers, faculty, and students navigating these dual expectations faced impossible schedules and unfeasible logistics, often with few to no external support mechanisms in sight.

Still more students experienced the loss of one or more jobs, given that many of them held positions in lower-wage hospitality and tourism industries that bore the brunt of widespread mandates to close (St. Amour, 2020). The jobs that remained stable, however, were those of "essential workers" who were confronted with exposure to the potentially deadly virus, struggled to obtain personal protective equipment (PPE) that was in short supply, and were assigned additional duties of carrying out enhanced sanitation protocols. The category of essential also expanded in ways that highlighted inequities around the world, but particularly drew attention to the lack of safety nets for minimum wage workers around the world: a synthesis drawing on relevant studies around the world ultimately supported

> the view that precarious workers have suffered profoundly from COVID-19 and merit special attention. Many precarious workers have been undertaking work deemed essential to society during the pandemic yet they risk their own well-being, and sometimes their lives, for low pay and few employment rights.
> (McNamara et al., 2021)

Many students simultaneously occupied these positions of precarity in the workforce and in the classroom—and arguably, so did many teachers. An autoethnographic analysis of the experiences of contingent communication instructors emphasizes the intensity of the challenges facing adjuncts and others serving the needs of what is effectively the "gig economy" of higher education:

> As the campus shut down, we helplessly terraformed our living space to workspace and our relationships to time, place, and people along with it. While all types of academic appointees were affected by the pandemic, we assert that contract instructors were the least protected from the ravaging storm as ERT [emergency remote teaching] unleashed a series of technological, social, psychological, and material nightmares upon us.
> (Stewart et al., 2021, p. 402)

These problems of precarity in higher education are echoed in the precarity of K–12 educators, particularly in countries where educators are systematically undervalued and underpaid. The scale of the problem in the United States is growing: a National Education Association survey found 32% of respondents considering an early exit from the profession—not surprising given "teachers are paid as much as 20 percent less than other college-educated workers with similar experience" (Walker, 2021). In England, the Department of Education noted a decline in recruitment compared to expectation as the pandemic continued into 2021, with shortages across disciplines predicted—creating problems amplified by absences and illness (Weale & Adams, 2021). Already stressful positions were made much worse.

The pandemic emphasized what we already knew (but often ignore) about the disparity between disadvantaged students and those of privilege. Predictably, it was the students who were already excelling in school who struggled the least in the pivot to online, though one survey found that 40% of students lost a job, an internship, or had a job offer revoked during the pandemic (St. Amour, 2020). The survey revealed that those who were already exhausting their limited resources to keep up with their peers, however, were more likely to withdraw from courses or delay graduation:

> Lower-income students were 55 percent more likely to delay graduation than their higher-income peers. COVID-19 also nearly doubled the gap between higher-and lower-income students' expected GPAs. Nonwhite students were 70 percent more likely to change their majors due to the pandemic compared to their white peers, and first-generation students were 50 percent more likely to delay graduation than students who have college-educated parents.

Even students who enjoyed stable home lives, sufficient resources, and reliable support systems struggled with the restructuring of their existence and the curtailment of their social practices. Going from an active, multifaceted campus community or school to not being able to leave one's home was not an easy transition for many students. The loss of a substantial number of mechanisms for coping with stress, from gyms to concerts, intensified the new stress of a virus that was not yet understood even by experts and left a lot of students unable to perform their best academically. A review conducted synthesizing 36 studies across 11 countries during the pandemic's first wave noted: "there was consistency in findings across studies, particularly for mental health, with almost all studies documenting poorer mental health and well-being" (Viner et al., 2022).

Compounding these difficulties was the haphazard design of their newly online courses. Rather than thoughtfully designing a cultivated virtual experience for our students, the overnight shift to distanced instruction meant that for many courses, the portions of the syllabus that remained intact were those portions that could be quickly and easily replicated online—and understandably so, given the abrupt nature and short timeline of the required transition. In-person lecture attendance and participation requirements translated into mandatory Zoom session attendance. As teachers struggled to navigate new virtual learning platforms, student-centered classroom activities and games were mostly dropped. Without the ability to meet in person and with a lessening of synchronous class meetings, group assignments were also frequently eliminated from the revised syllabus. Any pre-pandemic prejudice against online instruction was able to be justified in this mass scramble; these quick adjustments were (valiant) attempts to rescue a fraction of the learning that had been slated for the semester: stop-gaps to prevent a total erosion of content mastery necessary for students' next steps in academia and beyond.

This work is not a critique of the many creative ways educators found to engage students online or of any solutions that emerged as feasible through the pandemic: it is completely unreasonable to hold that intensive labor (which often went undersupported and unrecognized) to scrutiny. Our interest in this section is particularly on the solutions that educational technology offers educators, and the ways that the solutions we've baked into our systems underserve students and educators. We assert that the pandemic and its massive, labor-intensive shift to online instruction highlighted the already existing issues with many ways in which gamification has been implemented in formal educational settings. We see this as a catalyst for examining the ways that gamification and game-based learning have been used in education thus far and how the pandemic might offer us motivation to rethink our relationship with these solutions.

Badges for all

One of the many ways that gamification manifests within traditional instruction is with the use of visual credentials representing the embroidered patches on the scout's uniform: a badging system. Examples of education-targeted badging systems abound, but one notable example is "Badgr." Marketed as a "digital credentialing solution," the platform evokes game achievement systems with promise like "No Achievement Is Too Small" (Badgr, 2022). The system is designed for LMS integration, working with Blackboard and Canvas. Badgr has been brought into the classroom across disciplines, with educators investigating it both as a tool for recognizing skillsets developed along the way in coursework and as a mechanism intended to motivate student engagement (Gogel et al., 2020). Institutions transitioning to the system have noted its ease of use during the pandemic as part of online migration, and also its value as a surveillance tool providing analytics on otherwise less-visible milestones (Helmandollar, 2020). Dylan Barth engages such badges more pragmatically, noting the particular value of Badgr in online learning as a mechanism for affirmation a student is on track with distributed requirements (Barth, 2020).

Clements et al. divide the current categories of badges into categories based on intent of recognition: skills, knowledge, social or life skills, participation, identity, and certification badges (Clements et al., 2020). Philosophically, Clements et al. point to the ideal role of the badges as a mechanism for rethinking educational structures:

> the emphasis that open badging gives to micro certification, rather than larger scale certificates such as degrees and diplomas, can open up possibilities for a re-organizing of learning systems, where learning can happen from one institution or many, at one time or over time, and in this way perhaps break free from the tyranny of the one semester, "X" credit hour system that artificially constrains many learning experiences. In this way, open badges and micro-credentials may be the key to unlocking the potential of MOOCs, online modules, and open courseware by providing a credentialing option for these open resources. In addition, open badges could provide the opportunity to break down barriers between informal and formal learning, and professional education and academic education.
>
> (p. 166)

This call for a reexamination of educational structures and institutional assumptions is one that will echo throughout this work, and indeed is the call to action behind many attempts at gamified learning: we offer this critique not to dismiss the work of educators trying to harness badges toward these ends of reflective and critical pedagogy, but rather to critique the role of structured models and systems in shaping those endeavors. The integration of badges into opt-in systems that exist outside of traditional grade structures or institutional models makes more sense than the additive measure that these badges often play in higher education: they do not replace traditional assessment, but instead add on top of it.

The shift to home education brought new thinking about badging: a team in Indonesia looked to non-digital badging as a solution to recommend to parents trying to mediate the challenges of remote learning, and noted that even without technology it had a potential for impact on enthusiasm (Zainuddin & Keumala, 2021). However, such strategies place a burden of game mediation on the abruptly pivoted home educator, and are unlikely to be sustainable. Similarly, educators seeking to adopt gamified class systems have noted that "a one-size-fits-all approach demotivates a part of the students to participate," suggesting the need "to design a gamified system by using a user-centered design process with special attention to personal differences in motivational cues" (van Roy & Zaman, 2015, p. 5). This type of study is a reminder that gamification is no quick solution to the educator's fundamental challenge of building an inclusive classroom: rather, it is a motivational system structured around assumptions that value competition and incentive models. A survey of empirical studies on gamification in education conducted in 2015 noted that while the practice was still growing, it appeared to be "sliding down into the 'trough of disillusionment,'" with a growing "number of studies with inconclusive or negative results" (Dicheva & Dichev, 2015, p. 1445). A similar survey conducted in 2020 of 14 studies continues to "support the conclusion that educational gamification has a potential impact on the academic performance, commitment, and motivation of students," but the depth and range of that impact remains questionable at best (Manzano-León et al., 2021, p. 1). Other educators have centered on the negative effects, and point out that some of the most popular design elements (including the ubiquitous "Leaderboard") can be the most consistently demotivating (Toda et al., 2018).

While digital badges have been discussed in the context of higher education for some time, a study of 700 employers on awareness of badging (conducted before and during the pandemic) noted that 97% of respondents reported being "unfamiliar with the concept of digital badges," suggesting gamification's reach has been more internal than external (Perkins & Pryor, 2021, p. 29). And yet this isn't the last time we'll be discussing badges in the context of the pandemic—the concept has been renewed by those advocating for credentialing on the blockchain (Chukowry et al., 2021), as we will critique further in Chapter 4.

On gamification

The pandemic and its hardships forced many of us to take stock of our priorities, providing many of us with a new perspective on what really matters in life. We would do well to pause and take time to rejuvenate ourselves from the physical, mental, and emotional tolls that the 18+ months of pandemic survival have taken. As we return to whatever version of instruction our institutions deem "normal," the authors find themselves reflecting on the sudden conversions that took place, the resilience we saw from our students and colleagues, and the challenges that this once-a-century experience presented to humanity. It is from this vantage point that we work to assess what education has become and where it can—and should—go from here.

As we prepare for future semesters that might regain some semblance of "more normal" teaching and learning situations, we would be negligent to push forward without taking time to pause and refocus. What is our goal as educators? Which aspects of education are "essential," and which are simply there to fill time or keep students occupied? Are we teaching students what they need to learn, or are we just regurgitating the same stale "facts" we were fed as students? The calls to revolutionize education for modern times have been around for decades—and yet we continue to design our courses in largely the same way they have been run for centuries. This work is our attempt to do this reflecting and refocusing for game-based learning; why should we bother to do the work of incorporating games and playfulness into our lessons?

To reevaluate course emphases and classroom techniques, it is helpful to understand the full spectrum of game-based learning. A large part of this—the part that, in our opinion, has been misinterpreted and misapplied—is gamification. Problematically, this term is often conflated with well-designed game-based learning, frequently appearing in education conferences across fields as a positive descriptor of playful learning design. Gamification is commonly defined in the literature as "using game design elements in non-game contexts" (Deterding et al., 2011, p. 9), which is notably broad and includes a wide range of fragments of games applied intentionally (or not!) to an even wider range of contexts. The educational application of gamification, specifically the one that has been monetized and sold to well-meaning educators and administrators, is the form of gamification that is the focus of our critique here. This narrowed idea of gamification, then, we define as the use of game elements (such as rewards systems) applied superficially to existing educational tasks. Chapter 2 discusses some of these examples such as *Jeopardy!* and their shortcomings in more depth, but the takeaway lesson is if it could also be a worksheet, it probably isn't a well-designed educational game.

Gamification emerged in the scene in part as a response to Clayton Christensen et al.'s (2008) *Disrupting Class*—a seductive call to action meant to persuade educators to leverage technology to teach beyond the multiple-choice test by recentering education around the student. Unfortunately, it seems as though the main thing that many decision-makers chose to take away from this work was that technology in any form would improve learning by default—a successor to the historical approaches of reinforcement emphasized by Skinner's behavioralist approaches to learning and those of his successors (Watters, 2021, p. 19). We can particularly see the trail from Skinner to gamification in the focus on reward: in both instances, no pedagogical soundness for lasting learning and motivation holds. However, our experience with educational technology has resoundingly been that no soundness is required to profit from the same assumptions. And Silicon Valley has proved an attentive successor to earlier profiteers of education in the design of teaching machines, as Audrey Watters chronicles:

> as Silicon Valley has turned its attention to education reform, it has designed new teaching machines for "personalized learning" ... however, with the enhanced data extraction and analytical capabilities of modern computing, today's new teaching machines now claim to know more about each student, claim to be able to respond more rapidly, more intelligently, more efficiently than a human teacher or even a human tutor could. What we find in personalization today is not merely an outgrowth of some new sociopolitical system called surveillance capitalism; rather personalization is the pinnacle of a long-running dream of education technology.
>
> (Watters, 2021, p. 255)

Silicon Valley's iteration of "teaching machines" have been complicated by an assumption of digital centricity surrounding the most recent generations of students. The belief that all students born in the 1990s and beyond were "digital natives" and therefore adept at all things technology-related is in part what drove the gamification push in the early 2010s. The media expounded on how students were all somehow innately tech-savvy purely on account of their birth year and blamed students' educational failings on schools not catering to learners' video game-centric interests. Some administrations and manufacturers of educational content chose to blindly follow these broad claims, ignoring the fact that there is no such thing as innate ability to master any technology, and the ability to access technology is greatly dependent on the privilege of any given child's family. Much of this proved problematic, with one-to-one device initiatives rolling out into schools where teachers were underprepared to use the tools meaningfully and school Internet and power infrastructures incapable of supporting the technology without costly renovations (Weston & Bain, 2010). Such thinking also ignored the reality that the consumption of digital content is very different from the making and understanding of the digital—a challenge we revisit in Chapter 5, through the lens of critical making.

At the same time that technology was going to save education, video games were emerging as a widely popular pastime for children and adults alike. Educators such as James Paul Gee (2004) looked with envy at the ways players engaged with game content and were motivated to continue playing—and, like with all new technologies, many were quick to point to the perils of logging countless hours in front of a screen role-playing violent characters (such as Anderson & Dill, 2000). Despite this fretting, youth and adults of all genders continued to be drawn to games. Many educators sought ways to capitalize on the genre. Meticulous studies were conducted to determine which components of video games were doing the motivating and engagement work, with many of them pointing to the complex ways that video games were able to reward players for effort and persistence. Games showered players with points, trophies, badges, weapon upgrades, health points, extra lives, and the unlocking of new game areas to explore. Behavioral psychologists pointed to these rewards systems as "addictive" and while some continued to seek bans or limits on game playing (Bean et al., 2017), others worked to apply these isolated elements to the things they were already doing in class.

Textbook companies and other corporations seized this trend as a way to artificially incorporate game elements into existing content: cost-effective but educationally hollow and ineffective. In short, corporations gave "gamification" a bad name. The draw of games is, we argue, in part because games are interdisciplinary: most modern games incorporate a variety of skills and knowledge—even the rather simple mechanics of FPS (first-person shooter) games require players to use different strategies in different situations. The issue we have with most gamification attempts in education is the way that they seem to inject isolated elements from these given rich, multifaceted digital worlds into existing rote tasks. They return us to the Skinner box: systems of artificial motivation, but no meaningful play.

It should be noted that this application of rewards systems into mundane exercises can have some beneficial outcomes. One example is the i-Ready platform (*I-Ready*, 2021) adopted widely by K-12 schools in the United States at the time of writing. This platform is, at its base, a series of animated multiple-choice questions; digital worksheets intended to engage students in rote practice of isolated reading and math problems. Discussed elsewhere (Reich, 2020), this platform does the one thing it is supposed to do: improve standardized test scores. In this case, because the multiple-choice questions of standardized test scores in the United States are so decontextualized, the isolated rote practice provided by the i-Ready system is effective for this one (highly valued by policymakers) assessment metric.

The problem with gamification used in this superficial way, however, is that truly engaging games are complete ecosystems of goals, challenges, puzzles, and—yes—rewards and punishments, but they all work together to create a player experience that is far more than the sum of its parts. The immersion and flow are lost when elements are used in isolation; just as a teacher seeking to isolate what makes poetry compelling would be remiss to claim that all writing could be modified to include rhythm and rhyme and suddenly become as moving as poetry (even this metaphor is reductive and ignores the countless poems that do not contain rhythm and/or rhyming patterns). As has been expressed before, adding chocolate does not make broccoli any more palatable; it ruins the dish entirely.

Looking back to the popularization of gamification, with technology developing and becoming more obtainable, and with the dissection of games into their mechanics and elemental parts, many in the field of education believed they had discovered the secret recipe for student engagement. Educators far and wide set out to implement points systems in their own classrooms, apparently forgetting that they had already been doing so for decades. Complex rewards systems were already in place, at least in K–12 classrooms, through grades, daily behavior scores, Accelerated Reader points, and more—often with a currency that could be spent on novelty erasers and other trinkets in a class store. Literal badges and ribbons are regularly issued to students during honors assemblies for achievements in grade point averages, sports, clubs, and scholarships. Many local newspapers print leaderboards for high schools, under the heading of "honor roll," and the highest academic achievers win money in the form of scholarships. Pupils who fail to meet expectations are punished with detention, retained a grade level, enrolled in remedial courses (often viewed as a punishment—at least by the students forced to complete the additional coursework), or simply not awarded a diploma. Formal schooling has always emphasized achievement, rewarding and punishing learners with an arsenal of incentives and penalties: as educators who grew up with Pizza Hut reading rewards programs, we are not immune to their appeal, but note that such structures are part of the commercialization of schools: as Alex Molnar critiqued in noting the impact of such incentive programs, the ultimate goal is to promote consumption (Molnar, 2000).

Further, play is commonly thought of as the opposite of work, which is one reason many are hesitant to include games and play in postsecondary instruction. Game-based learning is frequently dismissed by university professors as not odious and therefore not rigorous. At the postsecondary level, gamification is seen only in moderation, often taking on more "serious" forms of simulations, exam preparation, and comprehension checks. Highlighting the distinction between game-based learning and gamification in 2016, Wiggins found that although the term "gamification" was not ubiquitously familiar to communications faculty in higher education institutions across Arkansas in the United States, many faculty were already employing game-based elements in their instructional activities, with 83% of respondents reporting they used games or simulations (27% digital and 56% non-digital) in their classrooms. Using Kapp's 2012 list of gamification strategies—levels, points, badges, feedback, storytelling, multiple attempts, goals, rules, leaderboards, sandbox, and time limits—Wiggins defined these on the survey in "educational contexts" rather than games. The leaderboard, for example, was defined on the survey as "a public display of student performance to motivate students to compete with one another to be at the top of the leaderboard" (Wiggins, 2016, p. 22). Given the large percentages of these elements that respondents indicated they used, Wiggins concluded that gamification was in fact "a re-working of previous traditional instructional strategies" (27). The use of game-design-specific jargon, Wiggins reasons, works to decontextualize these common classroom activities and made them seem foreign and new to even veteran instructors.

Much of gamification follows behavioralist learning theory. In *Punished by Rewards*, Alfie Kohn (1999) describes the problem with behaviorism: the idea that human behavior can be influenced by rewards and punishments. The originator of behavioral learning theory, psychologist B.F. Skinner (1958), monitored the behaviors of pigeons and rats to discover that they could be motivated to conduct or refrain from specific behaviors through punitive and reinforcing feedback, the most effective balance of which he termed operant conditioning. Kohn and a number of behavioral and educational psychologists after Skinner question the applicability of Skinner's research on animals to humans, leading to the more widely held belief that humans should be guided to construct their own meanings in the world (constructivist theory) or presented with increasingly complicated and difficult educational tasks in order to learn effectively (cognitivist theory) (Chalmers & Hunt, 2013). Therefore, using points, badges, and punishments in gamification views learning as a behavior, and human learners as animals whose behavior can be controlled or guided to a desired performance: selecting the correct answers on the class assessment. Chapter 2 will discuss the issues with these games in more depth.

Jesse Stommel's provocation "What if we didn't grade?" is a similar condemnation of the underlying assumptions of gamification: that is, both grades and gamification systems tend to assume that the best way to incentivize learning is to measure it (Stommel, 2020). He offers several follow-up questions encouraging educators to rethink the role of evaluation:

> Why do we grade? How does it feel to be graded? What do we want grading to do (or not do) in our classes (whether as students or teachers)?
> What do letter grades mean? Do they have any intrinsic meaning, or is the value purely extrinsic? Does assessment mean differently when it is formative rather than summative?

This might seem an odd topic to consider in a chapter on gamification, but given the similarities outlined above, a call to rethink our relationship with the structures of games must inherently come with reflection on how we have internalized practices of ranking and evaluation across the board. At best, grades indicate how much value the instructor places on any given aspect of the course, with rubrics guiding students' efforts to successful completion of meaningful learning tasks. At worst, they micromanage exploration and extinguish curiosity. What functions are grades performing in each of our courses? Similar scrutiny should be carried out on our use of games and gamification in the classroom: what do we badge, and why? How does it feel to be left out, or at the bottom of the leaderboard? What behaviors are we incentivizing, and what are we ignoring?

Student engagement as commodity

The pandemic and its online shift highlighted the shortcomings and failures of many gamification practices in part because of the way many companies in the education industry created and marketed one-size-fits-all student engagement packages. Globally, the gamification market was valued at US$5.5 billion in 2018 (Hurix, 2019), its value had doubled by 2020 to US$10.19 million (*Gamification Market Size, Trends*, 2021). The draw of this lucrative and rapidly growing sector is understandably enticing, but the commercialization of education is never without complications or strings attached. Both K–12 and higher education institutions around the world are heavily involved in ecosystems exploiting students as a captive audience.

Clearly, the commodification of gamification had begun prior to the pandemic. Despite the efforts of the MacArthur Foundation and Mozilla Open Badges to create platforms for open-source digital badging systems in 2011, textbook company Pearson filed two patents for badges for their proprietary online credentialing system Acclaim (later sold to Credly) (Young, 2019). The patents were granted in 2019, raising concerns about how something that had been in existence for so long could be patented and the implications for the future of open-source badging systems (Belshaw, 2019). Given the relative each with which textbook-driven systems can be implemented by faculty—at high cost to students—such trends are particularly alarming, and decidedly counter to the calls for more emphasis on access and open educational resources (OER) alongside pandemic library disruptions. A report documenting OER initiatives from Greece, Italy, Poland, Uruguay, and Brazil demonstrates the international impact of moves away from expensive textbooks: the OER model provides "resilience to educational systems" (Szczepaniak et al., 2020).

In February of 2021, about a year into the pandemic, after a semester of "hy-flex" (hybrid and flexible) modalities that attempted to provide the "university experience" to students in the modality required at whatever the state of the pandemic, Nearpod was purchased by Renaissance Learning for $650 million (Wan, 2021). Nearpod promises gamification activities and interactive videos along with integration with LMS systems, presentation and collaboration platforms, and "flex between classroom, distance learning, or hybrid" (*Nearpod*, 2021). This enticing all-in-one platform for all modalities of teaching certainly arrived on the market with excellent timing. The gamification elements advertised on the Nearpod website are *Time to Climb* (multiple-choice with student avatars racing to "climb" a mountain by answering correctly), *Matching Pairs* (word–image pairs), *Draw It* (a whiteboard where teachers and students annotate images like graphs by highlighting and adding images), and *Drag & Drop* (dragging images into category columns). These activities are content-agnostic, allowing for use over a wide variety of classrooms levels and course content, but they are at their base the same mundane worksheet activities students recognize as busywork.

Nearpod's website touts an "independent research" study to claim that using Nearpod with live instruction "prevents digital distraction and multitasking" (*Nearpod—How Nearpod Contributes to Better Learning Outcomes*, 2021). Arguably, the platform prevents digital distractions by providing students with digital distractions—but at least they are on the topic of the class. Nearpod has found the lucrative market of student engagement and is designing a plethora of surface learning exercises under the guise of games and interaction. After any sense of novelty wanes, students will no doubt see these "engagement activities" for what they are: digital babysitters of attention just like the paper worksheets that came before them. Making students jump through hoops with exercises, clickers, and interactive "games" that do not invoke deep learning robs them of their autonomy, curiosity, and will to learn. In primary and secondary grades, where the content mandated by legislators must be "covered," these gamification practices are no doubt a means to that specific end, but higher education should strive for loftier goals.

During the pandemic, especially in the early stages of sudden lockdowns and rapid pivoting to fully online instruction, much virtual instruction was hastily composed. As teachers swapped out carefully planned, in-person activities for online ones, much careful instructional design understandably went out the window. Eager for anything to ease the transition and engage students in the course (with some instructors desperate for students to turn their video on so they could speak to a person and not a screen full of black boxes with white names), many turned to educational technology companies and their engagement packages full of Zoom polls, PowerPoint quizzes, and other worksheet-style attention babysitters. This was pandemic pedagogy, and it was understandable; however, it should not become standard online pedagogy.

The tech startup model

Another platform identified as a "major player" in the gamification market is Cognizant (*Gamification Market Size, Trends*, 2021). Cognizant boasts a range of clients in education; their website categorizes them into three groups: education providers, education publishers, and testing/assessment providers. Cognizant also publishes a blog on their website with a variety of digital education topics. One in particular has the troubling title, "To Reimagine the Student Experience, Think Like a Tech Company" (Nerurkar, 2021). Targeted at higher-ed administrators, the article encourages them to "reimagine the college experience and make the transition to digital learning," using the perspective of a technology startup. The author's advice includes ushering in a culture change that views the students as consumers and therefore the first priority, be willing to take risks, and to empower the CIO make investments because "industry disruption will only accelerate." Additional suggestions include reassessing marketing strategies and adopt a flexible educational technology platform.

Although there is some sound advice encapsulated within this article, the business model of technology companies described here and used by many of current organizations includes the connotation of Facebook's motto to "move fast and break things" (Taneja, 2019) or the motto that Google used before somewhat ominously dropping it in 2018: "don't be evil" (Conger, 2018). The technology company metaphor is problematic because of the intense sexist (Hernandez, 2021), racist (Gray, 2020), and otherwise questionable practices (Birnbaum, 2020) commonly occurring at so many high-profile companies. The fact is that education should not be modeled after such historically exclusionary entities. We certainly don't want to recklessly move forward and "break things" – we seek carefully crafted learning experiences – and education should actively work toward the greater good, rather than passively not being evil (or actively doing "evil" things, which is what the removal of the motto signaled to some).

The field of game studies has worked to define the terms game, play, and even fun. An often-cited definition of "game" is "a system in which players engage in artificial conflict, defined by rules, that results in a quantifiable outcome" (Salen & Zimmerman, 2003, p. 80). Finally, no discussion of games, play, or gamification is truly complete without including mention of Huizinga's (1955) magic circle—a concept Salen and Zimmerman made ubiquitous thanks to its mention in their frequently used game design text. The idea that the area of play, as defined by the players, creates a sort of temporary parallel world, where societal norms and cultural conventions can be ignored and replaced with new, often silly or illogical ones for the sake of the game: players can embody fictional characters, alternate personalities, or not; an arbitrary goal is set with specific guidelines for achieving that goal that all players agree upon to not transgress. The concept of the "magic circle" has since been redefined and challenged, particularly because it relies upon a distinction between "real" and "virtual" that has proven decidedly unhelpful as games and play have evolved (Lehdonvirta, 2010). Certainly, pandemic play has reemphasized the futility of that distinction, as we will consider further in Chapter 3.

Aside from its connection with technology and corporations, another problem with the idea and application of "gamification" is the term's broad definition. Nieto-Escamez and Roldán-Tapia (2021) assert that web-based quizzes in and of themselves are "one of the simplest ways to gamify teaching" (p. 2). The definition Nieto-Escamez and Roldán-Tapia use to define gamification is broad and reveals a problematic misunderstanding of games that drives the misapplication of gamification, and they go through a number of theories from self-determination theory (which they define as including any one of the three psychological needs of autonomy, relatedness, or competence), to goal-setting theory, to flow theory. Huang and Hew (2018) conclude that gamification includes the use of any of these elements in an educational setting, asserting that these individual elements create gamification.

Goal-setting theory, as a parameter of gamification, is defined as including a challenge or objective, a way to measure progress toward the objective, feedback about performance, levels of achievement, and a sense of competition (Huang & Hew, 2018; Landers, 2014; Latham & Locke, 2007). Defining gamification using goal-setting theory alone results in the ability to claim that most traditional courses are in fact forms of gamification. All educators traditionally strive to include learning objectives, measurements of student progress in the form of assignments and assessments, graded indications of achievement levels, and the classic competition for top of the class, valedictorian, honor roll, etc. Education has always had badges (and pageantry)—gamification merely amplifies existing tendencies.

Looking at the idea of flow, which we discuss and critique in greater detail in Chapter 2, Huang and Hew (2018) include a sense of flow in their gamification definition. The elements Huang and Hew list as creating the feeling of flow are clear goals, timely feedback, achievement indicators, and a balance of student goals, ability, and sense that the activity is important. While flow is an oversimplified lens for understanding play, it is most helpful here for acknowledging how easily it can be disrupted. Most classes structure feedback and a sense of progression in the form of learning objectives, instructor comments, and grades: those mechanisms had to be reimagined rapidly during the pandemic, and their sustainability was decidedly conditional on instructor and student status. The persuasion of value at a moment of massive fear, anxiety, and suffering is even harder to achieve—and one that required more care and consideration to meet students in the moment. As Deborah Cohan reflects in her essay on letting go in pandemic pedagogy: "a crisis should not prompt us to add more; it should encourage us to distill things to an essence and to model for students how and what to prioritize"—a lesson we can and should take forward (Cohan, 2020, p. 25).

To summarize, the term gamification basically indicates the tacking on of superficial game-adjacent elements to existing traditional classroom activities or renaming those activities so that the activities *sound like* they are games or game-related. Gamification ultimately becomes synonymous with existing instructional frameworks in formal educational systems and has been around under other names for a long time in all levels of education, pointing to a deeper issue. Perhaps the problem with gamification is it is not the specific uses of these behavioral elements to superficially encourage learning but rather the structure of formal education in which it finds itself embedded. We assert that both are problematic. Gamification emphasizes the main issue of formal education: it is (still) no longer suitable for the students nor the needs of this century. Despite repeated calls for overhauling or disrupting schooling, the fact remains that the industrial assembly-line model of education still applies to what takes place in most classrooms today. Will technology fix everything? Definitely not. Will reinforcing systems of competition, reward, and repetition craft the space for reflection and care we most need in our classrooms going forward? Certainly not.

Playful and gameful learning can help take the sting and the stigma out of what has been done to education over the decades (and perhaps what has been done as a result of the overpopularizing of "gamification," given the term's ubiquitous use). We can and should inspect the ways we are teaching and the skills we are emphasizing, and whether or not we can and should change any of those. We can modify the style of the traditional lecture course from memorization of facts to a mode that fosters curiosity and exploration. We can shift the focus from a rigid lecture-and-regurgitate to scaffolding and coaching. Many people are already doing this in innovative, if isolated, ways. In the rest of this book, we outline additional issues with specific instances of gamification and different styles of game-based learning. We inspect the complex problems we face when we do bring games into the classroom, the ways in which learning can be simultaneously effective and playful (if not always "fun"), and why we think game-based learning—despite all of this—is worth doing.

Un-gamifying education

The greatest challenge of crafting playful learning environments prior to the pandemic was in undoing the damage caused by the corporate, educational technology-driven mechanisms of gamification. The pandemic has added another layer:

the need to reshape our relationship to that very definition of "play," and the assumptions of student needs encoded in its mechanisms. The necessary over-reliance of educators on the mechanisms of learning management systems during remote pivots has likely amplified that harm, as the platforms of online education became a too prominent force in the collective lives of educators and students. Frustration and fatigue on the part of students and faculty across learning environments has only begun to be documented: as we are closing our writing, survey-driven evaluations are starting to be published and discussed, with decidedly mixed results.

Indeed, many in the field of online learning have already raised concerns that the haphazard, remote instruction of the pandemic has forever damaged the reputation of distance learning. Unicef launched the #ReopenSchools campaign, asserting that "The cost of school closures on students' learning, health and well-being has been devastating" (*#ReopenSchools*, 2022). Worldwide, many schools (about a third, according to Unicef) were unable to provide remote learning, and many schools provided safety and food to primary and secondary students, so these claims are not without merit. But the cry to reopen schools because in-person learning is inherently superior to online learning has bled into the post-secondary realm where online instructional design has been a field of study and continued improvement for several decades now.

The design of effective online instruction is a field of study with robust, scholarly discussions of how to best engage students in quality instruction and meaningful learning activities. Many in this field are concerned that students will forever equate all online learning opportunities with the instant pivot to virtual instruction during the pandemic. These suddenly distant courses were created hastily—some of them literally overnight—as a necessity to the sudden widespread school closures. The *Teaching Online Podcast* (TOP-cast) even dedicated several episodes to the misconceptions of online learning, including episode 87 (released April 5, 2021), "Repairing Our Reputation Post-COVID;" episode 89 (released May 17, 2021), "Seven Slogans to Save Online Learning;" and episode 98 (released September 20, 2021), "'I Don't Ever Want to Do [Online] Again!'" These calls to restore or retain positive perceptions of online learning programs demonstrate the reputational damage many stakeholders in distant learning feel that the rapidly converted online courses have done to the field. Such discussions often point to underprepared educators: a study conducted on pivot practices and success in Spain noted that it was not the technology but the instructors' knowledge of and attitudes toward the technology that seemed to correlate with student success (Iglesias-Pradas et al., 2021).

However, our critique of gamification (and, more broadly, the assumptions underlying educational technology design for online education) highlights a greater tension between educators and their tools. A survey conducted as part of a dissertation at our own institution noted that those platforms (including Canvas, which we teach with) became an additional and unwelcome source of stress during pandemic teaching, thanks in part to their rigid structures and assumptions about what courses should look like, and what instructors need to know to run them (Kugelmann, 2021). The shift to online learning was particularly unintuitive for those used to the most active, dynamic classrooms: while traditional learning structures are easy to reproduce in learning management systems (and in gamification), educators seeking something more would have to work harder to create spaces for creativity and play within the learning management box.

References

Almanssori, S., & Hillier, K. M. (2020). Frontline workers from home: A feminist duoethnographic inquiry of mothering, teaching, and academia during the initial stages of the COVID-19 pandemic. *Journal of the Motherhood/Initiative for Research and Community Involvement Double Issue, 11*(2), 171–188.

Anderson, C. A., & Dill, K. E. (2000). Video games and aggressive thoughts, feelings, and behavior in the laboratory and in life. *Journal of Personality and Social Psychology, 78*(4), 772–790. https://doi.org/10.1037/0022-3514.78.4.772.

Badgr. (2022). *Badgr—Features and pricing*. Badgr. https://info.badgr.com/features-and-pricing.html.

Barth, D. (2020). Seven ways of engaging the online learner to develop self-regulated learning skills. *Journal of Teaching and Learning with Technology, 9*(1), 19–29.

Bean, A. M., Rune, K. L., van Rooij, A. J., & Ferguson, C. J. (2017). Video game addiction: The push to pathologize video games. *Professional Psychology: Research and Practice, 48*(5), 378–389. https://doi.org/DOI:10.1037/pro0000150.

Belshaw, D. (2019, March 13). What we need is an Open Badges community renaissance, free of IMS involvement | Open Thinkering. *Open Thinkering*. https://dougbelshaw.com/blog/2019/03/13/open-badges-community/.

Birnbaum, E. (2020, July 1). *A wall of silence holding back racial progress in tech: NDAs*. Protocol — The People, Power and Politics of Tech. https://www.protocol.com/nda-racism-equality-diversity-tech.

Bruk, D. (2020, March 31). *12 funny quarantine videos of people getting creative in isolation*. Best Life. https://bestlifeonline.com/funny-quarantine-videos/.

Chalmers, D., & Hunt, L. (2013). *University teaching in focus: A learning-centred approach*. Routledge.

Christensen, C., Johnson, C. W., & Horn, M. B. (2008). *Disrupting class: How disruptive innovation will change the way the world learns* (1st ed.). McGraw-Hill.

Chukowry, V., Nanuck, G., & Sungkur, R. K. (2021). The future of continuous learning– Digital badge and microcredential system using blockchain. *Global Transitions Proceedings, 2*(2), 355–361. https://doi.org/10.1016/j.gltp.2021.08.026.

Clements, K., West, R. E., & Hunsaker, E. (2020). Getting started with open badges and open microcredentials. *International Review of Research in Open and Distributed Learning, 21*(1), 154–172. https://doi.org/10.19173/irrodl.v21i1.4529.

Cohan, D. J. (2020). Rethinking what we value: Pandemic teaching and the art of letting go. In J. M. Ryan (Ed.), *COVID-19 volume II: Social consequences and cultural adaptations: Vol. II* (pp. 23–30). Routledge.

Conger, K. (2018, May 18). *Google removes "Don't Be Evil" clause from its code of conduct*. Gizmodo. https://gizmodo.com/google-removes-nearly-all-mentions-of-dont-be-evil-from-1826153393.

Deterding, S., Dixon, D., Khaled, R., & Nacke, L. (2011). From game design elements to gamefulness: Defining "gamification." *Proceedings of the 15th international academic*

MindTrek conference: Envisioning future media environments (pp. 9–15). https://doi.org/10.1145/2181037.2181040.
Dicheva, D., & Dichev, C. (2015). Gamification in education: Where are we in 2015? 1445–1454. https://www.learntechlib.org/primary/p/152186/.
Gamification Market Size, Trends. (2021). Industry research report 2021 to 2026 With COVID impact. Mordor Intelligence. https://www.mordorintelligence.com/industry-reports/gamification-market.
Gamification Services: Things you Must Know Before you Opt for. (2019, April 17). *Hurix Digital*. https://www.hurix.com/selecting-gamification-services/
Gee, J. P. (2004). *What video games have to teach us about learning and literacy*. Palgrave Macmillan.
Gogel, D., Eikenaar, J. H., & Rajabi, P. (2020). Badging for accreditation: Electronic credentialing in the undergraduate curriculum. *Proceedings of the Canadian Engineering Education Association (CEEA)*. https://doi.org/10.24908/pceea.vi0.14193.
Gray, K. L. (2020). *Intersectional tech: Black users in digital gaming*. LSU Press.
Helmandollar, M. S. (2020). Meeting students where they are: Implementing canvas for successful student outreach. *Inquiry*, *23*(1). https://eric.ed.gov/?id=EJ1265811.
Hernandez, J. (2021, July 22). *California sues gaming giant Activision Blizzard over unequal pay, sexual harassment*. NPR. https://www.npr.org/2021/07/22/1019293032/activision-blizzard-lawsuit-unequal-pay-sexual-harassment-video-games.
Huang, B., & Hew, K. F. (2018). Implementing a theory-driven gamification model in higher education flipped courses: Effects on out-of-class activity completion and quality of artifacts. *Computers and Education*, *125*, 254–272. https://doi.org/10.1016/j.compedu.2018.06.018.
Huizinga, J. (1955). *Homo ludens: A study of the play-element in culture*. Beacon Press.
Iglesias-Pradas, S., Hernández-García, Á., Chaparro-Peláez, J., & Prieto, J. L. (2021). Emergency remote teaching and students' academic performance in higher education during the COVID-19 pandemic: A case study. *Computers in Human Behavior*, *119*, 106713. https://doi.org/10.1016/j.chb.2021.106713.
I-Ready. (2021). https://www.curriculumassociates.com/products/i-ready.
Kapp, K. M. (2012). *The gamification of learning and instruction: Game-based methods and strategies for training and education*. John Wiley & Sons.
Kohn, A. (1999). *Punished by rewards: The trouble with gold stars, incentive plans, A's, praise, and other bribes* (2nd ed.). Mariner Books.
Kugelmann, C. (2021). *Canvas course design and the effects on faculty workload and stress during COVID-19* [Texts & Technology PhD, University of Central Florida]. https://stars.library.ucf.edu/etd2020/891.
Landers, R. N. (2014). Developing a theory of gamified learning: Linking serious games and gamification of learning. *Simulation and Gaming*, *45*(6), 752–768. https://doi.org/10.1177/1046878114563660.
Latham, G. P., & Locke, E. A. (2007). New developments in and directions for goal-setting research. *European Psychologist*, *12*(4), 290–300. https://doi.org/10.1027/1016-9040.12.4.290.
Lehdonvirta, V. (2010). Virtual worlds don't exist: Questioning the dichotomous approach in MMO studies. *Game Studies*, *10*(1). http://gamestudies.org/1001/articles/lehdonvirta.
Manzano-León, A., Camacho-Lazarraga, P., Guerrero, M. A., Guerrero-Puerta, L., Aguilar-Parra, J. M., Trigueros, R., & Alias, A. (2021). Between level up and game over: A systematic literature review of gamification in education. *Sustainability*, *13*(4), 1–14. https://doi.org/10.3390/su13042247.

Mcleod, S. (2020, December 29). *Maslow's hierarchy of needs*. Simply Psychology. https://www.simplypsychology.org/maslow.html.

McNamara, C. L., McKee, M., & Stuckler, D. (2021). Precarious employment and health in the context of COVID-19: A rapid scoping umbrella review. *European Journal of Public Health*, *31*(Supplement_4), iv40–iv49. https://doi.org/10.1093/eurpub/ckab159.

Molnar, A. (2000). Looking for funds in all the wrong places. *Principal*, *5*.

Nearpod: You'll wonder how you taught without it. (2021). http://nearpod.com.

Nearpod—How Nearpod contributes to better learning outcomes. (2021). https://nearpod.com/independent-research-from-dakota-state-university-about-nearpod.

Nerurkar, K. (2021, July 16). *To reimagine the student experience, think like a tech company*. Digitally Cognizant. https://digitally.cognizant.com/to-reimagine-the-student-experience-think-like-a-tech-company-codex6732.

Nieto-Escamez, F. A., & Roldán-Tapia, M. D. (2021). Gamification as online teaching strategy during COVID-19: A mini-review. *Frontiers in Psychology*, *0*. https://doi.org/10.3389/fpsyg.2021.648552.

Perkins, J., & Pryor, M. (2021). Digital badges: Pinning down employer challenges. *Journal of Teaching and Learning for Graduate Employability*, *12*(1), 24–38. https://doi.org/10.21153/jtlge2021vol12no1art1027.

Reich, J. (2020). *Failure to disrupt: Why technology alone can't transform education*. Harvard University Press.

#ReopenSchools. (2022). https://www.unicef.org/coronavirus/reopen-schools.

Salen, K., & Zimmerman, E. (2003). *Rules of play: Game design fundamentals*. The MIT Press.

Skinner, B. F. (1958). Reinforcement today. *American Psychologist*, *13*(3), 94–99. https://doi.org/10.1037/h0049039.

St. Amour, M. (2020, June 23). *Report: COVID-19 has hurt college students | Inside Higher Ed*. Inside Higher Ed. https://www.insidehighered.com/quicktakes/2020/06/23/report-covid-19-has-hurt-college-students.

Stewart, N. K., Rahman, A., Adams, P. R., & Hughes, J. (2021). Same storm, different nightmares: Emergency remote teaching by contingent communication instructors during the pandemic. *Communication Education*, *70*(4), 402–420. https://doi.org/10.1080/03634523.2021.1948084.

Stommel, J. (2020, March 3). *Ungrading: A bibliography*. Jesse Stommel. https://www.jessestommel.com/ungrading-a-bibliography/.

Szczepaniak, K., Biernat, M., Mirecka, M., Tarkowski, A., Panagiotou, N., Lazou, C., Uggeri, M., Rodés Paragarino, V., Díaz Charquero, P., Aquino Ribeiro, R., Śliwowski, K., & Piątek, T. (2020). Open education as a game changer – Stories from the pandemic. *Open Education Policy Network*. http://repositorio.cfe.edu.uy/handle/123456789/1139.

Taneja, H. (2019, January 22). The era of "move fast and break things" is over. *Harvard Business Review*. https://hbr.org/2019/01/the-era-of-move-fast-and-break-things-is-over.

Toda, A. M., Valle, P. H. D., & Isotani, S. (2018). The dark side of gamification: An overview of negative effects of gamification in education. In A. I. Cristea, I. I. Bittencourt & F. Lima (Eds.), *Higher education for all. From challenges to novel technology-enhanced solutions* (pp. 143–156). Springer International Publishing. https://doi.org/10.1007/978-3-319-97934-2_9.

van Roy, R., & Zaman, B. (2015, October 4). The inclusion or exclusion of teaching staff in a gamified system: An example of the need to personalize (workshop paper). *CHI Play '15 Workshop*. London, Great-Britain.

Viner, R., Russell, S., Saulle, R., Croker, H., Stansfield, C., Packer, J., Nicholls, D., Goddings, A.-L., Bonell, C., Hudson, L., Hope, S., Ward, J., Schwalbe, N., Morgan, A., & Minozzi, S. (2022). School closures during social lockdown and mental health, health behaviors, and well-being among children and adolescents during the first COVID-19 wave: A systematic review. *JAMA Pediatrics*. https://doi.org/10.1001/jamapediatrics.2021.5840.

Walker, T. (2021, June 17). *Educators ready for fall, but a teacher shortage looms*. National Education Association. https://www.nea.org/advocating-for-change/new-from-nea/educators-ready-fall-teacher-shortage-looms.

Wan, T. (2021, February 19). Renaissance learning to acquire nearpod in blockbuster $650M all-cash deal. *EdSurge news*. https://www.edsurge.com/news/2021-02-19-renaissance-learning-to-acquire-nearpod-in-blockbuster-650m-all-cash-deal.

Wanshel, E. (2020, March 23). *Just A few extremely funny ways people are passing the time in quarantine*. HuffPost. https://www.huffpost.com/entry/funny-quarantine-videos-coronavirus-social-distancing_n_5e750067c5b6eab77947b614.

Watters, A. (2021). *Teaching machines: The history of personalized learning*. MIT Press.

Weale, S., & Adams, R. (2021, December 3). Staff absences having 'massive impact' on pupils in England say head teachers. *The Guardian*. https://www.theguardian.com/education/2021/dec/03/staff-absences-having-massive-impact-on-pupils-in-england-say-head-teachers.

Weston, M. E., & Bain, A. (2010). The end of techno-critique: The naked truth about 1:1 laptop initiatives and educational change. *Journal of Technology, Learning, and Assessment, 9*(6). https://eric.ed.gov/?id=EJ873680.

Wiggins, B. E. (2016). An overview and study on the use of games, simulations, and gamification in higher education. *International Journal of Game-Based Learning (IJGBL), 6*(1), 18–29. https://doi.org/10.4018/IJGBL.2016010102.

Young, J. R. (2019, March 12). *Who owns digital badges? A company's patent on credential system raises questions - EdSurge News*. EdSurge. https://www.edsurge.com/news/2019-03-12-who-owns-digital-badges-a-company-s-patent-on-credentials-raises-questions.

Zainuddin, Z., & Keumala, C. M. (2021). Gamification concept without digital platforms: A strategy for parents on motivating children study at home during Covid-19 pandemic. *PEDAGOGIK: Jurnal Pendidikan, 8*(1), 156–193. https://doi.org/10.33650/pjp.v8i1.2174.

2 These aren't the games you're looking for

Pre-packaged play

The allure of quick fix gameplay seemed particularly strong during the pandemic: inevitably, educators in crisis turned to built-in solutions and readily available mechanisms for digital learning. This desire for premade solutions frequently leads educators back to a type of play that is rarely inclusive or transformative: instead, such games are frequently repetitive and tedious, echoing the monotony of the virtual classroom in a reliance on trite mechanics and interfaces. The challenges of meaningful play in the classroom predate the pandemic, but the pandemic amplified our awareness of them, while drawing critical attention to the existing limitations of common online learning platforms thanks to their widespread, rapid adoption.

In this chapter, we first frame the state of game-based education solutions pre-pandemic, and use this lens to understand the challenges of the educational pivot. The pandemic did not just create crises, it raised our collective awareness, asking more educators to take on the challenges of virtual learning, and in doing so, it revealed the limitations and possibilities. We argue that the collective challenges of pandemic learning (as particularly amplified in countries reliant upon virtual learning structures, such as the United States) expose a fundamental lack in these platforms, pushing against the feasibility of commercial solutions to learning through play.

Goaded on by the marketing-driven, rhetorically empty promise of gamification, the landscape of game design more broadly continues to evoke a type of play that is rarely inclusive or transformative. The history of games-driven engagement in the classroom is filled with attempts to reclaim studio titles, often amplifying the very narratives of settled discourse deeply embedded in their mechanics: consider history favorites *Civilization* and *Age of Empires*, for instance, each with its own variant on a savage–civilization dichotomy alongside a model that emphasizes progress and conquest. Such games can certainly be brought into the classroom thoughtfully, and educators have engaged with their limited models to create space for conversation and critique, but classroom use of these games also risks reaffirming biases and existing mindsets through their procedural representations.

However, the alternative to the commercial game—the customized or classroom-ready educational game—is similarly unrewarding, and particularly difficult

DOI: 10.4324/9781003281696-3

because of the expected scale associated with game production and aesthetics. One reason that gamification and educational games have failed to live up to their revolutionizing promises is because of the types of games being implemented and the ways they are being used in classrooms. As has been discussed elsewhere (Toda et al., 2018), the games that are most commonly adopted in classrooms are selected-response and competitive: frameworks easily adapted to a range of content, and minimal in their demands on a game engine, and thus simply built and polished for the course management system.

These selected-response games such as *Jeopardy!* parodies and quiz-bowls are, arguably, multiple-choice tests and worksheets being acted out as games. They are familiar and repetitive, even when accompanied by lavish graphics or the tools of casual games—what Jesper Juul refers to as "juiciness" (Juul, 2010). While these are not terrible educational choices because they can help the work feel less mundane to students than actual worksheets and quizzes, and the content practice certainly transfers to multiple-choice standardized assessments (Reich, 2020), they retain the constraints of limited-choice tasks. Despite decades' worth of calls for a collective move away from these types of assignments and assessments, they remain. Whether it is because of so-called teacher accountability measures (Frederiksen, 1984) or because it is simply quicker and easier to adapt to "games" that fit into the grammar of schools (Tyack & Cuban, 2009), selected-response questions remain in many gamification and educational game attempts.

It is widely agreed that critical thinking skills and the ability to analyze information are vital skills to learn and practice (Bell, 2010; Bellanca, 2010; Rotherham & Willingham, 2010; Saavedra & Opfer, 2012). Critics of high-stakes, selected-choice assessments are quick to quip "life is not multiple choice," but we have not yet been able to effectively use these types of games or playful instruction on a larger scale. Educator attitudes have begun to shift toward emphasizing constructivist activities, but it can be tempting to fall back on more comfortable, traditional methods that match the styles of educators' own teachers, a phenomenon Justin Reich terms the "curse of the familiar" compounded by the "trap of routine assessment" (Reich, 2020, p. 125), especially as increasing mandates on teachers erode more and more of their prep time.

Competitive games can also be problematic, exacerbating the existing issues in the classroom, with behaviorist leaderboards and badges threatening to undermine intrinsic motivation and self-esteem. Competition in the classroom naturally includes comparisons between students, which is detrimental to self-efficacy and has been shown to increase "imposter feelings" (Canning et al., 2020; Hutchins, 2015; Leary et al., 2000; Parkman, 2016). Minority racial and gender groupings are especially susceptible to feeling like imposters in the classroom (Cokley et al., 2013; Dancy & Brown, 2011; Peteet et al., 2015; Vaughn et al., 2020). The inclusion of commercial game titles, or games with mainstream mechanics such as real-time strategy, threatens to amplify this divide further between those with existing access to similar games and play.

Selected-choice and competition games that reward and punish follow behaviorist learning theory, which is why they feel so outdated. Alluding to the popular quote often attributed to William Butler Yeats, "education is not the filling of a pail, but the lighting of a fire," Reich (2020) asserts that these teacher-centric activities "draw pedagogical inspiration from pail fillers rather than flame kindlers" (p. 111). Our society and our technology are ready to move past rewarding and punishing specific student behaviors, and on to fostering exploration and more complicated, interdisciplinary problems. Some educators have attempted this by finding creative ways to adapt commercial entertainment games to the classroom. Though a noble effort, this practice has failed to become as common as the gamification attempts described above, for a number of reasons.

First, commercial entertainment games produced by large gaming studios, often referred to as AAA or commercial off-the-shelf (COTS) games, have narrow target audience demographics that are typically different than most educators. For example, the bestselling AAA game of 2019 was *Call of Duty: Modern Warfare* (Webb, 2019). This game is a first-person shooter (FPS), a genre of game where the primary mechanic is the shooting of enemies. It would be difficult and rather inappropriate to tie this game into a K-12 curriculum. Even with less brazenly violent games, it is likely that many attempts to adapt commercial games for educational purposes have fallen flat simply because their primary design purpose is entertainment, not education. The learning tasks teachers tend to combine with the assigned gameplay are tacked on and feel only somewhat related rather than integral to the gameplay.

Adding to the burden of finding a commercial game that is appropriate for the classroom audience is the cost. AAA games are often expensive and require costly gaming consoles or specialized computers to effectively play. *Call of Duty: Modern Warfare* sells for US$60 and is played on the PlayStation 4, which is US$300 (Partleton, 2019). The upgrade cycles of such systems are demanding, and their maintenance is similarly frustrating, as a console, once broken, is frequently irreparable. Even though consoles are typically sold at a loss to the company (Havens & Lotz, 2012), the bestselling game console in 2019, the Nintendo Switch, was still US$300 (*Buy Now—Nintendo Switch—Bundles, What's Included*, 2021). The hope of a classroom set of gaming consoles, or even gaming PCs, is out of reach for most.

Further obstructing the successful adoption of AAA games for education includes the fact that they are difficult to incorporate well into instruction in a meaningful way, requiring considerable time, effort, and creativity to tie a commercial game to instructional content. Charsky and Mims (2008) provide educators wishing to adapt AAA games to their curriculum with the advice to "play the game—extensively" (p. 38) reminding educators that the typical AAA game is designed to ensure 40–50 hours of gameplay. Beyond that, they assert that the educator must "learn the game—extensively" (p. 39) because playing is not sufficient to ensure that the game can be used effectively by the instructor without comprehensive knowledge of the game, recommending the purchase of manuals or joining online affinity groups to more fully understand the game. They discuss the need for debriefing or "crossover" activities to "complement the elements and game play and/or correct the errors and misconceptions that students will develop due to a game's inherent simplicities or outright mistakes" (p. 41). The amount of effort required to adapt the curriculum around an existing AAA game and "make" the gameplay educational does not seem worthwhile. Further, when used in a classroom, the connection between the educational content and the commercial game is almost always weak and feels added-on despite how much additional teacher time and effort have been spent to adapt the game to the curriculum.

For example, the puzzle-based games, *Portal* and its sequel *Portal 2*, published by Valve in 2007 and 2011, respectively, have been adopted into a number of classrooms (Adams & Mayer, 2013; Gee, 2008; Pittman, 2013). These games ask the player to solve increasingly more difficult puzzles using spatial reasoning and physics knowledge. The studio also published lesson plans (teachwithportals.com). The 18 lesson plans posted on its site, ranging in target age from grades 4–5 (ages 9–11) to grades 11–12 (ages 16–18), include concepts on math (parabolas, geometry, and statistics), physics (gravity, oscillations, conservation of momentum, velocity), and one lesson on English.

The English lesson has a target audience of seventh grade, which one of the authors used to teach. This ten-page lesson plan and worksheet packet uses the opening scene of *Portal 2* (Courtesy Call) to teach students how setting can influence the feelings a character has. The accompanying worksheets guide students through the analysis of narrative setting and characters. Although this is an innovative use of the game and undoubtedly a nice change of pace for students, the accompanying worksheet is remarkably dry, and even below the seventh-grade level as far as the concepts on narratives that it covers. Plot, setting, and characters are taught and mastered in the elementary grade levels, and as models of narrative in games go, *Portal 2* is far from exemplary.

Additionally, because of the nature of the text in question—the introductory level of *Portal 2*—the analysis must stop at just that; it cannot be extended to have students modify the example game to experiment with other narrative effects. It is a published, commercial video game, and the lesson is designed to take place in a traditional middle school classroom where students are not, at most schools, designing and developing their own narrative video games. Though a gallant effort, the main issue with this lesson is its isolated nature. The introduction to *Portal 2* may effectively teach these concepts, but the lesson does not even require students to *play* the actual game. The plans and worksheets feel like a shoehorn, attempting to shove this game into a place it was never meant to go.

Looking at the uses of the *Portal* games to teach physics, a subject area seemingly more suited to these games, the results are mixed. One study describes the use of *Portal* to prime participants for learning physics concepts before showing them a video on Newton's laws of physics. When compared to the other two conditions, where participants played *Tetris* or *Text Twist*, respectively, no significant difference in physics knowledge retention was found between the three groups (Adams et al., 2016). Another study with the similar sequel, *Portal 2*, did show improvement in spatial cognition, problem-solving, and persistence, but was not used to teach any specific content area that would need to be covered in a formal educational setting (Shute et al., 2015).

In a study describing a high school teacher's use of *Portal 2* to teach physics, students used the video game's puzzle builder for lab exercises to construct and assess virtual experiments (Pittman, 2013). The puzzle creator acts like a sandbox game where players can become level designers and create their own puzzle chamber (or multiple chambers) in the game world. Player-designed levels can then be published to the video game distribution platform Steam and played by others. Pittman did not use a control group but reported positive findings, adding that, in his view, video games "are not standalone educational tools" but rather "field trips, laboratories, and everyday experiences rolled into one, creating opportunities for students to draw connections and gain deeper understandings" (p. 358). They necessitate often excessive additional work by the teacher to ensure that they reach their full learning potential.

Valve also offers an education version (*Puzzle Creator*) available on Steam for Schools that allows teachers to create their own puzzles in the game (*Portal 2—Educational Version—Portal Wiki*, 2015). These isolated puzzles have the potential to create engaging lessons that are focused on specific physics concepts, but without a narrative or other contextualizing elements, they risk falling short of meaningfully engaging students in a deep way.

Unlike expensive AAA computer games or those that require proprietary consoles to operate, mobile games were expected to change the landscape of learning, in part because the devices are so ubiquitous, being much less expensive than a typical computer or laptop, containing numerous sensors, and connecting to the Internet easily. Giannakas et al.'s (2018) review of mobile game-based learning noted seven major challenges facing those who are creating effective educational mobile games. They advocate that a good mobile learning game must ensure the game's educational content is adaptive and flexible, allow for personalized learning, strike a balance between fun and learning, ensure player privacy and security, leverage the features of the technology, emphasize context-based learning activities, and develop standards between mobile platforms.

The use of mobile-based games in the classroom poses challenges as well. Like AAA console and computer games, mobile games are designed for entertainment and require extensive adaptations to be used as educational tools. Mobile games have the potential advantage of allowing each student to play simultaneously without waiting for a turn on the classroom console, but this assumes that each student already owns a mobile device. On top of that, the wide range of models of mobile devices that students will bring to class creates an additional hurdle for the playability of a mobile game: it must be available on both Apple and Android app stores, and the devices must be up to date enough to handle the game. This prevents all classroom teachers except the very few who have the specialized knowledge, time, and resources (hardware, software, and funds to maintain accounts on the proprietary app stores) to develop their own educational games for mobile devices.

We inspect these preexisting weaknesses in games recognizing that as educators across the globe struggled to pivot to fully online learning, the focus was understandably on course content, with games and activities designed to foster learner engagement falling to the background while "coverage" took center stage.

Those who did include playful elements did not have the time to invest in adapting commercial games to their suddenly online curriculum, and instead relied on the typical models like *Jeopardy!* and other similar question-and-answer competition style games, if they were able to include games at all. The issues in using games for formal education activities were reproduced and amplified across the newly digitally mediated courses.

Making as play

A counterexample to the cynical educational frameworks of the original *Portal* exists in *Minecraft*, arguably one of the most successful educational games in recent history. Powered in part by its robust "Education Edition," *Minecraft* has become inextricably linked with STEM learning, tied to efforts such as "Hour of Code" but also part of a more robust curriculum. The program boasts educators in 115 countries using the approach, made possible in part by the choice of low-fidelity, signature blocky models, with a correspondingly low demand on technology.

Educational subjects represented in *Minecraft*'s pre-built resources include Science, History and Culture, Computer Science, Math, Language Arts, and Art and Design: of these, some of the most tenuously linked are those outside the framework of STEM. However, the underlying model of the approach relies on crowdsourcing and, in doing so, has all the strengths and weaknesses of this type of participatory design model. Its greatest appeal is in the allure of the relatively mediated marketplace: unlike platforms dedicated to small games, such as itch.io, *Minecraft* offerings undergo content moderation if not quality control.

Is *Minecraft*—or, at least, the model *Minecraft* represents—the future of games in education? It is tempting to push back against such an argument in part because of the many ways in which *Minecraft* does not resemble a game: it is, more accurately, a virtual world, or rules-driven Lego set, with all the creative possibilities and constraints that implies. Certainly, the use of *Minecraft* as a tool to bring students into making is popular and compelling, and its use to introduce digital culture has proven successful (Checa-Romero & Gómez, 2018). The association with general skills (collaboration, organizing, problem-solving, and design) has been strongly correlated, and the game's popularity in the classroom seems unabated (Hewett et al., 2020).

The idea that players can construct their own worlds certainly smacks of the promises of constructivist learning theory, where learners are encouraged to build their own knowledge. A "sandbox" like *Minecraft* could be the ultimate digital learning environment that optimistic educators envisioned when embracing technology. The looming problem of what the digital environment will teach, however, remains: how can this game map onto the "knowledge" assessed by the standardized tests? The fact that players of *Minecraft* can build interesting castles and other structures in the game demonstrates how it can foster creativity, agency, and self-expression; however, few, if any, of these important characteristics are valued (i.e., assessed) in K–20 environments, and often, when *Minecraft* is used in the classroom, it is the *Minecraft: Education Edition* where student actions are dictated and the game environment is limited to keep students on task—reformatting this exploration-centric game into another familiar school assignment (*What Is Minecraft*, 2021), much like the isolated puzzles of the *Portal 2 Puzzle Creator*. Are games unable to keep up with education, or is education unable to keep up with games and the needs of students?

The pandemic drew out the creativity and playfulness of thousands of people who used window signs, sidewalk chalk, and TikTok videos to connect with and encourage one another. There were balcony concerts in cities from New York to Milan; public murals, virtual choral performances by celebrities, and elaborate demonstrations of the laws of physics with ping-pong balls, to name but a few. Humans are indeed creative and playful; however, none of these compelling, engaging opportunities for meaning-construction took place in virtual education settings: they all occurred in the newfound leisure time people faced during lockdowns. This is a recurring issue with education: too many people believe education and play are separate—and even opposite—entities. We disagree.

Representation

Minecraft's block figures allow it to escape another challenge of AAA games in the classroom: a lack of meaningful diversity and inclusion, both in representation and structure. The demographics of gamers are more diverse than ever, as an industry self-study conducted in 2020 notes: "women make up 41% of the 214.4 million total US gamers—and the average age range of video game players is now somewhere between 35-44 years old" (LaPierre, 2020). The report also notes that the AbleGamers Charity estimates there are approximately 46 million video game players with disabilities. However, the characters and avatars are predominantly able-bodied, straight, white, and male. This lack of diversity is problematic enough when these games are used for their intended purpose of entertainment, but when they are brought into the classroom, it becomes unacceptable. A report for the Association for Library Service to Children Board urges educators, "children's materials that accurately portray diversity in multiple languages and cultures can have a positive influence on a child's self-image and help him or her build bridges of cultural understanding," continuing, "all children want to see images that reflect themselves and encounter stories in their native language and within the context of their personal cultures" (Naidoo, 2014, p. 3)—and while the discourse of "own voices," and stories reflecting a range of authorship, has started to influence children's and young adult publishing, it is far less prevalent in the discourse of mainstream games.

It is logical to extend this need for students to see their own culture reflected in all educational materials, including video games. Historical surveys of representational choices in games have frequently centered on the availability of playable characters offering certain identities, and even by this simple metric, gaming is still far behind even Hollywood in available offerings. More crucially, this type of survey is limiting and superficial, and doesn't capture the staggering lack of diversity at work in the larger industry: according to an industry self-study, "74 percent of workers in the industry identify as cis males, 61 percent are white and 81 percent are heterosexual. By contrast, just one percent of survey respondents identified as Black while only 4 percent identified as Latinx" (Dellinger, 2020). Even where a variety of representation is included on the surface, it often fails the test of meaningful play, as particularly has been noted by scholars addressing the inclusion of queer games and the limitations of mainstream games in crafting meaningful queer play experiences (Ruberg, 2019).

Perhaps most troublingly, every step forward for the industry is accompanied by regression and often deeply misogynist, racist, and transphobic outcry from within the gamer base. Exemplary moments include the *Cyberpunk 2077* release, which paired an intensely detailed character generator (featuring customizable genitals and pubic hair) with transphobic content. Similarly troubling, the game othered players by including epileptic triggers, originally with no warnings (Favis, 2020). Such conversations offer little in the way of optimism for the mainstream industry's path. Likewise, the legacy of GamerGate is deeply embedded in the industry discourse, offering a reminder of how intensely gamer identity has been controlled and dictated by the perceived centricity of the cis white man. GamerGate itself is just one very visible symptom of the toxic core: the event is now infamous, but ultimately was started when one man decided to harness the existing toxic misogyny toward the abuse of his ex. In the wake of 2021's QAnon rampage most pronounced in the United States, widespread deplatforming has been attempted on social media, but meaningful regulation of gaming spaces is a more difficult challenge. Even incorporating the platforms associated with gaming communities, such as Discord, threatens to bring the toxicity of gaming culture iconography and memes into play. It is no wonder we don't see more educators putting time and effort into using games in their classrooms.

When people or representations of people are present in the context of the classroom environment, such as teachers and characters in books, students who are not represented in race or gender likely receive the message that they are not valued. One study found that teens who were not matched with race- and gender-based role models did not perform as well as their matched peers academically, did not set as many achievement-oriented goals, thought less about their futures, and looked to peers rather than adults for guidance (Zirkel, 2002). Similarly, the field of education has been touting the merits of teaching with multicultural literature for decades (Florez-Tighe et al., 1983), with research suggesting that it increases cultural awareness, understanding, and appreciation, and even promoting the use of multicultural literature as one way to better prepare preservice teachers to effectively understand diversity issues (Jetton & Savage-Davis, 2005). Similar discourse surrounds gaming, but in underfunded and fringe initiatives, such as the grant-funded or community-supported games spotlighted at the Games for Change festival each year (*Games for Change*, 2022).

This challenge is not unique to games, though games amplify it: even when print media being used in schools are examined, there is a striking lack of diversity. That decades-old call for using multicultural literature in the classroom (Florez-Tighe et al., 1983) has yet to be meaningfully answered. Even the problematic perception of what canonical or classic literature is or should include persists (Guillory, 2013; Stallworth et al., 2006), with an especially egregious lack of diversity in children's literature (Adam et al., 2017; Dennihy, 2017; Young, 2019), often a result of a variety of reasons that librarians and those responsible for purchasing literature for schools choose to over-censor their selections (Bulatowicz, 2017).

Games *could* work to alleviate this issue in part, through characters and game narratives that meaningfully include members or representations of diverse populations. Sadly, this has not been a focus of the industry, which still greatly limits the representation of minority populations in games. Video games are notorious for oversexualizing and overgendering player avatars and non-player characters (NPCs) (Ivory, 2006). This lack of representation has acted to signal to much of the gaming community that those who are not represented in games do not belong there, allowing toxic masculinity to pervade the community and spurring alarming behavior and activity like the aforementioned GamerGate.

This common and systemic misogyny is accompanied by bigotry, with few if any avatar representations of people of color, and when they are represented, they are minor characters or enemies (Šisler, 2008). The fact that the most popular AAA games are first-person shooters (FPS) where the player's primary activity is pointing and shooting a gun exacerbates the issue. The common military setting of these games mimics actual American military campaigns in Iraq and Afghanistan, and situates the citizens of those countries as the player's enemies. Šisler (2008) details the way Muslims and Arabs are othered and demonized through the way they are depicted in a variety of video games.

Though these are symptoms of systemic cultural issues and not problems introduced by the AAA gaming industry, the industry could be working harder to address these issues through and within games; however, they currently do not. Using games where these issues are apparent in a classroom, even with the best intentions, can have negative consequences. When inequities are emphasized in games, the cultural norms are reinforced, sending the damaging message to all students that the cis white male is somehow better or more important than the rest of the population. To return to the origin story of *Oregon Trail*, the frequently undercontextualized inclusion of the game's Western expansion narrative of progress in the classroom may have captured the attention of educators for its early potential to engage, but it did little for the teaching of history. Indeed, even its success in the classroom was, thanks in large part to mechanics of character-naming that allowed for filling carriages of explorers with classmates and teachers who frequently met their demise within the game, to the delight of the student-player who often included these names for this purpose.

The shift to fully online teaching brought with it new ways for marginalized groups to be harassed and stigmatized. From Zoom-bombing, to the inability of proctoring software to recognize non-white faces, to the brunt of the essential work falling on those in minority demographics, the pandemic highlighted the multitude of ways that these communities are treated by those in power: invisible except when made targets of hate or overworked underpaid labor that benefits others at their expense.

All games and no fun

Another obstacle educators face when trying to use games in the classroom is that games assigned by educators become homework—a *requirement* for a class rather than a chosen pastime. This can greatly erode the motivation and engagement that are a large part of the reason games were adapted for learning in the first place. When instructors treat games the same way as other educational tasks, the sense of play is lost and the games become a burden. Gamification is particularly prone to this reduction: the framing of work through gaming incentive mechanisms "changes the nature of play, making it a duty rather than a choice, a routine rather than a process of exploration" (deWinter et al., 2014, p. 109). In the same way that enthusiastic teachers can "sell" their students on what would otherwise seem mundane busywork, teachers who expect the games to magically engage the entire class in the content will not yield the best results. In education, especially K-12, the atmosphere of the room can be just as important as the structure of the lesson.

In this case, only using games sparingly, making the assigned game a rare occurrence, can work to prevent the game-work from becoming a dreaded task; but if games are to fulfill their promise of transforming education into something more effective and fun, then the rarity of a game, relying solely on the novelty effect, is not a means to achieve this end. Another partial solution that is used to increase the feeling (or mirage) of student agency could be allowing students to select from a few options of games or assigning a game that provides players with a large amount of agency. The drawback here, of course, is that it also increases the burden on the instructor.

A more effective strategy is to adopt the perspective of play in the classroom. When the instructional approach is playful, their basic emotional needs are met, making the instruction more effective. Rather than treating games as just another learning task, or worse, as busywork to keep students occupied, teachers can use a playful perspective approach to the learning activities. A recent article grapples with the busywork dilemma (Fowlin, 2021). Fowlin defines this dilemma as one where students do not see the connection between the work they are being assigned and the content of the class. These feelings seem to be exacerbated in online-only settings, especially "suddenly online" courses, where instructors are attempting to replace or replicate in-class teaching activities and students are unable to see the relevance of these assignments.

Another common feature of gamification activities and educational games that seems to fall flat even when educators do their best to set a playful classroom tone is the lack of engagement. When games are presented as isolated, "extra" activities and/or started and stopped abruptly—such as playing for the last 20 minutes of a class or assigning Level 2 as homework—the potential for the learner to feel immersed in the game is diminished. For games to compel players to continue playing, they must engage the player by creating a sense of immersion.

An often-cited feature of video games is Csikszentmihalyi's (1990) concept of flow. This concept is a result of qualitative studies where he interviewed people who were experts in various hobbies that required extensive practice to excel, such as rock climbing and painting. These participants reported how they felt during the activity where they experienced flow. When describing the experience, there were nine common feelings they mentioned, which Csikszentmihalyi defined as "flow." The issues with the historic underpinnings of Csikszentmihalyi's theory as well as the uncritical manner with which it is emphasized in game design have been discussed in detail elsewhere (Soderman, 2021), but the fact remains that the idea and term of "flow" that he popularized is still emphasized in game design programs and textbooks.

For example, Michailidis et al. (2018) assert that effective games, whether they are intended for entertainment or education, *must* allow the player to experience Csikszentmihalyi's nine feelings of flow, or at least many of them. Many excellent games do induce a sense of immersion, engagement, or another favorite concept of game design spheres: Huizinga's "magic circle" of a game world (Huizinga, 1955). The game elements that allow the player to set goals, feel a sense of autonomy, feel immersed or lost in a different world, lose track of time, etc. are indeed elements of well-designed, enjoyable games. When looking at the types of superficial gamification activities and games commonly used in formal education settings, the stark lack of these elements is obvious.

Taking Michailidis et al.'s list at face value and applying it to the typical classroom review game, *Jeopardy!*, highlights the issues with this behavioralist game. In a classroom, a teacher will display category names on a board, and students select the category and "value" (representing the actual money that can be won by contestants in the television game show). In the television version, contestants are presented with an answer to which they must supply the correct question. In the classroom, this is sometimes reversed, with students providing the answer to each question, better matching the exam format for which they are preparing.

Classroom *Jeopardy!* has a clear goal: correctly answer the most questions (or earn the highest number of "dollars"). The students also receive immediate, clear feedback on the accuracy of their answers. The rest of the elements of flow listed above are absent from the experience. The skill required to play the game is minimal (whether or not the players know all of the content-related answers, there is little skill or even strategy involved in selecting which category/question to select). The teacher is always in control of the activity, and despite that teacher's best efforts, in the classroom setting, students are rarely focused on the learning activity alone. This and the fact that students are seated beside their peers diminishes the student's feelings of immersion in the game, while increasing their awareness of their sense of self—or the identity they perform for their peers and teachers. Finally, as students are required to attend classes for specified amounts of time, they are typically keenly aware of time passing and not intrinsically motivated to participate in the review game.

The same can be said for other common classroom games: they follow behavioralist question-and-answer, right-or-wrong formulas. Whether it is "skinned" as a quiz bowl, *Who Wants to Be a Millionaire*, or any other game show that happens to be popular at the time, the standard classroom games are performances of worksheets. Students playing in these games are not partaking in creative problem-solving or "higher-order thinking" skills—they are regurgitating information they were tasked to memorize by an outdated school system. No wonder millennials and the generations that follow cringe at competitive games. They have been forced to play far too many terrible ones.

Narratives and role-play

Many learning games fail to engage students in the same way that entertainment games do for all of the reasons already mentioned as well as the lack of a unifying story arc. This problem with fragmented in-class or as-homework games, and the problem with artificial gamification in general, is the sense that the activities being packaged as games are isolated and have no sense of beginning, middle, or end. Incorporating a narrative could be one solution to the "gamification" problem; situating the assignments students may perceive as busywork to an overarching course narrative may be beneficial.

Humans have conveyed information to one another through storytelling throughout recorded history (and likely before that). We naturally find stories interesting, and the desire to learn how the story ends typically motivates us to continue listening, watching, reading, or playing. Narratives can convey mundane details and harrowing tales. We advise our job-seeking students to be sure that they "tell their story" in their job application materials as a way to capture the attention of potential employers. It should be obvious that the key to an immersive game is narrative. One study of 133 participants found that narrative, as well as aesthetics in a game, contributed to positive engagement and perception of learning (Alexiou et al., 2020). Of course, perception of learning may not ensure actual learning, but student engagement is a key factor.

This does not mean that all games must be hours long. The popularity of the social game *Among Us* demonstrates that even a minimal narrative of "discover the impostor among the players" is enough to be compelling. Depending on the number of players and their playstyles, one game can last only a few minutes but remain immersive. One of the most celebrated examples of social game success during the pandemic, *Among Us* relies upon social dynamics and collective investigation into power play, using those elements to reshape what could be predictable patterns into engaging, re-playable challenges (Lorenz, 2020). Rather than adding superficial game elements to a routine learning exercise, perhaps we should strive to envelop the activity in a narrative. Marketers and bloggers have already realized this and have begun to capitalize on it, adding "storification" to their ads and blogs in an effort to capture the attention of their audiences.

Storification uses narrative as motivation (Aura et al., 2021). To be effective in conveying information, the narrative must have seven key components

(Avraamidou & Osborne, 2009): purpose of helping us understand the human and natural world, connected events, identifiable structure, time, agency, narrator, and reader. Narrative-based instruction has been used with varying success in formal education settings (Armstrong & Landers, 2017; Browning & Hohenstein, 2015; Prins et al., 2017). One study found that students developed a better understanding of evolution from reading a narrative text than an expository text (Browning & Hohenstein, 2015). Another study investigated an entire school that had embraced storification—down to the detail of painting classrooms and hallways to mirror fictional settings such as *Star Wars* and physical landscapes like the Grand Canyon (Aura et al., 2021). The authors state that although each teacher implemented storification differently, the practice has the capability to "*empower* students, support their *academic performance*, and allow them and the teacher *personalized spaces*" (emphasis original, p. 9).

Without a grounding narrative, individual learning games or attempts at gamification rarely succeed in capturing students' attention for long. There is no suspense at how the game will end in *Jeopardy!* Someone will answer the most questions correctly, and the others will not. Even if the students in the class try to consider themselves to be characters in the story, there is no plot, just a repeated cycle of question-and-answer, exactly like a worksheet or exam. In an educational game with a narrative—even a simplistic one like *Among Us*—students are usually motivated to play until they discover the ending.

Interestingly, there is not much more of a narrative in *Portal 2* than there is in *Among Us*. The player is trapped in the building, and they must solve puzzles to escape. The series of differing and increasingly complex puzzles helps to keep the player engaged, like the popular (pre-pandemic) in-person escape rooms. In fact, educational escape room games have been used to teach research methods (Clarke et al., 2017) and potentially communication skills (Pan et al., 2017). Scholars have published frameworks and guidelines for educators who wish to create escape rooms for their own courses, touting the games' ability to foster critical thinking and practice problem-solving skills, emphasizing aspects that match well with traditional education such as time limits for class meetings and need for peer cooperation (Clarke et al., 2017; Nicholson, 2018).

Nicholson's (2018) escape room design advice includes focusing the rooms on engaging narratives that students will work to explore, rather than concentrating all of the student efforts on locked boxes and other common game room accessories. The locks should instead, he suggests, serve to verify if the student's answers are correct. His design model, the "Ask Why" model (2016), centers the escape room activities around challenges that further the narrative, and engage the players within the narrative itself. Of course, the primary issue with escape room lesson plans at the present time lies in the title: escape *room*. These games necessitate that students work together in a physical classroom; something that is not possible during lockdowns and remains impossible in social distancing phases.

Another way to fold a narrative into educational activities is to harness the power of role-play. One analog game with a strong component of role-playing that has been successfully played in school settings for years is *Model UN* (Best Delegate, 2020). Hailed as possibly the most popular technique for active learning (Crossley-Frolick, 2010), *Model UN* has students simulate a United Nations conference by researching real countries and real issues, making persuasive speeches, and setting the policies of their randomly assigned country. The game is intended for students from middle school to college to understand how the actions of individual countries can impact other countries around the world. By acting out the roles of officials with political power, students gain a firsthand understanding of the ways that nations interact, compromise, and handle international conflicts. This experience provides students with opportunities to practice critical thinking, problem-solving, writing, and public-speaking skills. Engel et al. (2017) incorporated *Model UN* into an International Relations course and found evidence of deep learning, showing the highest growth in the areas of conceptual and metacognitive knowledge. These strengths of the game also serve as its drawback: these vital skills lack overt value in the classroom—they are not typically tested. Standardized tests and typical course exams assess only the things students would learn as a by-product of participating in a *Model UN* game: geography, world leader names, and other dry facts that can be isolated in multiple-choice assessments.

Reacting to the Past (Carnes, 2014) also uses a successful role-playing game structure that is a similar simulation. Games center around actual historic issues, and players are assigned the roles of real historical figures. They have the opportunity to react to the historic events in a different way than their character did, rewriting history in a way, but the deep research involved in understanding the historical events as they happened from the perspective of a specific person in history can result in a rich understanding of the complex events students typically only read overly simplified summaries about in history books. The narrative depiction of historic events such as the French Revolution, combined with the ability to revise history based on what the player knows about how the event actually played out, has been successful at a number of different universities: as with *Minecraft*, their model of co-creative play is key to their resonance. Postsecondary education is removed from the pressure of the standardized test, which is perhaps why these games are successful here. A high school teacher would likely need to weigh the engagement potential in these games against the time required to prepare and play them, and would likely realize that lecture and textbook readings "cover" the tested facts more efficiently.

One health education game that contains an overarching narrative and proved effective in a large 375-participant study is *Re-mission* (Tate et al., 2009). This 3D, 20-level computer-based game was designed to teach children who were diagnosed with cancer about what different types of cancers do to the body, how chemotherapy works, and the side effects it has. The game has the player guide an avatar through the body of various cancer patients, shooting cancer cells with a radiation gun, demonstrating to the patient-player the way that chemotherapy destroys cancer colonies. The study was determined to be successful in two metrics. First, participants playing *Re-mission* learned the cancer-related knowledge that was tested 70% faster than the group playing the control commercial video game.

Additionally, researchers found that patient medication and treatment adherence (taking medications as prescribed and attending scheduled appointments) was three times greater than the control group. Participants playing *Re-mission* also reported feeling a sense of agency over their condition as they imagined themselves to be destroying the cancer in their own bodies as they played. The researchers assert that their results showed changes in self-efficacy, and that this, rather than increased medical knowledge, was the key influencer of patient behavior.

Role-playing games or live action role-playing games (LARPs) are common to many in-person K-12 classrooms, particularly the earlier grades. The act of taking on the role of a character—historical or fictional—and engaging in a make-believe scenario that simulates the behavior and choices someone else might make encourages empathy, sympathy, and understanding for others. Thinking about current or past events in the real world and literature from the perspective of someone who actually experienced them can increase interest and promote deeper learning. Chapter 3 delves into the ways that players of the popular role-playing game, *Dungeons & Dragons*, were able to continue to play and encourage community engagement virtually during the pandemic shutdowns.

Deterding (2016) emphasizes the make-believe as a key aspect of narrative, play, and games, asserting that make-believe can organize knowledge, increase interest, add relevance, allow for new perspectives, and persuade. Storification can help invoke the feelings of make-believe in the reader, learner, and player. Though these types of games are often dismissed because the critical thinking skills they teach are not overtly transferable to typical assessments (Reich, 2020), the use of make-believe to teach through narratives and role-play could be why games like *Model UN* and *Reacting to the Past* have been used in formal educational settings with such success. Other scholars (Lee et al., 2006) highlight four key benefits of using narrative themes in educational games: creating vicarious experiences, lessening cognitive load, increasing motivation, and providing a sense of presence.

Games that happen to have a narrative, however, are not guaranteed efficacy. For example, Adams et al. (2012) conducted a media comparison experiment with a narrative educational game (*Crystal Island*) and an informative slide show, and found that participants learned more effectively from the slide show than the game. Their follow-up study compared a narrative version of a discovery educational game called *Cache 17* where players solve a mystery about paintings that went missing during World War II to a non-narrative version of the same game. This time, they found no significant differences between the narrative and non-narrative versions, with the slide show group outperforming both. These were isolated laboratory studies, and the actual in-class use of a game like this may be more effective when combined with other instructional activities.

It is clear that the balance between specific narrative structure and purposeful presentation of the content to be learned is a delicate one that requires thoughtful design. Verswijvelen et al. (2020) advise instructional designers to use meaningful, immersive contexts in a narrative that includes "strong characters, a well-paced storyline interesting choices and relevant consequences" (p. 1551). Dickey (2006) also argues that narratives can be designed for educational purposes. She describes the ways that narrative video games can inform instructional design, citing the ability of narratives to support problem-solving and learning. Adventure games, she asserts, are essentially problem-solving environments, full of "plot hooks" that invoke player curiosity as to what might happen next (p. 251). Much of early edutainment took its lead from this model of play, and the exploratory narratives it allowed, offering patterns for puzzle-driven, situational engagement (Salter, 2014) that have led to the alternate reality games we explore in later chapters.

The type of narrative in the game will have an impact on its use for learning as well. Jenkins (2004) defines four types of narratives: those that are evoked from themed spaces, those that the players enact, those embedded in the game that player discovers as they play, and those that emerge from the players themselves in open-ended games like the *Sims* series or *Animal Crossing*. Logically, it is not likely that all types of narratives are conducive or effective for learning all types of content; just as all types of class assignments are not conducive to learning all types of content. Further studies are needed to discern what types of learning map best onto what types of games or gameful elements. Player types and learning styles, however out of vogue and dependent on the context they are, could also have some influence on the efficacy of games to teach.

Here again, we see the separation of learning as work and narratives as leisure: millions of us turned to narratives for a sense of escape during lockdowns—books, films, and television shows—in our newfound leisure time. Rather than maintaining that false dichotomy, we should perhaps take a moment to reflect on the power of story to transport our minds to different, captivating places, and how we can harness that power for playful learning. The rich history and culture behind novels as well as MUDs and MOOs should remind us that fancy graphics and sound effects are unnecessary for the construction of immersive virtual worlds. We can immerse our students in playful worlds where they can learn and grow with the minimal resources already at our disposal.

Toward a playful future

Much has been learned since the initial calls for games to "disrupt" education nearly 20 years ago. A great deal of advances in technology have expanded the options and capabilities of games for learning as well. Now that we have all become, out of necessity, more accustomed to digitally mediated spaces, it is to our advantage to reexamine education and games, and perhaps reconceptualize the very idea of what learning from, with, and through games can be. The hasty modifications to enable teaching to continue through a pandemic have been done, and life shows some signs of returning to "normal" post-pandemic. We have an opportunity now to build on our existing course structures by infusing play into them.

We should consider the possibility that this massive shift to digital learning could be leveraged to improve education with a playful perspective. This could finally be the catalyst for disruption that revolutionizes teaching and learning. The options for open-source, user-friendly platforms for game development and playful teaching continue to increase. We have put in half of the work already—digitizing our curriculum with corporate tools. We can reimagine and redesign this digital corpus around play: and, as we will explore later, follow the examples of K-12 successes with *Minecraft* in envisioning a much stronger co-creative role for our students, inviting them to reimagine education with us rather than relying upon an industry of struggling diversity and corporate release incentives to solve the problems for us.

The predictable failures of pandemic education as well as the unacceptable failures of commercial games have brought us hard-earned knowledge, as well as timely insights into what we and our students most value in both community and play. Though we cannot argue that the costs have been worth it on any front, we cannot change the past; we can only learn from it. Inclusivity and access are vital for education and for games. These issues cannot be addressed in an afterthought with updates or modifications, they must be central to the design. When spaces are created that exclude certain populations, toxic behavior is tolerated and even invited. Inclusion from the beginning that promotes and values diverse voices and thoughts will go a long way toward combating online cultures of prejudice.

Education, like game design, is more of an art than a science. Teachers constantly experiment with different assignments, activities, and approaches to learning, perpetually striving to perfect their craft and reach every student. As we return to face-to-face settings, we would be wise to adapt some of the more playful digital modifications to our traditional or hybrid classes. The slowly increasing sense of relief we feel as the waves, variants, and fears of COVID-19 finally subside can naturally seep into our classrooms. We can build from this and recenter our instruction on compassion, building for ourselves and our students a playful, learner-focused environment. We have the digital capabilities and authoring tools to create meaningful play—it is time to put them to use.

References

Adam, H., Barratt-Pugh, C., & Haig, Y. (2017). Book collections in long day care: Do they reflect racial diversity? *Australasian Journal of Early Childhood, 42*(2), 88–96. https://doi.org/10.23965/AJEC.42.2.11.

Adams, D. M., & Mayer, R. E. (2013). Can playing portal affect spatial thinking and increase learning in a STEM area? *Proceedings of the Annual Meeting of the Cognitive Science Society.* http://csjarchive.cogsci.rpi.edu/proceedings/2013/papers/0319/.

Adams, D. M., Mayer, R. E., MacNamara, A., Koenig, A., & Wainess, R. (2012). Narrative games for learning: Testing the discovery and narrative hypotheses. *Journal of Educational Psychology, 104*(1), 235–249. https://doi.org/10.1037/a0025595.

Adams, D. M., Pilegard, C., & Mayer, R. E. (2016). Evaluating the cognitive consequences of playing portal for a short duration. *Journal of Educational Computing Research, 54*(2), 173–195. https://doi.org/10.1177/0735633115620431.

Alexiou, A., Schippers, M. C., Oshri, I., & Angelopoulos, S. (2020). Narrative and aesthetics as antecedents of perceived learning in serious games. *Information Technology and People*. https://doi.org/10.1108/ITP-08-2019-0435.

Armstrong, M. B., & Landers, R. N. (2017). An evaluation of gamified training: Using narrative to improve reactions and learning. *Simulation and Gaming, 48*(4), 513–538. https://doi.org/10.1177/1046878117703749.

Aura, I., Hassan, L., & Hamari, J. (2021). Teaching within a story: Understanding storification of pedagogy. *International Journal of Educational Research, 106*, 101728. https://doi.org/10.1016/j.ijer.2020.101728.

Avraamidou, L., & Osborne, J. (2009). The role of narrative in communicating science. *International Journal of Science Education, 31*(12), 1683–1707. https://doi.org/10.1080/09500690802380695.

Bell, S. (2010). Project-based learning for the 21st century: Skills for the future. *The Clearing House: A Journal of Educational Strategies, Issues and Ideas, 83*(2), 39–43. https://doi.org/10.1080/00098650903505415.

Bellanca, J. A. (2010). *21st century skills: Rethinking how students learn.* Solution Tree Press.

Best Delegate. (2020). *MUN made easy: How to get started with model United Nations.* Best Delegate Model United Nations. https://bestdelegate.com/mun-made-easy-how-to-get-started-with-model-united-nations/.

Browning, E., & Hohenstein, J. (2015). The use of narrative to promote primary school children's understanding of evolution. *Education 3-13, 43*(5), 530–547. https://doi.org/10.1080/03004279.2013.837943.

Bulatowicz, D. M. (2017). Diverse literature in elementary school libraries: Who chooses and why? [Ph.D., Montana State University]. https://search.proquest.com/docview/1940481556/abstract/401D018C5CE3436EPQ/1.

Buy now – Nintendo switch—Bundles, what's included. (2021). https://www.nintendo.com/switch/buy-now/.

Canning, E. A., LaCosse, J., Kroeper, K. M., & Murphy, M. C. (2020). Feeling like an imposter: The effect of perceived classroom competition on the daily psychological experiences of first-generation college students. *Social Psychological and Personality Science, 11*(5), 647–657. https://doi.org/10.1177/1948550619882032.

Carnes, M. C. (2014). *Minds on fire: How role-immersion games transform college.* Harvard University Press.

Charsky, D., & Mims, C. (2008). Integrating commercial off-the-shelf video games into school curriculums. *TechTrends: Linking Research and Practice to Improve Learning, 52*(5), 38–44.

Checa-Romero, M., & Gómez, I. P. (2018). Minecraft and machinima in action: Development of creativity in the classroom. *Technology, Pedagogy and Education, 27*(5), 625–637. https://doi.org/10.1080/1475939X.2018.1537933.

Clarke, S. J., Peel, D. J., Arnab, S., Morini, L., Keegan, H., & Wood, O. (2017). EscapED: A framework for creating educational escape rooms and interactive games to for higher/further education. *International Journal of Serious Games, 4*(3). https://doi.org/10.17083/ijsg.v4i3.180.

Cokley, K., McClain, S., Enciso, A., & Martinez, M. (2013). An examination of the impact of minority status stress and impostor feelings on the mental health of diverse ethnic minority college students. *Journal of Multicultural Counseling and Development*, *41*(2), 82–95. https://doi.org/10.1002/j.2161-1912.2013.00029.x.

Crossley-Frolick, K. A. (2010). Beyond model UN: Simulating multi-level, multi-actor diplomacy using the millennium development goals. *International Studies Perspectives*, *11*(2), 184–201. https://doi.org/10.1111/j.1528-3585.2010.00401.x.

Csikszentmihalyi, M. (1990). *Flow: The psychology of optimal experience*. Harper Collins.

Dancy, T. E., & Brown, M. C. (2011). The mentoring and induction of educators of color: Addressing the impostor syndrome in academe. *Journal of School Leadership*, *21*(4), 607–634. https://doi.org/10.1177/105268461102100405.

Dellinger, A. J. (2020, January 24). A new report shows how far the video game industry still has to go on diversity. *Mic*. https://www.mic.com/p/game-developers-conference-2020-report-reveals-developers-attitudes-on-diversity-in-the-industry-21745574.

Dennihy, M. (2017). Beyond English: Linguistic diversity in the college English classroom. *MELUS*, *42*(4), 192–212. https://doi.org/10.1093/melus/mlx066.

Deterding, S. (2016). Make-believe in gameful and playful design. In P. Turner & J. T. Harviainen (Eds.), *Digital make-believe* (pp. 101–124). Springer International Publishing. https://doi.org/10.1007/978-3-319-29553-4_7.

deWinter, J., Kocurek, C. A., & Nichols, R. (2014). Taylorism 2.0: Gamification, scientific management and the capitalist appropriation of play. *Journal of Gaming and Virtual Worlds*, *6*(2), 109–127. https://doi.org/10.1386/jgvw.6.2.109_1.

Dickey, M. D. (2006). Game design narrative for learning: Appropriating adventure game design narrative devices and techniques for the design of interactive learning environments. *Educational Technology Research and Development*, *54*(3), 245–263. https://doi.org/10.1007/s11423-006-8806-y.

Engel, S., Pallas, J., & Lambert, S. (2017). Model United Nations and deep learning: Theoretical and professional learning. *Journal of Political Science Education*, *13*(2), 171–184. https://doi.org/10.1080/15512169.2016.1250644.

Favis, E. (2020, August 14). Playing remotely: The massive success of Jackbox Games during the pandemic. *Washington Post*. https://www.washingtonpost.com/video-games/2020/08/14/playing-remotely-massive-success-jackbox-games-during-pandemic/.

Florez-Tighe, V., Mohrmann, S., & García, J. (1983). *Multiethnic literature; supplements for basal readers*. (ED246391). ERIC. https://eric.ed.gov/?id=ED246391.

Fowlin, J. (2021, January 11). *Overcoming the "busywork" dilemma*. Vanderbilt University. https://cft.vanderbilt.edu/2021/01/overcoming-the-busywork-dilemma/.

Frederiksen, N. (1984). The real test bias: Influences of testing on teaching and learning. *American Psychologist*, *39*(3), 193–202. https://doi.org/10.1037/0003-066X.39.3.193.

Games for Change. (2022). *Games for Change*. https://www.gamesforchange.org/.

Gee, J. P. (2008). Cats and portals: Video games, learning, and play. *American Journal of Play*, *1*(2), 229–245.

Giannakas, F., Kambourakis, G., Papasalouros, A., & Gritzalis, S. (2018). A critical review of 13 years of mobile game-based learning. *Educational Technology Research and Development*, *66*(2), 341–384. https://doi.org/10.1007/s11423-017-9552-z.

Guillory, J. (2013). *Cultural capital: The problem of literary canon formation*. University of Chicago Press.

Havens, T., & Lotz, A. D. (2012). *Understanding media industries*. Oxford University Press.

Hewett, K. J. E., Zeng, G., & Pletcher, B. C. (2020). The acquisition of 21st-century skills through video games: Minecraft design process models and their web of class roles. *Simulation and Gaming*, *51*(3), 336–364. https://doi.org/10.1177/1046878120904976.

Huizinga, J. (1955). *Homo ludens: A study of the play-element in culture*. Beacon Press.

Hutchins, H. M. (2015). Outing the imposter: A study exploring imposter phenomenon among higher education faculty. *New Horizons in Adult Education and Human Resource Development, 27*(2), 3–12. https://doi.org/10.1002/nha3.20098.

Ivory, J. D. (2006). Still a man's game: Gender representation in online reviews of video games. *Mass Communication and Society, 9*(1), 103–114. https://doi.org/10.1207/s15327825mcs0901_6.

Jenkins, H. (2004). Game design as narrative architecture. *Computer, 44*(3), 118–130.

Jetton, T. L., & Savage-Davis, E. M. (2005). Preservice teachers develop an understanding of diversity issues through multicultural literature. *Multicultural Perspectives, 7*(1), 30–38.

Juul, J. (2010). *A casual revolution: Reinventing video games and their players*. MIT Press.

LaPierre, J. (2020, July 20). *Gaming's biggest demographics are changing – Here's why that matters*. Filament Games. https://www.filamentgames.com/blog/gamings-biggest-demographics-are-changing-heres-why-that-matters/.

Leary, M. R., Patton, K. M., Orlando, A. E., & Funk, W. W. (2000). The impostor phenomenon: Self-perceptions, reflected appraisals, and interpersonal strategies. *Journal of Personality, 68*(4), 725–756. https://doi.org/10.1111/1467-6494.00114.

Lee, K. M., Park, N., & Jin, S.-A. (2006). Narrative and interactivity in computer games. In P. Vorderer & J. Bryant (Eds.), *Playing video games: Motives, responses, and consequences* (pp. 259–274). Lawrence Erlbaum Associates Publishers.

Lorenz, T. (2020, October 14). Everyone's playing among us. *The New York Times*. https://www.nytimes.com/2020/10/14/style/among-us.html.

Michailidis, L., Balaguer-Ballester, E., & He, X. (2018). Flow and immersion in video games: The aftermath of a conceptual challenge. *Frontiers in Psychology, 9*. https://doi.org/10.3389/fpsyg.2018.01682

Naidoo, J. C. (2014). *The importance of diversity in library programs and material collections for children*. Association for Library Service to Children.

Nicholson, S. (2016). Ask why: Creating a better player experience through environmental storytelling and consistency in escape room design. Paper presented at *Meaningful Play 2016*, Lansing, MI, 1–17. http://scottnicholson.com/pubs/askwhy.pdf.

Nicholson, S. (2018). Creating engaging escape rooms for the classroom. *Childhood Education, 94*(1), 44–49. https://doi.org/10.1080/00094056.2018.1420363.

Pan, R., Lo, H., & Neustaedter, C. (2017). Collaboration, awareness, and communication in real-life escape rooms. In *Proceedings of the 2017 Conference on Designing Interactive Systems*, 1353–1364. https://doi.org/10.1145/3064663.3064767.

Parkman, A. (2016). The imposter phenomenon in higher education: Incidence and impact. *Journal of Higher Education Theory and Practice, 16*(1), Article 1. https://articlegateway.com/index.php/JHETP/article/view/1936.

Partleton, K. (2019, August 16). *Nintendo switch remains the best-selling console of 2019 in the US*. Pocketgamer.Biz. https://www.pocketgamer.biz/news/71416/nintendo-switch-remains-the-highest-selling-console-of-2019/.

Peteet, B. J., Brown, C. M., Lige, Q. M., & Lanaway, D. A. (2015). Impostorism is associated with greater psychological distress and lower self-esteem for African American students. *Current Psychology: a Journal for Diverse Perspectives on Diverse Psychological Issues, 34*(1), 154–163. https://doi.org/10.1007/s12144-014-9248-z.

Pittman, C. (2013). Teaching with portals: The intersection of video games and physics education. *Learning Landscapes, 6*(2), 341–360. https://doi.org/10.36510/learnland.v6i2.620.

Portal 2—Educational Version—Portal Wiki. (2015, November 14). https://theportalwiki.com/wiki/Portal_2_-_Educational_Version.

Prins, R., Avraamidou, L., & Goedhart, M. (2017). Tell me a story: The use of narrative as a learning tool for natural selection. *Educational Media International, 54*(1), 20–33. https://doi.org/10.1080/09523987.2017.1324361.

Reich, J. (2020). *Failure to disrupt: Why technology alone can't transform education.* Harvard University Press.

Rotherham, A. J., & Willingham, D. T. (2010). 21st century skills: Not new, but a worthy challenge. *American Educator, 17*(1), 17–20.

Ruberg, B. (2019). *Video games have always been queer.* New York University Press.

Saavedra, A. R., & Opfer, V. D. (2012). Learning 21st-century skills requires 21st-century teaching. *Phi Delta Kappan, 94*(2), 8–13. https://doi.org/10.1177/003172171209400203.

Salter, A. (2014). *What is your quest?: From Adventure games to interactive books.* University of Iowa Press.

Shute, V. J., Ventura, M., & Ke, F. (2015). The power of play: The effects of portal 2 and lumosity on cognitive and noncognitive skills. *Computers and Education, 80,* 58–67. https://doi.org/10.1016/j.compedu.2014.08.013.

Šisler, V. (2008). Digital Arabs: Representation in video games. *European Journal of Cultural Studies, 11*(2), 203–220. https://doi.org/10.1177/1367549407088333.

Soderman, B. (2021). *Against flow: Video games and the flowing subject.* MIT Press.

Stallworth, B. J., Gibbons, L., & Fauber, L. (2006). It's not on the list: An exploration of teachers' perspectives on using multicultural literature. *Journal of Adolescent and Adult Literacy, 49*(6), 478–489. https://doi.org/10.1598/JAAL.49.6.3.

Tate, R., Haritatos, J., & Cole, S. (2009). HopeLab's approach to ReMission. *International Journal of Learning and Media, 1*(1), 29–35. https://doi.org/10.1162/ijlm.2009.0003.

Toda, A., Valle, P. H., & Isotani, S. (2018). The dark side of gamification: An overview of negative effects of gamification in education. https://doi.org/10.1007/978-3-319-97934-2_9.

Tyack, D., & Cuban, L. (2009). *Tinkering toward utopia: A century of public school reform.* Harvard University Press.

Vaughn, A. R., Taasoobshirazi, G., & Johnson, M. L. (2020). Impostor phenomenon and motivation: Women in higher education. *Studies in Higher Education, 45*(4), 780–795. https://doi.org/10.1080/03075079.2019.1568976.

Verswijvelen, M., Sosa, R., & Martini, N. (2020). Designing game-inspired narratives for learning. *DRS Conference Papers.* https://dl.designresearchsociety.org/drs-conference-papers/drs2020/researchpapers/97.

Webb, K. (2019, December 15). Video game sales are down in 2019 as the industry prepares for the PlayStation 5 and Xbox Series *X,* but that didn't stop this year's best-sellers from setting new records. *Business Insider.* https://www.businessinsider.com/best-selling-video-games-of-the-year-2019-2019-12.

What is Minecraft. (2021). Minecraft: Education Edition. https://minecraftedu.westus.cloudapp.azure.com/how-it-works/what-is-minecraft.

Young, C. A. (2019). Interrogating the lack of diversity in Award-Winning LGBTQ-inclusive picturebooks. *Theory into Practice, 58*(1), 61–70. https://doi.org/10.1080/00405841.2018.1536915.

Zirkel, S. (2002). Is there a place for me? Role models and academic identity among white students and students of color. *Teachers College Record, 104*(2), 357–376.

3 Searching for meaningful pandemic play

A virtual third place?

The book *Higher Education in the Digital Age*, first published in 2002, opens with an alarmingly accurate prediction: "A Particularly Open Letter to the Faculty from the President on the Occasion of the Closing of a University's Doors Forever," addressed from a hypothetical future May 2020. The letter included this warning:

> When those pixilated patients first become available in the '90s—and I remember my 12-year-old daughter conducting simulated surgery, mask and all, on those ADAM and EVE anatomy programs—we should have simply sat down and spent some time with them ourselves. We would have seen how completely engrossing they were and that they actually did teach, a mixture we as professors struggle mightily to achieve in the classroom.
>
> (Duderstadt et al., 2002, pp. 5–6)

The letter (written by Frank DeSanto) also addresses changes in public funding, private and for-profit competition, and other dire predictions that mirror the realities of the several institutions that did close, permanently, in 2020: while DeSanto doesn't predict the pandemic, his timetable is not too far removed from our reality. However, DeSanto places the blame in part on the ability of the digital (and playful) to draw in players to learning in a way the classroom does not, echoing a dualism that the pandemic has helped in part to strike down. By reflecting on his imagined future, and considering the realities of virtual pandemic play, we seek in this chapter to reconcile the tensions between the imagined playful classroom and our lived experience and look for exemplars of gaming that served to sustain community at a time of social distancing.

We can understand this search for meaningful pandemic play as a quest to restore Ray Oldenburg's "third place": the spaces which "lend a public balance to the increased privatization of home life"—a balance fundamentally disrupted globally by the pandemic, and restored in pieces, unequally distributed, as different communities prioritized spaces of work or learning, while others (including Florida, where the authors reside) put their focus on the social sphere. According to one Nielsen study in the United States, 55% of residents were playing games

DOI: 10.4324/9781003281696-4

at the height of lockdown. In the April 2020 survey, players listed their top reasons for play as: "Combat boredom / fill time; Escape the real world; Substitute for unavailable entertainment; Stay in touch with friends/family; Socialize with strangers" (NielsenIQ, 2021). Education, unsurprisingly, does not make the list, but note the significance of the third place in this rhetoric: games opened a virtual door to other worlds.

Most importantly, the impact of these play experiences will last beyond the pandemic: socially distanced *Dungeons & Dragons* has brought gaming groups together outside of spatial limitations. The constraints of the physical tabletop, particularly given the economic investments often required for a rotating arsenal of figurines and tile sets, no longer seem worth accepting. Many have discovered what proponents of accessible, virtual, and hybrid modalities (in education and beyond) have long been arguing: that the physical is not inherently "realer." Indeed, the virtual can enable types of collaboration that compel and demand our continuing investment post-pandemic as we rethink the tabletops of both game night and classroom.

DeSanto predicted a shift from physical prioritization, arguing that the physical classroom would be displaced by the virtual engagement he saw in games and simulations. What we instead see in pandemic play is a deconstruction of the hierarchy, and a reinvention of the dominant third space born of necessity, but with lasting impact. The rejection of digital dualism is not a certain outcome of the pandemic in education (consider the op-eds calling for refunds for "inferior" online education, for instance)—but gaming lends us models of innovation and growth that will likely remain. The breakdown of this binary is already embedded in many virtual communities around gaming, as members of *World of Warcraft* guilds; EVE Online communities; *Second Life* art collectives; and so forth all have long shared stories of the wealth of what online connectivity through play can offer. Weddings, lifetime friendships, support communities – the list goes on, and play has enabled them.

Socially distanced community

The lockdown recommendations and mandates of the COVID-19 pandemic prevented many popular social events and activities that had become common. As individuals worked to navigate the divide between their need to socialize and their need to practice social distancing, virtual options became appealing. Video games such as *Among Us*, *Tabletop Simulator*, the suite of Jackbox games, and *Animal Crossing: New Horizons* were used to bridge this gap. These casual games each had unique affordances that positioned them as the logical choice to reinvent what it meant to be social during these unprecedented times. Several varieties of virtual representations of physical board games proliferated. These platforms enabled groups who had previously met in person to play board games to continue meeting and playing virtually. It also fostered the creation of new communities of virtual game playing, as even those who had not regularly met for game nights found the familiarity of board games an approachable way to engage in social activities safely.

Many of the entertainment platforms that adapted well to the pandemic already had styles and affordances which lent themselves to the task of replacing in-person social activities. The technology required to run these games was already owned and mastered by a large popular audience. No new equipment was needed to participate in many of these suddenly viral games, and those that seemed to gain the most popularity during the pandemic were socially based and required little to none of the hand–eye coordination or controller mashing stereotypical of the AAA games and their emphasis on the FPS genre. One well-known social game that had a robust community well before the pandemic was *Dungeons & Dragons*: this is the flagship tabletop role-playing game, but also exemplifies a broader interest in shared narrative genres.

The distanced models of *Dungeons & Dragons* rely upon well-structured community resources for play, which remove some of the challenges of sharing materials and collaborating at a distance. The structure of one of the leading platforms, *D&D Beyond*, evoked the learning management system: players join different campaigns, gaining access to materials shared by their fellow players and dungeon master, and allowing updates to their character sheet and stats in real time. Wizards of the Coast fueled interest with their "Stay at Home. Play at Home" campaign, featuring free resources and promising to keep education in mind:

> with schools closed around the world, many parents and caregivers are at home with their kids, including many in the *D&D* community. If you are in need of fun & educational material to share and/or play with your kids, you can check back here for *D&D* materials to help during this time. And if you (or someone you know) is a younger gamer, we're also releasing resources to make it even easier to get into *D&D*.
>
> (Wizards of the Coast, 2020)

Examples of the family-oriented materials included the free "Monster Slayers: Champion of the Elements" adventure focused on younger gamers, while material for everyone included extensive options for Zoom digital backgrounds, short adventures, and similar content.

D&D Beyond connects through a browser extension to virtual tabletop systems such as *Roll20*, *Tabletop Simulator*, and *FoundryVTT*. These tools in turn replace the game map and miniatures of a traditional in-person campaign, offering a shared screen simulation that all players can manipulate simultaneously. Acting as the perfect virtual markerboard, these systems can even handle information transference directly from the correlated texts.

Such collaborative models evoke the browser-based collaborative tools under development in education: the virtual whiteboard, or Jamboard, brings the platonic ideal of the markerboard to the screen—without fussing over spatial dynamics, users can simultaneously fill it and re-envision its contents. Digital solutions of this kind have been an allure of the smart classroom, but the reality is frequently expensive and frustrating—Microsoft's PixelSense, for instance, promised a future of smart tables adaptable to multiple tasks that has gone largely unrealized.

D&D executive producer Ray Winninger notes the suitability of the current game to this type of play:

> Fifth Edition has been the most successful version of the game … It, fortunately, happened to land in a place where it's easy [to play] in situations we find ourselves now. When we're all isolated, *D&D* is a great opportunity to maintain a connection with people you're close to.
>
> (Francisco, 2020)

Notably, *D&D* has been criticized for its lack of inclusivity in enabling those connections, but recently has been working toward the corrections of fantastical stereotypes that often rely on highly gendered, binary norms as well as racist notions of "evil" and "dumb" races.

The owner of one of the platforms, Doug Davidson of Fantasy Grounds, said he noted a spike of "about tenfold" in usage early in the pandemic. Speaking in a March 2020 interview, he observed: "We have seen a huge spike in users …. It's becoming a mandatory thing where that's the only way people can still get together and game" (Grebey, 2020). Another platform leader, Adam Bradford of *D&D Beyond*, noted the appeal at preserving some of the lost contact during isolation:

> The thing that you're clearly going to be missing when playing remote during this crisis is human interaction … You're going to miss the little side-conversation jokes that happen, you're gonna have to slow down the pace of the game. It's going to be missing some of the physical body language interactions and elements that make this game so great. But, again, I think it's absolutely better than not being able to play at all, and we all need a little entertainment as we're self-isolating.
>
> (Grebey, 2020)

Notably, this was an international trend: platforms noted a particular early increase from users in Italy before lockdowns spread. At the time, the expectation was that physical play would return soon. As it stands, use statistics on one platform, *Tabletop Simulator*, demonstrate strong increases aligned with the pandemic, but overall strong patterns of continued use (Table 3.1).

Unsurprisingly, March and April 2020 are outliers in this usage: however, the appeal of the platform continues.

Precursors to these platforms often emphasized asynchronous play: forum-based and PBEM (play by email) games have been sustained since the early web. However, the mechanisms described here provide a much stronger focus on recreating the shared space of play: the physicality is emphasized even as platforms take advantage of digital affordances. For instance, *FoundryVTT* (Virtual TableTop) allows for "rolling" directly to the tabletop. Rolls are displayed alongside the

Table 3.1 Use statistics on Tabletop Simulator

Month	Avg. Players	Gain	% Gain	Peak Players
Last 30 days	5,881.5	–618.7	–9.52%	15,168
April 2021	6,500.2	–534.5	–7.60%	16,536
March 2021	7,034.7	–710.6	–9.18%	18,872
February 2021	7,745.4	–792.9	–9.29%	20,653
January 2021	8,538.3	+1,668.8	+24.29%	21,781
December 2020	6,869.5	+398.0	+6.15%	17,721
November 2020	6,471.5	+1,055.0	+19.48%	17,222
October 2020	5,416.5	+272.9	+5.31%	14,692
September 2020	5,143.6	–1,113.4	–17.79%	12,503
August 2020	6,256.9	–521.0	–7.69%	14,829
July 2020	6,777.9	+297.2	+4.59%	15,529
June 2020	6,480.7	–2,815.0	–30.28%	16,169
May 2020	9,295.7	–3,698.0	–28.46%	27,108
April 2020	**12,993.7**	**+7,752.9**	**+147.93%**	**36,793**
March 2020	**5,240.9**	**+2,800.2**	**+114.73%**	**26,141**

map, and the feed of activity is recorded for the DM navigating choices like the calculation of combat order from initiative or deciding the outcome of an encounter (Figure 3.1). To recall Jamboard, this offers a manipulable, shared physicality with some affordances that are beyond the physical.

Platforms like *D&D Beyond* seek to meld the convenience of the digital with the familiarity of the material: for example, players can roll the correct dice for a character check without making the calculation by clicking an option directly on their character sheet. Rolls are vividly material (the die bounces, with accompanying noises) even as the calculations are algorithmic. This blending demonstrates the best of what "blendflex" and "hybrid" modalities struggled with during pandemic conversions: finding the balance in digital and physical, and preserving the essential aspects of play (or learning) while eliminating unnecessary labor. The need to track every change's impact on a character's development, for instance, is handled by the system – players are left to focus on the affordances of growth, not the tedium.

Socially distanced socializing

Other social games that required little prior knowledge, skill, or sophisticated gaming technologies also found new customer bases. The browser-plus-mobile phone platform of Jackbox games allowed groups of friends to play a variety of casual games with one another on only one purchased license. With a wide range of game styles ranging from trivia to t-shirt drawing, the platform saw a 251% increase in players, with approximately 250 million people playing from March 1, 2020, to mid-February 2021 (Jackbox Games, 2021)—often following up with players after the game with offers to sell them some of the t-shirts they had made

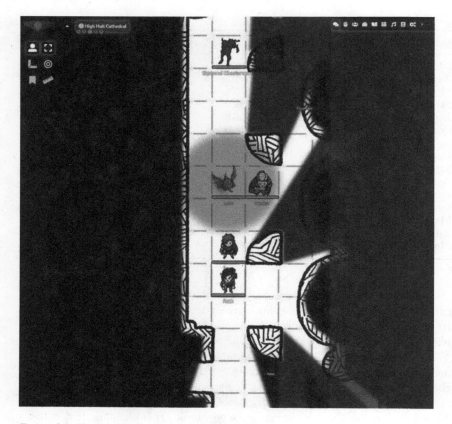

Figure 3.1 Shared play on a "virtual table top."

in the game with their friends. The co-creation and in a way, co-crafting, that these games engaged players in together provided a humorous, creative outlet for players to explore with their friends.

Jackbox games predate the pandemic, and their distinctive structuring previously invoked the living room as a site of play. Some of the game's mechanics are based on carefully watching other players, for instance, while others assume the frenetic pace of communication around the room. The trivia-style games are particularly well-suited to display on a large monitor or TV, eliminating the need for expensive consoles and creating opportunities for social play without additional fiscal costs. The striking suitability of the format to Zoom predates the pandemic and is thus perhaps unintentional: streamers immediately caught on to the value of showing a "big screen," and the addition of an "audience" mode for large parties seems remarkably fortuitous for streaming.

The history of these types of social games is notably indebted to physical spaces and game modalities: the physical party game, and the model of trivia night competitive gatherings, heavily influences the game modalities of the Jackbox "Party Packs," which nominally suggest an in-person gathering. However, the integration of remote play mechanisms to the Jackbox play experience invites the players to view the screen as the "site" of the party, assisting in the crafting of a much-needed "third place" within the confines of social distancing. Ray Oldenburg notes the importance of third places as "community-builders": the closure of so many physical third places (including campus libraries, cafes, computer labs, bookstores, and parks) left a void (Oldenburg, 2013).

Some of the most compelling examples of Jackbox gameplay recall Jamboard and other physical play in their affordances. For instance, the popular *Draw Something* game mimics a party game along the lines of *Pictionary*, but allows all players to draw in unison, using the distributed play mechanisms to decrease time spent waiting, and increase the speed of transmission of that which has been created. Variants on this theme (such as *Tee KO*, a vaguely martial arts themed competition game for designing T-shirts, as shown in Figure 3.2) emphasize collaboration: one player writes a slogan for another's art, trying to capture the imagination of other players through the juxtaposition. The results of such play can be satirical, absurd, or simply odd, but the act of collaborating occurs with far less friction than the average classroom exchange.

Similarly, Jackbox games engage players in meaningful dialogue regarding powerful questions of current digital literacy: the many iteration of the *Fibbage* series, for instance, asks players to engage both in the crafting and the deconstruction of misinformation, while offering reminders about the assumptions we make in seeking truths. Another game, *Faking It*, asks players to engage in social manipulation. Such structures combine the best aspects of collaboration and competition to encourage engagement.

Figure 3.2 An example of co-creative play in Jackbox.

The most obviously educational games in Jackbox resemble gamification in their use of sensationalized trivia: in addition to variants on the classic *You Don't Know Jack*, models such as *Trivia Murder Party* intersperse minigames and sarcasm with multiple-choice quizzes, offering no apologies for the repetitive nature of their main content thanks to the expressive play offered by the competition. While this model is not necessarily immediately adaptable for the future classroom, it certainly offers a reminder of how the interface and interaction around a design can fundamentally shift the player's (or student's) relationship with it. In an era of static, overly uniform, learning management systems, the retro animation and playful sound design of Jackbox games offer a compelling alternative.

Another suddenly popular social game was *Among Us*. This inexpensive computer download that was published in 2017 is part *Clue* and part playground tag, taking place on a damaged spaceship. The game features a randomly selected person out of the four to ten players to be the impostor, whose job is to sabotage the ship and murder the crew. (If there are six or more players, two impostors will be randomly selected and can conspire with one another.) The non-impostor crew members are given a number of tasks to complete to repair their spaceship, all the while on the lookout for the impostor. Crewmates can meet and vote to remove a player from the ship—an action which reveals, after the fact, whether or not the booted member is in fact the impostor. The crew wins if they boot the impostor and save their ship; the impostor wins if they eliminate the crew or destroy the ship.

Notably, the retro, nostalgic graphical choices highlighted by both *Among Us* and Jackbox games may work toward potential inclusion:

> the depersonalized player characters in *Among Us*, lacking in facial features as well as in indicators of gender, race, or any other identity, have become iconic. This removal of positionality perhaps speaks to a white liberal exhaustion with being asked to consider race and gender, recalling the classic tech utopianism discourse of "on the Internet, no one knows you're a dog" in its elimination of identity personalization that results in a white default.
> (Stanfill et al., 2021)

If we recall the discussion in Chapter 2 regarding the settler mindset often embedded in popular historically framed games, *Among Us*'s representation offers an opposite case study, creating a space for playful avatar personalization (through the purchase of hats and companion pets) while simultaneously removing visual positionality.

Among Us became so popular that even celebrities and politicians were playing and streaming the game. With the shutdowns and US Center for Disease Control's advice to avoid crowds continuing throughout the campaign cycle, politicians sought alternative, digital ways to connect with voters. In October, House of Representatives members Alexandria Ocasio-Cortez and Ilhan Omar livestreamed a game of *Among Us* on Twitch, a popular video game streaming platform. This play-centric outreach resonated with many people—meeting voters on a platform where they already spent time and playing a game rather than giving a speech or lecture on the divisive political topic of the day seemed to be an effective way for these politicians to demonstrate their capability of, as a writer from *The Guardian* put it, "acting normal" (Rivera, 2020). Again, this moment serves as a reminder of the potential of a shift in platform and context to shift receptiveness to discourse: several educators have adopted the Twitch stream approach, suggesting similar potential for reshaping the classroom (and enabling introverts to participate through a different modality)

Post-pandemic education could take some notes from this event and others like it: play can help disarm people of their preconceptions and prime them for listening, learning, and understanding. Educational psychologists point to a set of basic psychological needs that must be met in order for individuals to even be capable of meaningful learning, part of Maslow's Hierarchy of Needs, which identifies belongingness, esteem, and self-actualization (Mcleod, 2020). Games can help instill these feelings in the learners and players—by engaging in a game, a player enters the "magic circle," a term used to define the imaginary boundaries creating an area where players engage in game-driven rules that differ from the social conventions and norms of the non-game world (Huizinga, J., 1955). This game area creates a group of players, invites belongingness, along with the interaction with the game and other players, which can also convey a sense of esteem and self-actualization.

For a more utopianesque escape, many turned to *Animal Crossing: New Horizons* (*ACNH*), which was released on the Nintendo Switch during March 2020, a period where there were widespread global lockdowns in an unsuccessful attempt to stop the epidemic from reaching the level of a pandemic. *ACNH* predates the pandemic as a franchise, but the release of the game during the pandemic will inextricably tie it to the context of distant play. Images of *ACNH* facilitating reunions, weddings, conferences, and even funerals circulated to demonstrate the platform's success at a visually compelling and non-toxic alternative to the tedium of Zoom. Sullivan, Salter, and Stanfill argue that this affirms the significance of such play to our understanding of the pandemic distancing:

> that our experience of *ACNH* has been shaped by COVID-19 as much as the game has been an outlet during the experience of social isolation; while Zoom might be the headline-stealing technology for the times, *ACNH* is the platform where our new relationships with the domestic have been tested, challenged, and re-imagined.
>
> (2021, pre-print)

This positioning is global: *Animal Crossing* invited everyone to the island, even as it was amplified to particular significance by American popular culture and political stress.

Here as well, because of the widespread bans on large in-person crowds, we saw political hopefuls meeting voters in a virtual, playful space. The Biden-Harris campaign created a campaign headquarters on its own island in *ACNH* (Kelly, 2020). The island included decorated areas for players to take photos, a campaign field office, and a polling station. A Joe Biden avatar also walked the island, posing for virtual selfies and responding to every player question or comment with his signature phrase, "no malarkey!" Like Ocasio-Cortez and Omar, the Biden HQ island enjoyed a virtual tour livestreamed on Twitch. The campaign even paid to create virtual Biden-Harris yard signs for players to place in their *ACNH* lawns. Taking this playful approach to campaigning again seemed to resonate with voters. The Biden-Harris campaign worked to leverage playful spaces similar to Shira Chess's advice that feminist protesters, "find more room for play and laughter in the fight" (2020, p. 83).

A brief history of the virtual gaming world

In the 1990s, text-based worlds attracted the imagination of educators experimenting with their potential for global communities and explorable spaces: as a collection capturing the state of the field in 1998 opened:

> the MOO is not just a place to manipulate code, text, and the designs of engineers or programmers but can be, as our authors show, a space for bricoleurs, for those who create from what they have on hand, constructing and recycling imaginative murmurings in archi*textual* ways. MOOs reinvent the notion of education, and their users reconceive this space to accommodate radically different genres of discourse and pedagogies.
> (Haynes & Holmevik, 2001, p. 4)

These platforms look at lot like the group texts of today, but with environmental design and opportunities for movement through text—in many ways, they are a reminder of how text has been one of the most efficient forms of collective online education from the start of the web.

The pathway from MOOs to more robust online worlds was filled with interesting experiments, some of which found their way into the classroom. One of the earliest visions of an animated, avatar-driven virtual world was Lucasfilms project *Habitat*, which was described by designers Chip Morningstar and F. Randall Farmer in a postmortem in 1990 as an ambitious project for creating a fully realized third space:

> The system we developed can support a population of thousands of users in a single shared cyberspace. Habitat presents its users with a real-time animated view into an online simulated world in which users can communicate, play games, go on adventures, fall in love, get married, get divorced, start businesses, found religions, wage wars, protest against them, and experiment with self-government.
> (Morningstar & Farmer, 2008)

Successors to this project's vision would frequently focus on social and playful usages, but interest in virtual worlds for education would increase with the power and affordability of the technology. A taxonomy of virtual world usage conducted a decade ago in 2012 already noted the interest in virtual worlds for supporting collaborative and experiential learning (Duncan et al., 2012). While many platforms had captured the imagination of educators by that point, *Second Life* was the first to truly offer a vision of a future campus. Coverage in 2007 focused on the exciting opportunities offered by its pre-cryptocurrency "real" economy, and certainly the platform profited from the interest of universities in establishing a presence: private islands required not only in-game resources, but also rent, costing universities hundreds or thousands of dollars a month to establish customized terrain. The idea of virtual goods as a commodity was still new (DLC and Ian Bogost's expensive cows were not yet on the horizon), and the economics of what Martin refers to as "virtual commodities as symbols of status, individuality, and belonging" were on the rise (Martin, 2008). These in turn became hosting grounds for events and even classes, though those suffered from extensive logistical issues: *Second Life*'s interface is opaque at best, relying upon comfort with avatar-driven exploration and even flight to navigate the expansive world. *Second Life* was also a site of extensive disruption and trolling.

A journalist revisiting the islands in 2015 noted the landscape was entirely abandoned, and strange:

> the college islands are bizarre. They mostly are laid out in a way to evoke stereotypes of how college campuses should look, but mixed in is a streak of absurd choices, like classrooms in tree houses and pirate ships. These decisions might have seemed whimsical at the time, but with the dated graphics, they just look weird.
>
> (Hogan, 2015)

Time has not been kind to these spaces, belonging as they do to an era of 3D that has not, as of yet, evoked the nostalgia of earlier, more constrained graphical systems such as pixel art.

For those who never experienced *Second Life*, Mark Stephen Meadows's ethnographic study of the world offers a compelling description of it in 2006:

> the virtual online world also dedicated to profitable automation, easy luxury, inexpensive fun, and independence. Itself a product of the American Dream, *Second Life* produces hordes of Kens and Barbies we call avatars. Like vehicles driven through an online landscape, they float blank-eyed in their magic kingdom, each hoping to strike it rich, become a star, find a friend, or simply explore new possibilities.
>
> (Meadows, 2007)

Note the early conceptualization of avatar (a term at this time mostly associated with games) and the sense of virtual worlds as a space not just for possibility but for profit: this same desire would shape the economics of massively multiplayer worlds, but would become a driving aspect of *Second Life* as an aspirational platform. Julian Dibbell described this progression as inevitable, noting the influence of gold farmers, eBay sellers, and other "enemies of the virtual state" on fictional currency in 2006 (Dibbell, 2006).

Of course, this same type of mingling would bring with it an excessive culture of trolling and "griefing," a "subversive practice" involving everything from disrupting environments and harassing others to crafting phallic objects in every possible space (Bakioglu, 2008). No platform can escape trolling, but *Second Life*'s customizable items and wealth of craftable material made it a particularly inviting space for such play. Notably, the *Second Life* creators decided to allow all play to be anonymous: as Tom Boellstroff describes in his ethnography of the platform:

> Influenced by everything from the history of games and roleplaying to the Burning Man festival, the creators of *Second Life* decided at the outset to delink avatar accounts from physical world identities ... one valuable lesson from *Second Life* is that pseudonymity is not the same thing as anonymity,

as the avatar name "has a reputation ... if a *Second Life* resident is a member of various friendship networks and groups, that resident is not 'anonymous' at a collective level" (Boellstorff, 2015).

Researchers particularly looked at early *Second Life* for its potential for rapid design, both by learners and by educators building simulations:

> Simulations enable learners not only to see how a place looks, but also "feel" what it is like being part of it. To date, simulations have been a very expensive part of educational provision. *SL* makes them cheap and highly accessible, and they could become a key "killer application" of the future.
> (Salmon, 2009)

Second Life's "communal world-building" and potential for what Axel Bruns termed "produsage" in 2008 particularly captured the imagination of educators at the time (Bruns, 2008). The suitability of this type of shared, reshapable, space for certain types of education, such as critical media literacy, captured some educators, as Jennifer deWinter and Stephanie Vie noted the potential but also the risks:

> Though *Second Life* can force students into situations where they must consider how difference and inequality operate even (and perhaps especially) in virtual communities, such situations help them become more aware of how online technologies help maintain hegemonic power structures. At the same time, *Second Life* creates a space for the important work of teaching critical media literacy in the composition classroom by asking students not only to participate in a virtual world but also to help shape it.
> (deWinter & Vie, 2008)

Successors to *Second Life* continue: VR company VirBELA provides the virtual campus for an online certificate program at Stanford, which is marketed with an emphasis on the avatar-driven experience of place once promised by its predecessor:

"It's really important to us that not only do our participants get the content from our faculty," said Marineh Lalikian, director of the LEAD online business program, "but also develop a sense of community with their peers and maintain that high-touch relationship building and connections with other people they would otherwise benefit from if they were here on campus."

(Burke, 2019)

In spite of the demonstrated frustration of many of these highly fussy interfaces, the idea that avatar-based connection will enhance learning persists.

These "high touch" relationships are part of what the pandemic disrupted—or, at least, interrupted—with the closure of campus third places globally: even in countries that prioritized returns to the classroom, the other shared spaces essential to community-building frequently remained shuttered as the very characteristics that make them desirable were noted globally as risk factors. It is thus no surprise that companies and institutions around the globe turned to these ambitious models from the past for inspiration on how to solve the problem of disconnection—and are building new iterations that we will discuss further in Chapter 4—even though they we would be better served turning to the retro animation and team dynamics of Jackbox and *Among Us*.

Low-tech, high-touch play

One of the more surprising collective play experiences of the later waves of the pandemic, *Wordle*, is also one of the most low-tech, and least graphical: it thus offers us insights into how a minimalist, thoughtful experience can circulate and create space for communal play. There is nothing particularly unfamiliar about *Wordle*; in the manner of *Mastermind* style code games, it presents users with a word to guess every day. As with the play experiences of Jackbox, some of its cleverness lies in this connection to familiar physical play—but unlike Jackbox, it doesn't seek to augment or extend that tradition. Its minimalist web interface allows the player to focus, and notably forgoes any of the features or visual enticements we typically associate with gaming today: there are also no advertisements, no logins, and no data collection.

Designer Josh Wardle saw the game's popularity rise almost overnight, from 90 players to 2 million a day in January 2022, and credits it in part with the impact of the Omicron wave of COVID-19, as he said to a reporter:

> I get emails from people who say things like "hey, we can't see our parents due to Covid at the moment but we share our Wordle results each day." During this weird situation it's a way for people to connect in a low effort, low friction way.
>
> (Hall, 2022)

This echoes similar discussions of success around *Animal Crossing* and Jackbox games, but notably describes a game that has even lower barriers to entry—no expense, nothing to download, and a transparent, typing-based interface. The game is a global phenomenon (with a particularly high player base in New Zealand) thanks in part to its shareability without the need for opting into a platform: "In a massive unifying moment across the Internet, it's the same word for all of us," making the shared experience particularly resonant (Brandon, 2022).

Naturally, it has inspired many imitators: a collection as of January 2022 noted the existence of *Sweardle, Queerdle, Letterle, Absurdle,* and *Hello Wordl*—each with its own gimmick (and of course, forks for different languages abound) (Vincent, 2022). Most of these imitations have stuck to the free model, attributing the source and forgoing advertisements, but unsurprisingly others have taken to commercial modification: Zack Shakked attracted instant criticism for trying to mislead players with a blatantly plagiarized release to the app store, complete with in-app purchases (DeAngelo, 2022). We cannot help but see parallels to other efforts at commercialization in educational technology's often parasitic relationship with games (as discussed at greater length in Chapters 1 and 2).

The incredible success of *Wordle* is something any educator would envy: a simple language-driven experience that players are visiting daily. It is but one of many such games to occupy this type of viral position over the years, but it is particularly striking in how it recalls a much older version of the web. Other than its intuitively shareable results—which brilliantly includes no spoilers but allows comparison through illustrating successful guesses without letters—it is an example of success through rejection of almost every affordance of the modern web. As the shadow of the so-called "Web3" looms over us (as we will discuss at length in Chapter 4), it is a well-timed reminder of the power of simple play.

Virtually no play

The stories in this chapter are success stories for the preservation of the third place, and for the sustainability of community through online mechanisms: they reflect what we already know from years of virtual community examination and ethnographic observation, but also indicate the potential for the expansion of access through such platforms of play in the future. But we are left to wonder: given how many entertainment games adapted deftly to the "pivot to online" throughout the pandemic, why hasn't digital pedagogy also adapted as easily? Where can we find the educational, playful, equivalents to the play experiences documented here—experiences that learn from the physical, social play environments that the traditional classroom used to be well-suited for? The answer is likely that they are everywhere, scattered in experiences built by teachers and students working together—and unlike *Wordle*, they are unlikely to go viral without intentional search.

However, we also cannot ignore the ongoing challenges of trauma, and the value of these games during the pandemic in offering players and students a third space away from the crushing weight of the home as office as classroom, particularly for those sharing their spaces and restricted in their travel and movement. In many palpable ways, the charade of the work-life balance came crashing down during the pandemic, with the locations previously associated with "work" and "home" merging while we worked from home. The separation of "work" and "life" vanished, and we were left with only worklife. The games noted here work to decontextualize and reframe the desktop or phone into a compelling third place: they offer temporary relief to an ongoing strain.

Meanwhile, the technologies these games share screenspace with frequently undermine our play. Microsoft's "habits" analytics dutifully report workers' so-called "quiet hours" the definition of which (and the "productivity" taking place during these times) the employer can be left to presume or question. The belief that workers needed to constantly be productive during a lockdown during a global pandemic pervaded daily life around the globe and bled into education. As Chapter 2 details, surveillance software exacerbated this feeling and made it tangible. Already overworked and overwhelmed, teachers found themselves crisis teaching.

As discussed in Chapter 2, the pandemic forced faculty to quickly materialize entire courses mid-semester with almost no warning. The courses were pasted into LMS systems as rapidly as possible, and expectations were adapted and lowered accordingly. As projections for "only two weeks" of closed campuses stretched to the remainder of the spring, summer, and fall semesters, we continued to teach in crisis mode. Nobody asked for this. It is unreasonable to expect faculty to innovate digital pedagogy in any sort of playful way while also dealing with prolonged, additional burdens with the shutting down of K-12 schools, massive layoffs, and extra precautions necessary for a number of high-risk demographics. In May 2020, the US Department of Labor estimated that nearly 90 million adults were "forced home" by COVID-19 shutdowns, with two out of five of these adults were also caring for children, nearly one half with another "forced home" adult, and more than two thirds shared their home with another adult who was not in the workforce (retiree or stay-at-home spouse) (Van Dam, 2021).

As the months wore on, the arguments between administrators and faculty over questionable interpretations of student demands for the "college experience" exacerbated the already overwhelming stressors of higher education. Many faculty (and often adjuncts and instructors with less job security and lower pay) were forced to teach in person, all the while being told to be flexible and accommodate student absences and student requests to attend the physical classes remotely like never before.

The corporate surveillance of education was fully realized in the University of Florida's modifications to the university's student-facing public safety app to facilitate student reporting of who were not holding in-person classes (Flasherty, 2021). Yet further evidence that the higher education institutional focus views employees and students as income-generating numbers above all else, the selected-response options under "report course concerns" include:

Instructor was not in the class.
Instructor modified the class to virtual.
Instructor cannot be reached.
Instructor does not hold virtual lectures during the class period.

Though these options were modified after massive outcry on social media, the demoralizing seeds of mistrust between faculty, students, and administration were sown.

These surveillance technologies obviously did not foster innovation or playful pedagogy. Indeed, these circumstances made it impossible for innovation—these circumstances required every resource available just to survive them: this was teaching in crisis mode. As others have highlighted, crisis mode teaching is not the same as well-designed, intentional online instruction (Hodges et al., 2020). As we emerge on the other side of this terrible period in history and dig ourselves out from the trauma and stress we have all endured in varying ways and degrees, we can create an atmosphere of healing. We can rediscover the joy of teaching and learning. While we rethink what it means to teach and learn, as we redesign our courses to emphasize the essential activities and weed out the busywork, let us embrace playful classroom atmospheres, role-play, and engagement.

Imagining a playful future

We owe it to ourselves and our students to take the hard-earned lessons learned from emergency remote instruction and apply them to the intentional design of educational environments in the future—across modalities. What might a course or learning activity look like if it were modeled after *Among Us*, the Jackbox games, or distant *Dungeons & Dragons*?

The suspicion-based collaborative (and at times competitive) problem-solving nature of *Among Us* lends itself well to educational activities. The subject areas educators strive to "cover" in any given class period or semester are filled with complex problems, mysteries to uncover, facts to discover, and connections to make between ideas. Presenting these built-in mysteries as engaging, imagined worlds and assigning learners various roles in those worlds, especially roles where students take on expert perspectives, could be one way to integrate play into the classroom.

Education researchers have explored the impact of encouraging learners to view content from an "expert perspective," they adjust their performance and behavior accordingly, often demonstrating increased understanding of the subject. Common in classroom discussions, where teachers ask students to "think like a scientist" or consider what an expert in the field might ask or look for to solve a particular problem, the idea of encouraging learners to "try on" the role of an established figure in the field is rather common. More formal investigations in the scholarship of this type of perspective taking are sometimes referred to as a "professional vision" (Goodwin, 1994) or "disciplined perception" (Stevens & Hall, 1998). This literature highlights the ways that novices to certain sophisticated fields gain experience, expertise, and nuanced understandings of specialized skills like archeological digging, engineering, etc. from working closely with an expert in the field.

Specifically, *Among Us* requires the player to make observations and inferences while carrying out assigned tasks. Players also hold meetings to discuss their hypotheses about which player is the impostor (though the meeting includes all players, including the impostor), and if players agree on the hypothesis that one specific player is the impostor, they can test that hypothesis by voting that player off of the spaceship. This collaborative and at times competitive style of gameplay is well-suited to classroom activities, as students must learn to work together toward common goals. The "impostor" aspect adds interest and intrigue, although it should be noted that it has a slight potential to be misused, creating a dodgeball-like situation where groups gang up on one student. The same tensions that make it so appealing for social play make its mechanics more difficult to imagine in the classroom.

Social-constructive problem-based learning (Savery & Duffy, 1995) has a rich body of research indicating that classroom activities designed using this learning theory are effective and promote deep learning (Gallagher, 1997). Originating in a Canadian medical school in the 1960s (Camp, 1996), problem-based learning follows key characteristics of facilitating self-directed learning by providing students with an ill-structured problem to solve collaboratively (Graaff & Kolmos, 2003). There is a large database of peer-reviewed problems and instructor guides on the University of Delaware's Problem-Based Learning Clearinghouse website (https://www.itue.udel.edu/pbl/problems). By asking students to solve ill-structured problems collaboratively, instructors are simulating real-world situations and experience working with others to construct solutions and knowledge.

The step from problem-based collaborative problem-solving activities to engaging games is a small one: many popular games, such as *Among Us*, are designed around complex challenges that players must cooperate to solve. As mentioned in Chapter 2, escape room pedagogy is increasing in popularity, as these styles of games had been (pre-pandemic) spawning in-person escape room venues as well as video games in this genre, such as *Among Us*. Engaging students in escape room-styled learning activities, where they must work together to solve a multifaceted problem is likely to be an engaging educational experience. Introducing the problem in an escape room or another playful approach could encourage student motivation and engagement while also working to build classroom community.

Looking closer at the Jackbox platform, initially designed to facilitate in-person social night style games, adapted well to the remote play necessitated by the pandemic. The games use one central computer for the host player, and other players join the game by entering a game code in a website on their mobile devices. The popularity of this platform during the pandemic is likely due to its ability to be played on non-specialized device already commonly owned as well as the wide variety of game genres and styles. Similarly, Jackbox games require little prior game knowledge, specialized genre literacy, or hand–eye coordination that many AAA games (especially those in the FPS genre) require, lowering the barrier to entry and making it easy and manageable for novice players to understand and play.

The Jackbox style of play is similar to other in-class review games like *Kahoot*. *Kahoot* is an educational game platform that specializes in trivia-style quiz games. These games follow the genre and style of the lower-tech PowerPoint based *Jeopardy!* review game, which, before PowerPoint, was run with sets of question-and-answer cards or papers. The issues with this game genre have been discussed in Chapter 2, but it is popular and has also evolved to increase its compatibility with the massive shifts to online-only learning, and thus it warrants a closer look.

To play *Kahoot,* the teacher prepares a set of selected response questions (multiple-choice, multiple answer, or true/false), arranges them in a desired order, and saves them to the website's database. In class, the teacher logs into the website and clicks "play" next to the list of questions they made, and their computer (presumably connected to a projector) runs the game by displaying the prepared questions in the order they were arranged. Students connect to the game by navigating to a companion website on their phones or laptops and entering the game code. They then resister their answers by clicking the appropriate option. The platform includes the typical gamification elements of digital games like this, such as a timer counting down the limited allotted answering time, points awarded for accuracy and speed of answering, leaderboard displays with motivational messages for students who are improving or on a "hot streak," etc. At the end of the game, the teacher can download a log of student participation and, if the teacher knows the student's chosen screenname, they can even assign a grade for the student's efforts or accuracies.

Likely due to the pandemic and widespread shifts to online-only education, *Kahoot* has iterated and optimized its products to allow for classes that are in-person, remote, or a hybrid of both. Interestingly, prior to this shift, the game was geared toward exclusive in-class use: students who were not physically present in the classroom were intentionally excluded from participating, to facilitate typically strict pre-pandemic attendance requirements. Even if a classmate were to send their absent peer the game code, the questions did not appear on the device the student was using to answer them—it was assumed that if the student could not see the projector in class, they were not eligible to participate. The shift in perspective is apparent on the platform's website, as it touts a blog post titled, "Based on popular requests: Now students can see questions and answers on their devices in a live kahoot!" (*How to Display Kahoot! Questions and Answers on Students' Devices*, 2021).

Finally, the fantasy worlds of tabletop role-playing offer us another playful way to engage students' creativity and establish a playful tone in the course. Like the successful role-playing of *Reacting to the Past* and *Model UN*, discussed in Chapter 2, fabricating a fictional setting for the class—collaboratively with students or not—is another way to bring play and games to education. Worldbuilding is taught explicitly in game design and creative writing courses, while also being a popular activity that people from all disciplines and walks of life engage in during leisure time: Trent Hergenrader's *Collaborative Worldbuilding for Writers and Gamers* suggests paths forward for bringing this approach to the classroom. We will consider other pandemic educational successes following in these traditions in Chapter 5.

Making a third place for communal learning

Prior to the "online shift," institutions were already redefining what and how learning could be conducted. Back in 2012, Tom Cavanaugh asserted we were living in a "postmodal era" while citing course enrollments across modalities; student enrollment data showed students enrolling in a mix of online, in-person, and hybrid modes that he interpreted as indicating that higher education students are "increasingly unconcerned with the labels of modality and location" (Cavanaugh, 2012). Faculty had to, out of necessity, revise attendance requirements throughout the pandemic, and in doing so, have begun to redefine the concept of attendance, as well. Student-centered learning and play-centric activities have always privileged participation over attendance. We have the opportunity to rethink participation requirements and to create inviting, playful learning environments that motivate our students to engage with the course and to excel, modeled on community-first, social successes of pandemic play.

To reimagine coursework, we can remove, scale back, or rethink the attendance requirement. How can our students best engage with the material to foster a more complete understanding of—and perhaps even a deeper curiosity for—the subjects or fields that we teach? One common approach is to replace daily attendance with daily participation activities. Though a baby step toward fostering student-directed learning, this minor switch can indicate to the university student that the course requires something more than their mere physical (or virtual) presence. Engaging students in an active way with the content of each course meeting—or, at least once a week in asynchronous online courses—is likely the goal for most educators anyway. This first step is good, but ideally the engagement is meaningful and more often than only during class.

It would be all too easy to take the wrong lessons from pandemic play: to say that the platforms that thrived, from Jackbox and *Among Us* to *ACNH*, were poor substitutes rather than compelling learning platforms to consider with our gaze to the future. But in games, the influence of these successes is clear;—the call for wholesome games, for instance, holds *ACNH* up as an exemplar. *ACNH* also draws our attention to creative play as communal. The community-building style of *ACNH* can be used to build playful, student-centric classroom environments and learning activities.

Among Us and Jackbox games also demonstrate a point mentioned in Chapter 2: the fact that games can be successful—that is, immersive and enjoyable—without elaborate 3D worlds. The relatively basic graphics and minimal special effects reveal that the key element in enjoyable games is engagement with other players, and the expensive and time-consuming special effects that the AAA industry prides itself on are no guarantee of meaningful play.

The thoughtfully designed but often relatively minimalist graphics of both of these pandemic hits demonstrate the appeal of the retro and nostalgic. To return to DeSanto's posited future at the start of this chapter, it's not the immersive, realistic virtual worlds that make the compelling third place: it's the community interactions, collaboration, and friendly competition those places enable.

The autonomy afforded to the player in *ACNH* as well as prior popular games like the *Sim City* series is routinely and almost mechanically squashed in standard education. Likely for understandable pragmatic reasons, the typical course structure revolves around everyone in the class performing the same learning task at the same time. But is this something that playful pedagogy and even perhaps technology could change to allow for greater learner autonomy? Asynchronous online pedagogy already allows at least portions of this. Self-paced MOOCs permit the learner to select when and which assignments to complete. Can we envision a more playful, autonomous design for learning than even that? Can we create a utopic supportive community in our courses?

Humans are natural community-builders. With this pandemic, we have experienced how deeply we really need one another and how the things we once thought of as trivial, like social engagement, are in fact essential to our mental health and overall well-being. The games that brought us together to foster these community needs are the types of playful pedagogy that we should be working to harness and instill into our learning environments. Games can help create a learning community that puts students—and their humanity (rather than their ability to multiple-guess)—at the center of education. Playful teaching can provide students with safe places to try, learn, fail, and grow. It can encourage them with a supportive community, arm them with the guidance of instructors and peers alike, and trust them with the autonomy to direct their curiosity. These are the factors we should be designing our post-pandemic courses to include. Our cues need to be taken not from AAA games with graphics that only a few can ever program into their own games, but from the engagement and interactions fostered by the collaborative storytelling and world-building of *Dungeons & Dragons*; the simple narrative behind *Among Us*; the absurd juxtapositions and competitive thinking embedded in Jackbox games; the wholesome community-building of *ACNH*; and even the simple, low-tech shared play of *Wordle*. Bringing the right games into our classes can allow us to build our own supportive learning communities, complete with the social elements of play and the potential to reimagine and rebuild third spaces together.

References

Bakioglu, B. S. (2008). Spectacular interventions of second life: Goon culture, griefing, and disruption in virtual spaces. *Journal for Virtual Worlds Research, 1*(3), Article 3. https://doi.org/10.4101/jvwr.v1i3.348.

Boellstorff, T. (2015). *Coming of age in second life: An anthropologist explores the virtually human.* Princeton University Press.

Brandon, J. (2022, January 18). It only took a single tweet from Jimmy Fallon to make Wordle: A massive hit. *Forbes.* https://www.forbes.com/sites/johnbbrandon/2022/01/18/it-only-took-a-single-tweet-from-jimmy-fallon-to-make-wordle-a-massive-hit/.

Bruns, A. (2008). *Blogs, Wikipedia, second life, and beyond: From production to Produsage*. Peter Lang.

Burke, L. (2019, November 22). *Stanford conducts classes in a virtual world*. Inside Higher Ed. https://www.insidehighered.com/digital-learning/article/2019/11/22/stanford-conducts-classes-virtual-world.

Camp, G. (1996). Problem-based learning: A paradigm shift or a passing fad? *Medical Education Online*, *1*(2), 1–7. https://doi.org/10.3402/meo.v1i.4282.

Cavanaugh, T. (2012). The postmodality era: How online learning is becoming learning. In D. Oblinger (Ed.), *Game changers: Education and information technologies*. EDUCAUSE. https://library.educause.edu/resources/2012/5/chapter-16-the-postmodality-era-how-online-learning-is-becoming-learning.

Chess, S. (2020). *Play like a feminist*. MIT Press. https://mitpress.mit.edu/books/play-feminist.

DeAngelo, D. (2022, January 12). Wordle rip-off apps appear and fans aren't happy. *Game Rant*. https://gamerant.com/wordle-rip-off-apps-fans-unhappy/.

deWinter, J., & Vie, S. (2008). Press enter to "say": Using second life to teach critical media literacy. *Computers and Composition*, *25*(3), 313–322. https://doi.org/10.1016/j.compcom.2008.04.003.

Dibbell, J. (2006). 8. Owned! In *The state of play* (pp. 137–145). New York University Press. https://www.degruyter.com/document/doi/10.18574/9780814739075-008/html.

Duderstadt, J. J., Atkins, D. E., Houweling, D. E. V., & Houweling, D. V. (2002). *Higher education in the digital age: Technology issues and strategies for American colleges and universities*. Greenwood Publishing Group.

Duncan, I., Miller, A., & Jiang, S. (2012). A taxonomy of virtual worlds usage in education. *British Journal of Educational Technology*, *43*(6), 949–964. https://doi.org/10.1111/j.1467-8535.2011.01263.x.

Flasherty, C. (2021, January 21). *Snitch switch: U of Florida asks students to report professors who aren't teaching in person*. https://www.insidehighered.com/news/2021/01/21/u-florida-asks-students-report-professors-who-arent-teaching-person.

Francisco, E. (2020, April 27). *How Covid-19 is changing "Dungeons & Dragons," maybe forever*. Inverse. https://www.inverse.com/gaming/dungeons-and-dragons-online-coronavirus-zoom.

Gallagher, S. A. (1997). Problem-based learning: Where did it come from, what does it do, and where is it going? *Journal for the Education of the Gifted*, *20*(4), 332–362. https://doi.org/10.1177/016235329702000402.

Goodwin, C. (1994). Professional vision. *American Anthropologist, New Series*, *96*(3), 606–633.

Graaff, E. D., & Kolmos, A. (2003). Characteristics of problem-based learning. *International Journal of Engineering Education*, *19*(5), 657–662.

Grebey, J. (2020, March 25). *Dungeons & Dragons players turn to virtual tabletops in record numbers due to coronavirus*. SYFY WIRE. https://www.syfy.com/syfywire/dungeons-dragons-roll20-fantasy-grounds-virtual-tabletop-online-coronavirus.

Hall, R. (2022, January 11). Wordle creator overwhelmed by global success of hit puzzle. *The Guardian*. https://www.theguardian.com/games/2022/jan/11/wordle-creator-overwhelmed-by-global-success-of-hit-puzzle.

Haynes, C. A., & Holmevik, J. R. (2001). *High wired: On the design, use, and theory of educational MOOs*. University of Michigan Press.

Hodges, C., Moore, S., Lockee, B., Trust, T., & Bond, A. (2020, March 27). *The difference between emergency remote teaching and online learning* [Educause Review]. https://er

.educause.edu/articles/2020/3/the-difference-between-emergency-remote-teaching-and-online-learning.

Hogan, P. (2015, August 13). *We took a tour of the abandoned college campuses of second life*. Splinter. https://splinternews.com/we-took-a-tour-of-the-abandoned-college-campuses-of-sec-1793849944.

How to display Kahoot! Questions and answers on students' devices. (2021, March 4). Kahoot! https://kahoot.com/blog/2021/03/04/questions-answers-on-students-devices/.

Huizinga, J. (1955). *Homo ludens: A study of the play-element in culture*. Beacon Press.

Jackbox Games. (2021). *Press kit*. Jackbox Games. https://www.jackboxgames.com/presskit/.

Kelly, M. (2020, October 16). *The official Biden HQ in animal crossing has poll booths, ice cream, and no malarkey*. The Verge. https://www.theverge.com/2020/10/16/21519505/joe-biden-animal-crossing-new-horizons-biden-hq-campaign-election.

Martin, J. (2008). Consuming code: Use-value, exchange-value, and the role of virtual goods in second life. *Journal of Virtual Worlds Research, 1*(2), 1–21.

Mcleod, S. (2020, December 29). Maslow's hierarchy of needs. *Simply Psychology*. https://www.simplypsychology.org/maslow.html.

Meadows, M. S. (2007). *I, Avatar: The culture and consequences of Having a second life*. New Riders.

Morningstar, C., & Farmer, F. R. (2008). The lessons of Lucasfilm's habitat. *Journal for Virtual Worlds Research, 1*(1), Article 1. https://doi.org/10.4101/jvwr.v1i1.287.

Nielsen, I. Q. (2021, January 6). The future of video gaming is bright—Even as real experiences return. *NielsenIQ*. https://www.nielsen.com/us/en/insights/article/2021/the-future-of-video-gaming-is-bright-even-as-real-experiences-return.

Oldenburg, R. (2013). The café as a third place. In A. Tjora & G. Scambler (Eds.), *Café society* (pp. 7–21). Palgrave Macmillan US. https://doi.org/10.1057/9781137275936_2.

Rivera, J. (2020, October 22). AOC played among us and achieved what most politicians fail at: Acting normal. *The Guardian*. http://www.theguardian.com/games/2020/oct/22/alexandria-ocasio-cortez-ilhan-omar-among-us-twitch-stream-aoc.

Salmon, G. (2009). The future for (second) life and learning. *British Journal of Educational Technology, 40*(3), 526–538. https://doi.org/10.1111/j.1467-8535.2009.00967.x.

Savery, J. R., & Duffy, T. M. (1995). Problem based learning: An instructional model and its constructivist framework. *Educational Technology, 35*(5), 31–38.

Stanfill, M., Salter, A., & Sullivan, A. (2021, August). Orange is Sus: Among us and political play. In *The 16th international conference on the foundations of digital games (FDG) 2021* (pp. 1–9).

Stevens, R., & Hall, R. (1998). Disciplined perception: Learning to see in technoscience. In M. Lampert, M. L. Blunk & R. Pea (Eds.), *Talking mathematics in school: Studies of teaching and learning* (pp. 107–150). Cambridge University Press.

Van Dam, A. (2021, February 16). Analysis | We've been cooped up with our families for almost a year. This is the result. *Washington Post*. https://www.washingtonpost.com/road-to-recovery/2021/02/16/pandemic-togetherness-never-have-so-many-spent-so-much-time-with-so-few/.

Vincent, J. (2022, January 11). *Done your Wordle for the day? Try out these spoofs instead*. The Verge. https://www.theverge.com/tldr/2022/1/11/22877996/wordle-spoofs-alternatives-letterle-sweardle-queerdle.

Wizards of the Coast. (2020, April 6). *Stay at home. Play at home*. Dungeons & Dragons. https://dnd.wizards.com/remote/freematerial.

4 Confronting the perils of play

Into the metaverse?

In August 2021, over a year into the pandemic's impact on technology, Mark Zuckerberg announced his vision for our collective future in a familiar space: the metaverse. The accompanying press conferences and hype promised everything from avatars gathering to deal cards around a virtual poker table to people decorating a virtual birthday cake for a hypothetical—and apparently, foodless—party (CNET Highlights, 2021). The images Facebook – now Meta – has offered thus far are more *Wreck It Ralph* than *Ready Player One*: highly cartoony and frequently featuring an apparent set of disjointed character references occupying the same space as figures only one step removed from Nintendo's *Miitopia*'s exaggerated selfies. One journalist captured the familiarity of Zuckerberg's expressed work, but with an important warning about the economic implications and restrictions that accompany this new iteration of virtualized life:

> Zuckerberg's comments brought to my mind an earlier iteration of online life, a game and social space called *Neopets*. *Neopets* launched in 1999; I remember playing it in middle school, trading strategies with friends. In the game, the player takes care of small digital creatures, feeding and grooming them as well as buying accessories with "Neopoints" earned from in-game activities…In the metaverse Facebook envisions, however, you are the Neopet, and your in-game activities may affect every sphere of life that Facebook already touches: careers, relationships, politics. In Zuckerberg's vision, Neopoints become Facebook dollars, only usable on the platform; your self-presentation online becomes a choice limited to options that Facebook provides. A blue-and-gray virtual universe looms. The more immersive it is, the more inescapable it becomes, like an all-encompassing social-media feed, with all the problems thereof.
>
> (Chayka, 2021)

Neopets was a formative "metaverse" for geriatric millennials who are now educators: it offered an early preview of the impressive scale of community possible on even the most limited of social platforms, and also demonstrated early expertise at the manipulation of users through mechanisms like the slow starvation of one's pets if the player ventures away from the platform for too long. In a world revitalized for platforms of amiable social reckoning (likely spurred in part by the success of games like *Animal Crossing* during the pandemic, as discussed in Chapter 3), *Neopets* is experiencing a resurgence: the game has particularly been cited by long-time users as providing positivity and a relief from pandemic anxiety (Kurtzleben, 2021). Chayka's pointed acknowledgment that we are now the "Neopet" is a reminder of how dependent upon these platforms for connections and relationships we already are—and a warning of the influence that those same platforms might have as we move into a more mediated model of education.

Unfortunately, it's not only the platforms of our past that are evoking the metaverse: Zoom's CEO has also pointed to use cases for the metaverse, promising a "Whiteboard" for virtual reality that recreates the warmth of a conference room in virtual reality (Ion, 2021). Bill Gates has similarly invested in the vision of the metaverse, viewing it as the "revolutionized" consequence of COVID-19: "Within the next two or three years, I predict most virtual meetings will move from 2D camera image grids … to the metaverse, a 3D space with digital avatars" (Huddleston, 2021). This vision has not been met with widespread enthusiasm, particularly by those of us who have already had the experience of sitting in awkward avatar-driven chatrooms of the past: by contract, low-fidelity Gather.Town has proven to be a hit of the pandemic with 2D graphics and retro rooms. Meta's advertising has pushed back on both platforms like Gather.Town and competitors like Zoom, offering the tagline "Imagine connecting with colleagues beyond 2D screens" with the ad for their vision of "Work in the metaverse,"—which apparently features a lot of avatars staring at 3D models together (Meta, 2021).

Interestingly, 2021 also saw the release of *The Matrix: Resurrections*, a film that encapsulates both some of the challenges of the historic toxicity of virtual spaces and some of the potential solutions. This latest iteration of the film series turns to video game culture for its metaphors, repositioning its hero as a game designer unknowingly recreating his own understanding of the simulated reality through games. Alongside other game narratives released during the pandemic, such as *Free Guy*, this new vision of *The Matrix* points to how significant games are for our navigation of reality and community: both also, through very different mechanisms, push back on the historic centricity of casual violence in game narratives,—which themselves are already the "metaverses" of choice for many, as our discussion of pandemic gaming has noted.

Launching only a few months after Mark Zuckerberg's announcement, this new iteration in the *Matrix* franchise drew attention to its own history and fandom with new intention. *The Matrix* franchise already features prominently in the mythology of the Internet, though perhaps not in the way its creators, the Wachowski sisters, intended: red pill "philosophy" online signifies a commitment to often violent antifeminism and a perception of masculinity as under attack (Ging, 2019). The new *Matrix Resurrections* takes on that subtext and appropriation of a progressive narrative head-first, and does so with more than a nod toward the role of game development and game designer culture—the former hero of the franchise, Neo, is entrapped in a narrative in which his own attempts at rebellion have been trivialized, reduced to a video game about escapism. The new film reads as a warning against the complacent allure of the metaverse, while also warning against the ways that the very narratives of progressive cyberpunk are co-opted to fuel industry fantasies.

Matrix Resurrections offers a new character, The Analyst, who presents as a therapist and suggests that people are more comfortable with his metaverse than they will ever be with reality: his words hold echoes of Zuckerberg's exaggerated confidence from *the Social Network*. In a pivotal confrontation, he points out the futility of Neo's goals: "The sheeple aren't going anywhere. They like my world. They don't want this sentimentality. They don't want freedom or empowerment. They want to be controlled. They crave the comfort of certainty" (Wachowski et al., 2021). The parallels to Zuckerberg today are inescapable: a *Fortune* article covering the launch was appropriately entitled "Facebook wants to be The Matrix" (Dugan, 2021). The film has been criticized for the heavy-handedness of this message, but as one reviewer quipped, "if you were Lana Wachowski and you'd spent nearly twenty years watching the world's worst people hijack your ideas, you'd probably opt for placards over puzzles, too" (Pappademas, 2021).

Moderating the metaverse

That same metaverse looms large in cyberpunk;—since Zuckerberg's announcement of Facebook's rebranding (another consequence of the pandemic-era mishandlings and misinformation now forever associated with the company's major platform), plenty of ink has already been spilled drawing comparisons to the virtual worlds of William Gibson et al.'s imagined virtual dystopias. For us, the literary warning that looms large is M.T. Anderson's *Feed*, a cyberpunk-influenced young adult novel imagining a fully integrated social media platform with a gamified twist governing education, commerce, and more, directly wired into one's brain. One of the more resonant descriptions of education within the novel forecasts a future of sponsored content:

> When no one was going to pay for the public schools anymore and they were all like filled with guns and drugs and English teachers who were really pimps and stuff, some of the big media congloms got together and gave all this money and bought the schools so that all of them could have computers and pizza for lunch and stuff, which they gave for free, and now we do stuff in classes about how to work technology and how to find bargains and what's the best way to get a job and how to decorate our bedroom.
> (Anderson, 2004, p. 110)

Those of us already teaching online prior to 2020's more widespread pivot have wrestled with the challenges of classroom moderation since the days of the first course discussion posts. To recall the flying phalluses and harassment of *Second Life*, new platforms (and game-like spaces) only amplify the problems already all-too-familiar to anyone who has spent time online—realities amplified by marginalization. Whitney Phillips's reminders of the mundanity of trolling resonate across contexts: "while trolling behaviors might fall on the extreme end of the cultural spectrum, the most exceptional thing about trolling is that it's not very exceptional" (W. Phillips, 2015, p. 10). Studies of successful trolling note that trolls can make use of behaviors that appear discursive—"ignoring, mismatching, and challenging"—and in doing so disrupt conversation (Paakki et al., 2021). Any utopian vision of online education by necessity wrestles with these forces: for example, when the "MOOC," or Massively Open Online Course, was tested in practice, the format frequently suffered from the intentionally disruptive behavior of trolls, to the point where some studies noted participants felt "unsafe" and retreated from participation (Mackness et al., 2010).

In his examination of the challenges plaguing both MOOCs and *Second Life*, Siva Vaidhyanathan observed that the "disruptive" potential of these so-called "cutting-edge" platforms quickly falls in the face of users (Vaidhyanathan, 2017, p. 287). As he succinctly summarizes: "The biggest threats to MOOCs are the biggest threats to any online venture: bots and trolls" (292). We've come a long way from the days of dire headlines like Moshe Y. Vardi's "Will MOOCs destroy academia?"—an article that, in 2012, pointed to the dire financial situation of US colleges in particular, a situation that has only been amplified by 2020 and its sequels (Vardi, 2012). The reality of MOOC's disappearance from the spotlight was less dramatic than that, and in many ways echoed the fallout of favor of *Second Life* itself.

It is impossible to look at the hype surrounding MOOCs and *Second Life* without acknowledging the similar hype currently focused on the metaverse, a rebranded vision for virtual reality as a more ubiquitous experience platform that might play a role in the next iteration of educational technology. However, the lessons of MOOCs, *Second Life*, and the pandemic experiments in online education writ large do not offer much optimism for this next iteration of virtual world as classroom.

The pandemic has without doubt accelerated our trajectory toward the fully mediated classroom—if not, we fervently hope, to the "metaverse," though Mark Zuckerberg may disagree. Already, the discussions of an "education metaverse" in EdTech publications point toward familiar language. Unsurprisingly, proponents tout "personalized learning"—recalling teaching machines (Watters, 2021)—and of course, gamification, described depressingly in one editorial as a virtual scavenger hunt for coins and upgrades (Kongslip, 2022). One *Inside Higher Ed* article notes the familiarity of the model from now-abandoned *Second Life* islands, but still asks readers:

> Where will higher education be located in the emerging metaverse? Will colleges and universities host their own "islands" of campuses? Will virtual megamalls of storefronts offer certificates and certifications hosted by a plethora of institutions? Will your institution be represented—welcoming virtual students from around the real word to engage in 3-D learning around the clock?
>
> (Schroeder, 2021)

Yet Schroeder also looks to a warning from Tom Wheeler of other questions to come: questions of "personal privacy, marketplace competition, and misinformation" (Wheeler, 2021). It is to those challenges, among others, that we turn our attention in this chapter as we look at the long history of perilous educational play, and its magnification during the pandemic years.

Alongside some of the opportunistic educational technology projects we've already examined in this book, the shift in the rhetoric of social media platforms and the renewed interest in the "metaverse" suggests that the mainstreaming of virtual gatherings has prepared a broader population to be receptive toward increasing reliance on interfaces. While as educators who have seen the rise and fall of many such initiatives, we are inherently skeptical of these claims, there is no doubt that the financial investment in this vision of the future is already staggering, and likely to bring with it increased affordability of virtual reality technologies for the classroom. What, then, can we learn from the pandemic acceleration to prepare us for this envisioned future? Some of the most compelling lessons wait in the darkest corners, where the realities of managing and moderating large-scale platforms are revealed in spite of desires to treat content moderation as a solved problem.

Scholars working to address these challenges have emphasized the importance of "community-driven moderation," as Brewer, Romine, and Taylor address: "while significant attention, both from academia and industry, has been paid to developing algorithmically-driven moderation systems that automatically filter content, far less emphasis has been placed on designing interventions to proactively cultivate meaningful change in user behavior on social media" (Brewer et al., 2020, p. 766). Given the speed and scale of interactions looming in a future of even-more-virtual learning, such problems may well be coming to a metaverse classroom near you.

These problems are already familiar to educators who have been using games of scale—which are, like *Second Life*, their own type of "metaverse" in design structure and in difficulty of moderation. Educators working with platforms we've noted that rely upon multiplayer, such as *Minecraft*, are called upon to engage in significant mediation of this kind: as Slovak, Salen, and Ta note, such attempts to create "safety" can be at the detriment of community growth: "in trying to 'keep peace' … the online moderators monopolized the conflict resolution process, essentially preventing the children from actively working with and learning from the experiences of conflict" (Slovak et al., 2018). Yet such efforts have been met with continual difficulties. In this chapter, we will contextualize some of these core challenges through the lends of gaming in the classroom—harassment and toxicity; toxicity across technical platforms and gaming; and misinformation—while considering educator-driven, feminist, and anti-racist interventions and their challenges at scale.

Harassment and trolling

As the COVID-19 pandemic rapidly moved business and education activities online, requiring a massive amount of people to learn the intricacies and idiosyncrasies of new platforms as digitally literate as possible, groups already engaging in toxic behavior capitalized on the inexperience of this audience. Zoom bombing, discussed in the introduction, is just one of these instances, where gaps in security were exploited for real emotional harm in virtual classrooms and workplaces. Those who study digital culture were not surprised, but the rest of the population was caught off guard, and the technical knowledge of new platforms required to navigate these challenges took time and energy on the part of overwhelmed educators—thus making these methods more effective, and perhaps therefore more satisfying to the people performing them, collectively frequently referred to as trolls. The Internet's lack of traditional gatekeeping mechanisms like publishers and editors was once hailed as a democratic way to "level the playing field"—allowing anyone to access information anywhere, anytime. However, while the lack of rules and constraints did mean anyone could access information, it also meant that anyone could publish it. Whitney Phillips examines the malintent of numerous online communities (trolls) who leverage this access in order to bring emotional (and possibly physical) harm to vulnerable individuals and groups just for "lulz" (W. Phillips, 2013).

A time of widespread stress and more extended time online is inherently a time for trolls. Further, the pandemic hit at a time when social media had already been playing an important role in the spread of polarizing political groups across the globe (Bradshaw & Howard, 2018; Hall et al., 2018). With nationalistic movements on the rise, different groups took advantage of the virtual spaces to spread misinformation. Games-related platforms such as Discord have been particularly central to the spread of extremism, as Daniel Heslep and PS Berge's research on Disboard critically notes: "It is worth remembering that the presence of extremism on Discord has real, deadly consequences beyond virtual spaces, as the violent events of the 'Unite the Right' rally grimly illustrates" (Heslep & Berge, 2021, p. 18). Those same platforms began advertising to educators alongside the pandemic: Discord now has an entire classroom server support section and corresponding templates (Librarian, 2020), encouraging educators seeking online community solutions to turn to a platform that still abounds with everything from extremist gifs and memes in the chat to a cultural history of white supremacist servers.

This is not to suggest that the challenges of harassment should be understood as platform specific, or even that Discord is particularly unique in this history of extremism—though some of its affordances have certainly played a role in encouraging toxicity. Kevin Veale's work illuminates the important challenges of anyone hoping to solve these problems in the classroom or elsewhere through technology: drawing on the parallels between ARGs and harassment campaigns, he argues that any system we create is a system for these communities to "game" (Veale, 2020). This is critical to understanding the parallels between games and the classrooms where trolls are concerned: both offer rules to be bent, broken, and turned against other players.

The patterns connecting creative play on the web with "trolling" are historically well-established, and the online classroom has never been exempt from this trend. Online courses are often hailed as increasing diversity and participation across demographics, especially in higher education. With the ability of asynchronous assignments that can be completed within flexible timeframes, more students than ever before now have access to higher education regardless of where they live and what their work schedules or family responsibilities. Furthermore, because students are not facing each other in the same physical room, asynchronous online courses can impart a feeling of anonymity, with students being identified often with only their name, occasionally accompanied by small profile photo of their choosing. This is widely thought to encourage greater participation in class discussions by students who would otherwise not speak up in a physical classroom (e.g., Warschauer, 1995). However, even in online courses where student names are displayed next to each post, inappropriate posts still occur and are a valid concern for distance educators (e.g., Buffington, 2010), as students frequently require redirection and direct instruction as to what terms and phrasing are appropriate for a variety of issues.

Given these structures, any platform is an opportunity for trolling "play," but Discord and other platforms already equipped with referential memes and white supremacist visual language offer more tools than most for that play. Perhaps one of the greatest challenges meme-based communication presents is that of moderation: a reference decontextualized requires significant knowledge to interpret. Even the most notorious of meme figures, such as Pepe, is inscrutable to one unfamiliar with digital cultural discourse (Glitsos & Hall, 2019). Whitney Phillips' essential examination of trolling reminds us that trolls act as "agents of cultural digestion," noting that "if you want to understand the contours of the contemporary media environment, then study the content trolls adopt, the jokes trolls make, and the groups trolls most frequently target" (W. Phillips, 2015, p. 135). Specific cases (such as #YesAllWomen) particularly "illustrate memes' ability to spur meaningful conversation, as well as the inescapably political standpoint of participants" (W. Phillips & Milner, 2017). Given that depth and reliance on intertextuality and of-the-moment knowledge, some types of harassment and trolling in the virtual classroom can go unnoticed by the classroom's moderator—particularly when that person is a single, already overextended educator with an endless amount of visual and textual language to track.

Even platforms that have attempted more intensive moderation struggle to handle such visual communication, particularly as their efforts are met with more creative subversion: as the Twitter rules have grown in attempts at specificity, so too have the strategies for bypassing their restrictions. For instance, the "Hateful Conduct" policy as of 2019 prohibits hateful imagery and display names:

> You may not use hateful images or symbols in your profile image or profile header. You also may not use your username, display name, or profile bio to engage in abusive behavior, such as targeted harassment or expressing hate towards a person, group, or protected category.
>
> (Staff, 2019)

Such regulations raise more questions than they answer: what is "hateful," and who decides? In a society of continually co-opted memes, where Pepe and Gritty can become respectively the alt-right and anarchist figureheads regardless of their creator's intentions, where do we—or Twitter's moderators—draw the line? Insider knowledge is often crucial in understanding certain types of hateful imagery or references, and when certain queues (such as the notorious "OK" symbol) are brought into popular media discourse, they are still rarely well-understood.

Misinformation and altered realities

Similarly, the association of gaming with the spread of misinformation and counterfactual knowledge has been particularly cemented in popular understanding with the rise of QAnon in the United States: thriving alongside the heart of the pandemic (perhaps in part due to the rise in online time collectively, as well as the widespread challenges of communication and leadership in the US pandemic response). Several game designers recognized the connection to the mechanics of alternate reality games specifically in its clue-driven, narrative mystery, as designer Reed Berkowitz warned: "When I saw QAnon, I knew exactly what it was and what it was doing. It was the gamification of propaganda. QAnon was a game that played people" (Berkowitz, 2021). As Berkowitz described:

> In ARGs, people do a lot of the same things QAnon followers do, but they don't call and report fictional crimes as if they are real. They don't break laws. They may show up in mobs, but they understand it's all pretend. Q is the opposite: People report crimes, or they swamp emergency phone lines with false reports about their enemies setting wildfires. They break the law. They show up in mobs for causes they think are very real—like the Jan. 6 insurrection at the Capitol, where QAnon figures were pivotal actors.

Historically, ARGs have been structured on the same features of online collaboration: "voluntary, collective problem solving is an intriguing phenomenon wherein disparate individuals work together asynchronously to solve problems together" (Kim et al., 2009). A collaborative team examining digital literacy learning in ARGs noted the game's development of the ability of "metaliteracy," or to "MAKE SENSE" (analyzing, synthesizing, and reflecting): "The ability to make sense of information through analysis, synthesis, and interpretation; and to aggregate dispersed components into a coherent framework" (Bonsignore et al., 2012, p. 34). This form has incredible educational value (as we'll explore in Chapter 5)—unfortunately, that same power applies to its use for misinformation.

Perhaps most dismayingly for those looking at education as a remedy to similar conspiratorial thinking, the nature of QAnon's storytelling makes it, as Matthew Hannah summarizes, "nearly impossible to debunk" (Hannah, 2021). Hannah notes that efforts to convince QAnon supporters they are "misinformed" are particularly doomed to failure: "Anons believe they are actually *more* informed than the regular population." This recognition of game-like conspiracy theorizing is hardly unique to the US political scene: the same platforms where QAnon thrives are host to endless similar, if smaller, communities reshaping reality collectively. The loosely tied international community that makes up what has been termed the "manosphere" is an exemplar, and like QAnon, they are continually in search of new targets. As Marwick and Caplan describe: "networked misogyny is often organized in subcultural online spaces such as Reddit, 4Chan, and chat rooms, where participants collectively frame feminists like Sarkeesian as 'villains'"—a label which in turn justifies their continued abuse (Marwick & Caplan, 2018).

These narratives are particularly powerful because of how they are shared and co-created. Ethan Zuckerman dubbed QAnon "the radically participatory conspiracy," noting that QAnon fully takes advantage of the desire of the community to co-create the narrative (Zuckerman, 2019). Zuckerman's description recalls early scholarship of the participatory web: Lawrence Lessig, for instance, viewed the web's structures through the lens of "remix culture," suggesting that "read/write culture" would transform cultural production (Lessig, 2009). However, even he has refocused his work away from the web of potentialities to the challenges of what it has become. Similarly, Henry Jenkins was among the first to chart out the potential impact of fan communities, which are vital to shaping participatory culture on the web: his more recent work examines the impact of "spreadable media," a term that can encompass content made to circulate (like memes) for both information and disinformation (Jenkins et al., 2013). QAnon and its ilk are a warning of participatory culture and spreadable media write large: in an examination linking QAnon to its roots, Aleena Chia et al. argue "the internet supercharges perennialism, providing a connective medium for New Age ideology of manifesting: the belief that we create our own reality" (Chia et al., 2021). Such beliefs are difficult to challenge or moderate.

Notably, such shared narrative construction also plays a role in the online community construction of hate groups such as "incels" (short for "involuntary celibates"), who have built their framework around a misappropriation of *The Matrix*:

> incels consequently see themselves as destined to be ignored or dismissed by women with no hope or prospects of change. The incels call the epiphany taking the "black pill"—a derivative of the "blue pill/red pill" binary adopted from the 1999 science fiction film, *The Matrix*.
> (Hoffman et al., 2020)

Such groups are even more strongly tied to the history of gaming masculinity—a mindset inescapable when thinking about the challenges of game environments in and as classrooms, which also returns us to Phillips and Milner's warning (2017) about the continual referentiality and repurposing of trolling's toxic messages.

Gaming culture and toxic masculinity

Elsewhere, we have written more specifically about patterns of toxic masculinity in gaming culture (Salter & Blodgett, 2017). To summarize here, the events of

GamerGate, a social media fueled hate mob targeted at Zoe Quinn but expanding to attacks on the perceived threats of feminism in gaming development and journalism, amplified awareness in academia of the fundamental challenges gaming can bring to discourse (Chess & Shaw, 2015). The work of feminist games studies has been reshaped by the ongoing culture wars, as Phillips notes in *Gamer Trouble*: "our relevance is now justified by the emergence of a virulent harassment campaign rather than the self-evident value of nuanced conversations about the politics of gamers and video games" (A. Phillips, 2020, p. 21). Such work has become even more pressing in the wake of the pandemic, as the increased reliance on platforms associated with gaming must come with intense scrutiny and wariness.

Historically, the connection of gaming culture to toxic masculinity (and in the United States particularly, to a centering of whiteness and heteronormative experiences, though this framework varies when we consider the gaming industry as a global phenomenon) is rooted in the workplace. Self-studies within the gaming industry were conducted by the Game Developers Conference in 2020, with 75% of respondents identifying as male, 21% identifying as female, 2% as other, and 2% declining to answer the demographic question. Previous years demonstrated an even higher prevalence of men (77% in 2019, and 80% in 2018). This is not a comprehensive global study (a little over half the respondents are from North America), but it does provide an important insight into the tendencies of the industry. Notably, many titles produced within this space hold international sales prominence, and are inescapably a part of the global "education" of youth even if they are not formally incorporated into the classroom.

Alongside the pandemic, we noted increased scrutiny on gaming workplaces as sites of harassment and discrimination: a lawsuit in California against Activision Blizzard in July 2021 centered on the "frat boy culture" and was filed "after a two-year investigation into the company revealed discrimination against women generally and pregnant employees, sexual harassment, retaliation and unequal pay" (Betancourt, 2021). The company's demographics as reported at the time skewed similarly to the industry's overall diversity—"the company's workforce was just 20% female, while all executive level positions are held by white males" (Paul, 2021). This whiteness is also inescapable in gaming, and the work of scholars such as Kishonna Gray has drawn critical attention to the attacks on black gamers, as well as community efforts at resistance and claiming space in gaming culture (Gray, 2020).

Interestingly, as we close this study, Activision Blizzard's acquisition by technology titan Microsoft has been announced. In their own press release, Microsoft's CEO Staya Nadella promised that through this acquisition, "We're investing deeply in world-class content, community and the cloud to usher in a new era of gaming that puts players and creators first and makes gaming safe, inclusive and accessible to all" (Microsoft News Center, 2022). This framing is particularly troubling given Microsoft's hold on the educational market is already intense, thanks in part to their 2014 acquisition of *Minecraft* (discussed in Chapter 2). While Activision Blizzard has not been associated with educational gaming in any major way, the reach of their titles makes the company a powerful force in digital culture.

Minecraft is a particularly notorious example of a now-mainstream "edutainment" title whose history cannot be separated from GamerGate and the culture wars of gaming generally: the game's creator Markus "Notch" Persson has never rescinded his GamerGate positions, including referring to "feminism as a 'social disease'" (Bonazzo, 2017). While we can certainly separate a work from its creators, it is important to recognize that concerns regarding *Minecraft*'s structure and moderation have been amplified by the pandemic, and *Minecraft*'s built-in misogyny has attracted coverage in the context of education previously. A free playable feminine avatar was only added to the game in 2015, a year after Microsoft's acquisition, at which time a journalist covering the change noted the game's historical emphasis on men:

> Nearly all of the characters, like villagers, are male, with the exception of the villainous witch. And for a long time it appeared that Mojang wasn't interested in adding female characters. Mojang's founder, Marcus "Notch" Persson, said in 2012, "I've tried making a girl model in *Minecraft*, but the results have been extremely sexist" He added: "Blocky things are more masculine."
>
> (Harwell, 2015)

This rhetoric of the representation of women being too "difficult" is not unfamiliar, and has shown up as an excuse for exclusionary practices in franchises repeatedly (see Guins et al., 2022 for an examination of this trend in the EA Sports *FIFA* franchise.) It is based on assumptions about who will play games, but is perhaps best understood as a reflection of who is shaping the culture of their production.

Perilous playbour

Some of the most influential examples of educational games have been the subject of disturbing revelations during this time of increased scrutiny. Perhaps the most dismaying for educators interested in gaming as a space for creative work are the allegations around Roblox, which like *Minecraft* offers a collaborative toolkit for creative work, including built-in tools for programming, audio, and graphic development. Initially, the platform didn't include any models for profit from the development of experiences—rather, like *Little Big Planet* and *Mario Level Designer*, the platform allowed for sharing but not profiting at its launch in 2006. However, that changed with the addition of in-game transactions: Roblox takes as much as 70% and the rest goes to the creator (Roblox, 2021). This is anomalous even in the world of digital platform fees, which are exemplified by the excessive profiteering of the Apple store—which, at 30%, looks minor by comparison. As a sidenote, tensions over the impact of these models on creative work distribution raised by the 2021 *Epic v. Apple* trial led Roblox to reclassify their platform as an "experience" creation tool, with one spokesperson offering the new description centering the metaverse:

> The term "experiences" is consistent with how we've evolved our terminology to reflect our realization of the metaverse ... *Roblox* is an online community where people do things together in virtual worlds, and over the years, we began referring to these worlds as experiences, as they better represent the wide range of 3D immersive places – from obbys to virtual concerts – that people can enjoy together with their friends.
>
> (Robertson, 2021)

During the pandemic, the platform took off in popularity, and its potential for abuse was magnified: in July 2020, the company reported that "over half of US kids and teens under the age of 16 play the game," a dramatic rise from one-third of that same population only three months prior (Lyles, 2020). The company took advantage of the interest in the platform for community to launch extended "Play Together" services and events, including concerts (Lyles, 2020). Simon Parkin and other journalists and developers working to document the abuses underlying the platforms' façade of child-friendly creativity have revealed problems ranging from financial and labor abuses to sexual harassment and grooming. Quintin Smith's essential YouTube investigation into the company's exploitation of young developers particularly demonstrates the significant financial profits made off the labor of children involved in no formal contracts, with no oversight (People Make Games, 2021). As Parkin summarizes the debate:

> Supporters argue that Roblox provides a helpful introduction to game-making. The company provides the tools to make games, the servers to host games, an audience to find and play games and the financial ecosystem to enable young developers to profit from them. Yet Roblox also reflects many of the challenges and shortcomings of the wider commercial games industry: the risk of exploitation, of abusive managers, of miserly revenue splits and, most prevalently, of worker burnout, all of which Roblox claims fall outside its responsibilities.
>
> (Parkin, 2022)

The closed ecosystem of Roblox, and its extensive internal tools, encourage children to invest significant labor into a platform whose moderation is insufficient to the scale. The platform has struggled with problems familiar to any creative content ecosystem—they particularly drew criticism for their failure to remove recreations of the 2019 Christchurch mosque shooting. The researcher who flagged the problem, David Kelley, warned that

> Each game on *Roblox* is a potentially a social platform in and of itself, and can potentially give refuge to players of all ages who are flirting with or fully engaged with hateful ideologies online ... Every space that allows for the

veneration of hateful ideologies ... contributes to the normalization of these ideologies and their spread.

(Brandom, 2021)

Cecilia D'Anastasio's investigations of the platforms echo these findings: Nazi role-plays continue on the game's servers in spite of bans—"One, called Innsbruck Border Simulator, received more than a million visits between mid-2019 and late May or early June of this year" (D'Anastasio, 2021). Exploring one of these types of play experiences with one of the leaders of a Rome simulation with intensely fascist structuring, D'Anastasio describes the Roblox game's discriminatory rules and structures:

> Parthian society was a product of Malcolm's increasingly bigoted politics and his fierce need for control, three former members say. The outpost's laws classified support for race-mixing, feminism, and gay people as "degeneracy." They also required one player in the group, who is Jewish in real life, to wear "the Judea tunic or be arrested on sight." Inside Parthia, *vigiles* patrolled the streets. We'd be stopped, Ferguson said, for having the wrong skin tone. (My avatar's skin was olive.) The players voted overwhelmingly to allow Malcolm to execute whomever he wanted.
>
> (D'Anastasio, 2021)

Other reports have predictably found problems with adult content, noting that "those looking to act inappropriately on the site are constantly finding new ways to bypass moderation systems," and the ease of creating what are colloquially referred to as "condo games" means that they are returned to live servers as quickly as they are eliminated (Breen, 2021).

None of these problems are new, they are simply problems that have been amplified: amplified by the scale of participation brought on by the pandemic, certainly, but also by the struggles of platforms grown beyond their originally envisioned scale. Sarah Roberts published an essential study just before the pandemic drawing attention to the crisis of social media content moderation (and moderators): in a post-pandemic preface to the 2021 edition, she noted that "the world is in an informational crisis," with the social media's model of speed and "quick and rather thoughtless circulation of material" at the heart of the struggles (Roberts, 2019, p. ix).

Warnings for the metaverse

The popularity of platforms such as Roblox during the pandemic has contributed to the rising interest in what has been unfortunately dubbed "Web 3." Facebook's name change to "Meta" marks a shift in the imagined future of social media, and with it the predicted corporate future of the virtual classroom. The vision of increased reliance on immersive virtual reliance magnifies existing problems: as OASIS Consortium founder Tiffany Xingyu Wang observed:

> You can think of the Jan. 6 insurrection as a result of not having safety guardrails 15 years ago ... This time in the metaverse, either the impact will be much bigger, or the time to get to that catastrophic moment will be much shorter.
>
> (Chow, 2022)

She reminds us that the speed of this damage is only increasing: "Immersiveness increases the impact of any toxicity. Persistence increases the velocity of toxicity. And the interoperability part makes content moderation very hard, because toxicity is very industry-specific" (Chow, 2022).

An unexpected consequence of the pandemic's reduction in physical gathering spaces, and ongoing financial damage to in-person venues, is the ongoing search for new models of capital bridging digital and material. Roblox's financial model has taken advantage of the desire for digital personalization: it effectively already acts as a metaverse, with events like Lil Nas X's Roblox concert attracting 33 million dancing avatar viewers (Peters, 2021).

The drive toward purchasing real estate in the metaverse is deeply reminiscent of the widespread adoption of *Second Life* as a platform for everything from universities to corporations. As one journalist cynically describes the craze:

> If the metaverse is meant to encompass everything that exists virtually, from digital art to virtual worlds, then the real estate parcels that are being snapped up can be seen as just one type of metaversal investment, often listed as NFTs. These virtual worlds—The Sandbox, Decentraland, Cryptovoxels, Earth2, Nifty Island, Superworld, Wilder World—each offer different things to users: hyper-realistic graphics, gaming options, communities of specific types of early adopters. (Snoop Dogg, for instance, staked out a home for himself in The Sandbox; Paris Hilton has an island in Roblox.)
>
> (Bruner, 2022)

The early shadows of university engagement are already present: Berkeley and Miami, seeking new ways to engage with fundraising, have already auctioned off NFTs (Whitford, 2022). It is hard not to see the shadow of every abandoned *Second Life* island campus in each of these careless transactions—a specter made worse by the economic tightening and resource shortages in campuses around the world.

Universities are just beginning to invest in various metaverse models of education: Queen Mary University of London has touted the introduction of virtual reality lectures using the metaverse for medical education, and is particularly counting on them to sustain elements of in-person learning made more difficult by shifts online, as their press release brags:

> Teaching students in the metaverse helps solve one of the key challenges that has arisen from online learning – a lack of tools in place to enable scientific

experiments or any practical, hands-on activities in much the same way that would be possible in-person.

(Queen Mary University of London, 2022)

Stanford is similarly touting VR classes, perhaps predictably focused on communication in VR. As professor Jeremy Bailenson described:

In Virtual People, the students don't just get to try VR a handful of times. VR becomes the medium they rely on ... Nobody has networked hundreds of students with VR headsets for months at a time in the history of virtual reality, or even in the history of teaching.

(I. B. L. News, 2022)

Such work builds on the traditions of using platforms like *Second Life*—and similarly introduces incredible challenges of access equity, moderation, and sustainability.

Feminist interventions and gaming futures

Educators who build, or even select, games for their classrooms have an opportunity to reject these trends. In her powerful call to action *Play Like a Feminist*, Shira Chess offers a provocation embracing GamerGate's accusation that feminists are out to "destroy the video game industry":

I want to annihilate the toxic cultures, mediocre products, and public reputation of this industry. In turn, I would like to see a better industry making products for a larger audience. I want to see a mass scale of games that captivate, enrapture, and educate. I want to destroy the industry, disrupt the playground, and find ways to make games better. To do this, we need more feminists playing games, on the front lines of gaming culture, and making games.

(Chess, 2020, p. 86)

Chess gestures to the work of games education scholar Karen Schrier for part of the motivation to do this labor, even in the face of the industry's hostility and existing challenges. Karen Schrier's own recent work responding to the pandemic similarly offers a call to action drawing on games, noting that games "remind us that we are all connected. We are dependent on each other for our community, for our play, and our future" (Schrier, 2021, p. 225). She points to the power of games to enable us to teach, and practice, ethical decision-making in the face of these networked challenges.

Such ethical challenges are likely to become even more pressing, and difficult to navigate, as the platform behaviors discussed here move through new mechanisms. Already, new models of exploitation are on the rise in the games industry: to return to a moment to *Neopets*, even the most comforting of social platforms has turned to NFTs. For those fortunate enough to be unfamiliar, NFT is short for

"Non-fungible token," and it has effectively become a way of claiming ownership over ephemeral digital archives through an environmentally costly process of recording one's ownership on the blockchain—which is itself effectively a fancy linked list. NFTs are particularly alluring to game designers as another potential avenue for microtransactions, which Ian Bogost has already mercilessly mocked through his social media gamification parody "Cow Clicker" and its many colors of cow (Bogost, 2010). One hopes there won't be a need for NFT update of his parody: certainly, the move by *Neopets* to turn pets into tokens was met with immediate criticism, and as one journalist observed: "NFTs are a predator of last resort, sucking the remaining dregs of value from brands big and small in the name of financial efficiency" (Vincent, 2021). The static, unplayable, *Neopets* NFTs are certainly a dark harbinger of such a future.

Lest NFTs seem like a sidenote in this chapter on toxicity, it's important to recognize that the discussions of this form are already raising new questions about gamification and badges: one advocate for the form published an article arguing that "micro-credentials" should be moved to the blockchain, predicting a future where "all forms of credentialing like diplomas, degrees, and PHDs can also be tokenized, and likely stored in some kind of digital wallet that serves as a person's educational profile" (DelSignore, 2021). An EdSurge article even attempted to use the NFT form to sell a .jpg version and demonstrate the potential utility of the form, noting the potential applicability for everything from re-sellable digital textbooks to diplomas (Young, 2021).

A future of numbered eBooks or otherwise limited digital editions may sound a tad absurd, and yet such speculations area already in progress. Such a proposition must be alarming, particularly from an environmental standpoint. An article in *The New York Times* in 2021 calling out Bitcoin for using "more electricity than many countries" is just one example of investigations into this problem (Huang et al., 2021).

Interestingly, even game developers (an industry associated with early adoption) are not sold—the GDC developers survey found 70% of respondents were not interested in NFTs (*2020 State of the Game Industry Report*, 2020). This may not matter, as more and more companies are announcing their intentions to dive into the model in search of profits: a *PC Gamer* article surveying the expected terrain of 2022 NFTs noted Ubisoft's emphasis on "more play-to-earn that will enable more players to actually earn content, own content, and we think it's going to grow the industry quite a lot"—a model that sounds particularly troubling in light of the types of exploitation uncovered in *Roblox* (Fenlon, 2022).

As discussed in Chapter 1, when attempting to include or adapt mainstream games in the classroom, educators are presented with issues of representation and marginalization, along with possibilities of harming intrinsic motivation through behavioralist game designs. We described that despite all of these challenges, we continue to love games and use them for teaching. What about these new perils raised here? Can play in the classroom transcend this history of discrimination in gaming? Can informed teaching help prevent this in the future? Certainly, abandoning and ignoring the influence of these platforms—and their corresponding toxicity—will not make it go away, and the best hope for taking a critical lens to the "metaverse" and other sales pitches of future educational technology is found in drawing upon this history.

This is a conversation in which our students must be engaged: when confronted with the platforms and challenges discussed herein, it is incumbent upon us to prepare them to examine and challenge power and to rethink binaries and hierarchies—two of the key principles of data feminism (D'Ignazio & Klein, 2020). Collective awareness and resistance is critical, particularly as those most negatively affected by platforms, policies, and practices are typically the people who have the least control over the decision-making (Costanza-Chock, 2020; D'Ignazio & Klein, 2020). Our vision of better experience design for the classroom may not look much like Mark Zuckerberg's eerie metaverse conference rooms, but if such spaces are to become as potentially inescapable as Zoom, Shira Chess's call to action for feminist pedagogy definitely holds. Through co-creation, selection, critique, challenge, and conscientious moderation, we can bring these games and platforms into our classrooms while pushing for games to become better. It will not be easy, but a critical mass of interested and invested teachers and game designers dedicated to creating inclusive, representative, pedagogically effective games can absolutely join forces and improve choices for game-based learning. The example games and features discussed in the next chapter are a good place to start.

References

2020 state of the game industry report. (2020). Game Developers Conference. https://reg.gdconf.com/e/f2?LP=3114.

Anderson, M. T. (2004). *Feed.* Candlewick Press.

Berkowitz, R. (2021, May 11). Perspective | QAnon resembles the games I design. But for believers, there is no winning. *Washington Post.* https://www.washingtonpost.com/outlook/qanon-game-plays-believers/2021/05/10/31d8ea46-928b-11eb-a74e-1f4cf89fd948_story.html.

Betancourt, S. (2021, July 22). Video game company Activision Blizzard sued over 'frat boy culture' allegations. *The Guardian.* https://www.theguardian.com/us-news/2021/jul/22/activision-blizzard-sued-frat-boy-culture-allegations.

Bogost, I. (2010, July 21). *Cow clicker.* Bogost.Com. http://bogost.com/writing/blog/cow_clicker_1/.

Bonazzo, J. (2017, June 13). Minecraft creator tells women on twitter 'act like a cunt, get called a cunt.' *Observer.* https://observer.com/2017/06/minecraft-gamergate-markus-persson-notch-zoe-quinn/.

Bonsignore, E., Hansen, D., Kraus, K., & Ruppel, M. (2012). Alternate reality games as platforms for practicing 21st-century literacies. *International Journal of Learning and Media, 4*(1), 25–54. https://doi.org/10.1162/IJLM_a_00086.

Bradshaw, S., & Howard, P. N. (2018). The global organization of social media disinformation campaigns. *Journal of International Affairs, 71*(1.5), 23–32.

Brandom, R. (2021, August 17). Roblox is struggling to moderate re-creations of mass shootings. *The Verge.* https://www.theverge.com/2021/8/17/22628624/roblox-moderation-trust-and-safety-terrorist-content-christchurch.

Breen, K. (2021, October 20). *Experts, users warn about explicit content on Roblox.* TODAY.Com. https://www.today.com/parents/roblox-experts-users-warn-about-inappropriate-content-t235027.

Brewer, J., Romine, M., & Taylor, T. L. (2020). Inclusion at scale: Deploying a community-driven moderation intervention on twitch. In *Proceedings of the 2020 ACM Designing Interactive Systems Conference*, 757–769. https://doi.org/10.1145/3357236.3395514.

Bruner, R. (2022, January 20). *Investors are sinking real money into Virtual Real Estate, with no guarantees.* Time. https://time.com/6140467/metaverse-real-estate/.

Buffington, M. L. (2010). Redirecting discussion: Challenges related to the social aspects of online educational environments. In S. J. Hoffman (Ed.), *Teaching the humanities online: A practical guide to the virtual classroom* (pp. 99–111). Routledge.

Chayka, K. (2021, August 5). Facebook wants us to live in the metaverse. *The New Yorker*. https://www.newyorker.com/culture/infinite-scroll/facebook-wants-us-to-live-in-the-metaverse.

Chess, S. (2020). *Play like a feminist*. MIT Press. https://mitpress.mit.edu/books/play-feminist.

Chess, S., & Shaw, A. (2015). A conspiracy of fishes, or, how we learned to stop worrying about #GamerGate and embrace hegemonic masculinity. *Journal of Broadcasting and Electronic Media*, 59(1), 208–220. https://doi.org/10.1080/08838151.2014.999917.

Chia, A., Ong, J. C., Davies, H., & Hagood, M. (2021). "EVERYTHING IS CONNECTED": Networked conspirituality in new age media. *AoIR Selected Papers of Internet Research*. https://doi.org/10.5210/spir.v2021i0.12093.

Chow, A. (2022, January 6). *Here are the first comprehensive safety guidelines for the metaverse.* Time. https://time.com/6133271/oasis-safety-metaverse/.

CNET Highlights. (2021, October 28). *Watch Mark Zuckerberg's vision for socializing in the metaverse.* https://www.youtube.com/watch?v=b9vWShsmE20.

Costanza-Chock, S. (2020). *Design justice: Community-led practices to build the worlds we need.* The MIT Press.

D'Anastasio, C. (2021, June 10). How "Roblox" became a playground for virtual fascists. *Wired*. https://www.wired.com/story/roblox-online-games-irl-fascism-roman-empire/.

D'Ignazio, C., & Klein, L. F. (2020). *Data feminism*. MIT Press.

DelSignore, P. (2021, September 15). NFTs in education. *The Future of Learning*. https://medium.com/the-future-of-learning-and-education/nfts-in-education-957ce434047c.

Dugan, K. T. (2021, October 28). *Facebook wants to be The Matrix*. Fortune. https://fortune.com/2021/10/28/facebook-matrix-metaverse-mark-zuckerberg-meta/.

Fenlon, W. (2022, January 24). What to actually expect from NFTs in games this year. *PC Gamer*. https://www.pcgamer.com/what-to-actually-expect-from-nfts-in-games-this-year/.

Ging, D. (2019). Alphas, betas, and Incels: Theorizing the masculinities of the Manosphere. *Men and Masculinities*, 22(4), 638–657. https://doi.org/10.1177/1097184X17706401.

Glitsos, L., & Hall, J. (2019). The Pepe the Frog meme: An examination of social, political, and cultural implications through the tradition of the Darwinian Absurd. *Journal for Cultural Research*, 23(4), 381–395. https://doi.org/10.1080/14797585.2019.1713443.

Gray, K. L. (2020). *Intersectional tech: Black users in digital gaming*. LSU Press.

Guins, R., Lowood, H., & Wing, C. (2022). *EA sports FIFA: Feeling the game*. Bloomsbury Academic.

Hall, W., Tinati, R., & Jennings, W. (2018). From Brexit to trump: Social media's role in democracy. *Computer*, 51(1), 18–27. https://doi.org/10.1109/MC.2018.1151005.

Hannah, M. (2021). QAnon and the information dark age. *First Monday*. https://doi.org/10.5210/fm.v26i2.10868.

Harwell, D. (2015, April 27). Minecraft is finally fixing its huge gender problem. *Washington Post*. https://www.washingtonpost.com/news/the-switch/wp/2015/04/27/minecraft-is-finally-fixing-its-huge-gender-problem/.

Heslep, D. G., & Berge, P. (2021). Mapping discord's darkside: Distributed hate networks on disboard. *New Media and Society*, 14614448211062548, https://doi.org/10.1177/14614448211062548.

Hoffman, B., Ware, J., & Shapiro, E. (2020). Assessing the threat of incel violence. *Studies in Conflict and Terrorism*, *43*(7), 565–587. https://doi.org/10.1080/1057610X.2020.1751459.

Huang, J., O'Neill, C., & Tabuchi, H. (2021, September 3). Bitcoin uses more electricity than many countries. How is that possible? *The New York Times*. https://www.nytimes.com/interactive/2021/09/03/climate/bitcoin-carbon-footprint-electricity.html.

Huddleston, T. (2021, December 9). *Bill Gates says the metaverse will host most of your office meetings within 'two or three years'—Here's what it will look like*. CNBC. https://www.cnbc.com/2021/12/09/bill-gates-metaverse-will-host-most-virtual-meetings-in-a-few-years.html.

IBL News. (2022, January 5). Stanford University launches its first full class in metaverse virtual reality. *IBL News*. https://iblnews.org/stanford-university-launches-its-first-full-class-in-metaverse-virtual-reality/.

Ion, F. (2021, September 13). *Zoom preps for the dystopian hellscape of working in the metaverse*. Gizmodo. https://gizmodo.com/zoom-is-getting-ready-for-the-dystopian-hellscape-of-wo-1847666978.

Jenkins, H., Ford, S., & Green, J. (2013). *Spreadable media: Creating value and meaning in a networked culture*. New York University Press.

Kim, J., Lee, E., Thomas, T., & Dombrowski, C. (2009). Storytelling in new media: The case of alternate reality games, 2001–2009. *First Monday*. https://doi.org/10.5210/fm.v14i6.2484.

Kongslip, S. (2022, January 23). Metaverse and edtech: How do they work together? *Education Technology*. https://edtechnology.co.uk/e-learning/48961/.

Kurtzleben, D. (2021, November 14). Neopets, an online game popular in the 2000s, is having a resurgence. *NPR*. https://www.npr.org/2021/11/14/1055640620/neopets-an-online-game-popular-in-the-2000s-is-having-a-resurgence.

Lessig, L. (2009). *Remix: Making art and Commerce thrive in the hybrid economy* (8/30/09 edition). Penguin Books.

Librarian. (2020, September 25). *How to use discord for your classroom*. Discord. https://support.discord.com/hc/en-us/articles/360040613072-How-to-Use-Discord-for-Your-Classroom.

Lyles, T. (2020, July 21). *Over half of US kids are playing Roblox, and it's about to host Fortnite-esque virtual parties too*. The Verge. https://www.theverge.com/2020/7/21/21333431/roblox-over-half-of-us-kids-playing-virtual-parties-fortnite.

Mackness, J., Mak, S. F. J., & Williams, R. (2010). The ideals and reality of participating in a MOOC. *Networked Learning*, *10*, 266–274.

Marwick, A. E., & Caplan, R. (2018). Drinking male tears: Language, the manosphere, and networked harassment. *Feminist Media Studies*, *18*(4), 543–559. https://doi.org/10.1080/14680777.2018.1450568.

Meta. (2021, October 28). *Work in the metaverse*. https://www.youtube.com/watch?v=uVEALvpoiMQ.

Microsoft News Center. (2022, January 18). *Microsoft to acquire Activision Blizzard to bring the joy and community of gaming to everyone, across every device*. Stories.

https://news.microsoft.com/2022/01/18/microsoft-to-acquire-activision-blizzard-to-bring-the-joy-and-community-of-gaming-to-everyone-across-every-device/.

Paakki, H., Vepsäläinen, H., & Salovaara, A. (2021). Disruptive online communication: How asymmetric trolling-like response strategies steer conversation off the track. *Computer Supported Cooperative Work (CSCW)*. https://doi.org/10.1007/s10606-021-09397-1.

Pappademas, A. (2021, December 30). "The Matrix Resurrections" is a crucial Keanu Reeves movie. *The New Yorker*. https://www.newyorker.com/culture/culture-desk/the-matrix-resurrections-is-a-crucial-keanu-reeves-movie.

Parkin, S. (2022, January 9). The trouble with Roblox, the video game empire built on child labour. *The Observer*. https://www.theguardian.com/games/2022/jan/09/the-trouble-with-roblox-the-video-game-empire-built-on-child-labour.

Paul, K. (2021, August 8). Activision Blizzard scandal a 'watershed moment' for women in the gaming industry. *The Guardian*. https://www.theguardian.com/technology/2021/aug/08/activision-blizzard-lawsuit-women-sexual-harassment.

People Make Games. (2021, August 19). *Investigation: How Roblox is exploiting young game developers*. https://www.youtube.com/watch?v=_gXlauRB1EQ.

Peters, J. (2021, July 7). *Roblox, explained*. The Verge. https://www.theverge.com/2021/7/7/22457264/roblox-explainer-game-app-faq.

Phillips, A. (2020). *Gamer trouble: Feminist confrontations in digital culture*. New York University Press.

Phillips, W. (2013). The house that Fox built: Anonymous, spectacle, and cycles of amplification—Whitney Phillips, 2013. *Television and New Media*, *14*(6), 494–509. https://doi.org/10.1177/1527476412452799.

Phillips, W. (2015). *This is why we can't have nice things: Mapping the relationship between online trolling and mainstream culture*. MIT Press.

Phillips, W., & Milner, R. M. (2017). Decoding memes: Barthes' punctum, feminist standpoint theory, and the political significance of #YesAllWomen. In S. Harrington (Ed.), *Entertainment values: How do we assess entertainment and why does it matter?* (pp. 195–211). Palgrave Macmillan UK. https://doi.org/10.1057/978-1-137-47290-8_13.

Queen Mary University of London. (2022, January 19). *Queen Mary students receive first lecture in the metaverse*. Queen Mary University of London. https://www.qmul.ac.uk/media/news/2022/pr/queen-mary-students-receive-first-lecture-in-the-metaverse.html.

Roberts, S. T. (2019). *Behind the screen*. Yale University Press.

Robertson, A. (2021, May 14). *Apple said Roblox developers don't make games, and now Roblox agrees*. The Verge. https://www.theverge.com/2021/5/14/22436014/apple-roblox-epic-fortnite-trial-what-is-game-name-change.

Roblox. (2021). *Developer economics*. Roblox Developer. https://developer.roblox.com/en-us/articles/developer-economics.

Salter, A., & Blodgett, B. (2017). *Toxic geek masculinity in media: Sexism, trolling, and identity policing*. Springer.

Schrier, K. (2021). *We the gamers: How games teach ethics and civics*. Oxford University Press.

Schroeder, R. (2021, October 20). *Is the metaverse finally emerging?* Inside Higher Ed. https://www.insidehighered.com/digital-learning/blogs/online-trending-now/metaverse-finally-emerging.

Slovak, P., Salen, K., Ta, S., & Fitzpatrick, G. (2018). Mediating conflicts in Minecraft: Empowering learning in online multiplayer games. In *Proceedings of the 2018 CHI Conference on Human Factors in Computing Systems* (pp. 1–13). Association for Computing Machinery. https://doi.org/10.1145/3173574.3174169.

Staff, T. (2019, October 29). *Hateful conduct policy*. Twitter FAQ. https://help.twitter.com/en/rules-and-policies/hateful-conduct-policy.

Vaidhyanathan, S. (2017). 18. MOOCs, second life, and the white man's burden. In *18. MOOCs, second life, and the white man's burden* (pp. 287–299). University of Chicago Press. https://doi.org/10.7208/9780226469591-020.

Vardi, M. Y. (2012). Will MOOCs destroy academia? *Communications of the ACM*, *55*(11), 5–5. https://doi.org/10.1145/2366316.2366317.

Veale, K. (2020). Gaming the rules. In K. Veale (Ed.), *Gaming the dynamics of online harassment* (pp. 87–106). Springer International Publishing. https://doi.org/10.1007/978-3-030-60410-3_4.

Vincent, J. (2021, October 1). *Neopets are being turned into NFTs because of course they are*. The Verge. https://www.theverge.com/2021/10/1/22703881/neopets-nfts-crytpo-trend-raydium-solana.

Wachowski, L., Reeves, K., Moss, C.-A., & II., Y. A.-M. (2021, December 22). *The matrix resurrections* [Action, Sci.-Fi]. Warner Bros., Village Roadshow Pictures, Venus Castina Productions.

Warschauer, M. (1995). Comparing face-to-face and electronic discussion in the second language classroom. *CALICO Journal*, *13*(2/3), 7–26.

Watters, A. (2021). *Teaching machines: The history of personalized learning*. MIT Press.

Wheeler, T. (2021, September 30). The metachallenges of the metaverse. *Brookings*. https://www.brookings.edu/blog/techtank/2021/09/30/the-metachallenges-of-the-metaverse/.

Whitford, E. (2022, January 20). *Berkeley and Miami auctioned NFTs. Who's next?* Inside Higher Ed. https://www.insidehighered.com/news/2022/01/20/colleges-cash-nfts-new-fundraising-mechanism.

Young, J. (2021, August 9). *We wondered if NFTs could change education, so we decided to sell this article on the Blockchain—EdSurge News*. EdSurge. https://www.edsurge.com/news/2021-08-09-we-wondered-if-nfts-could-change-education-so-we-decided-to-sell-this-article-on-the-blockchain.

Zuckerman, E. (2019). QAnon and the emergence of the unreal. *Journal of Design and Science*, *6*(6). https://doi.org/10.21428/7808da6b.6b8a82b9.

5 Designing playfully for a distant future

Introduction

The ineffective games assessed in prior chapters all have similar downfalls. They propagate issues already pervasive in society in and out of schools. The lack of diversity in video games is a direct result of the dominant culture in the places where video games are made (again, primarily the United States), where the default player is assumed to be a white, straight, cis male. Toxic communities across the globe have been created by those who received the message that they were the rightful default players and have used the Internet to target, harass, and discriminate against women, people of color, and any group threatening their mirage of dominance. The use of games in schools that lack diversity sends the message to students who do not fit the identity of the presumed default player that they are not valued in society nor in the classroom: a message educators are in danger of sending unconsciously if these games are used without a discussion of these issues.

Another issue with the ineffective games analyzed in this book is the way that most of them follow the outdated behaviorist learning theory and reward correct answers while punishing failure. This, as noted previously, emphasizes accuracy and already knowing specific answers rather than helping students to learn and grow from their failures. It is also a replication of the existing problems in the culture of schools, where students are almost expected to already know—or at least quickly memorize—the narrow range of facts that are tested on the high-stakes standardized assessments. This is inevitable in the United States, where school funding is tied to test scores and the tests themselves are created by for-profit companies with teams of lobbyists, but similar education structures are in place around the globe.

However, play is worth pursuing: an examination of gaming during the pandemic found a majority of players found games to be positive, with impacts including "providing cognitive stimulation and opportunities to socialise, and a variety of benefits related to mental health, including reduced anxiety and stress" (Barr & Copeland-Stewart, 2022, p. 122). Given the corresponding rise in gaming around the world and the visibility of COVID-19 in player communities and events in the wake of campaigns like #PlayApartTogether (Hjorth et al., 2020), play is also more

DOI: 10.4324/9781003281696-6

Table 5.1 Framework for meaningful play in education

Ineffective games	Playful pedagogy
Lack diversity	Is inclusive and diverse
Perpetuate problematic dominant culture	Questions dominant culture; provides opportunities to think beyond it
Punish failure	Deemphasizes or promotes failure
Reward success and winning	Defines success as improving or learning from failure
Promote memorization	Promotes questioning, exploration, creative solutions
Have rigid, correct answers	Presents unstructured, complicated problems to solve
Follow behaviorist or cognitivist learning theory	Follows constructivist or similar (socio-constructivist, humanist, or connectivist) learning theory

present in daily life than it was even prior to the pandemic (recall the enthusiasm around *Animal Crossing: New Horizons* at the pandemic's start, as discussed in Chapter 2). This chapter looks at playful pedagogy that invites students to engage more meaningfully in their learning. Building from the framework contrasting ineffective games and playful pedagogy in Table 5.1, we identify elements of playful learning that can be incorporated naturally into courses, along with some examples of potential platforms that teachers and students might use to create rich learning experiences. By looking to co-creative models, such as alternate reality games and "Netprov," we reveal the importance of invested students in the design of their own play (and learning.) We also suggest gameful learning environments where students are responsible for their own learning and can create unique interactive narratives and games. Finally, we recommend critical making projects that provide students with opportunities for creativity and expression as well as serious critique of issues that they identify in their environment and speak to from their own perspectives.

This chapter particularly responds to the ongoing trends in higher education noted in Chapter 4: an emphasis on scale and technological complexity puts us continually in the hands of the start-up approach to learning, with all its associated pitfalls. Collectively, the solutions we hold most valuable are those that are least technical. The unpolished, imperfect, co-created methods of play discussed here rarely or never involve 3D graphics, or platforms of extensive coding. They are often low-tech, and low-cost, minimizing the amount of corporate mediation and intervention required to run them. These are a subset we selected because we find them inspirational for thinking through the challenges of crafting educational community going forward, but we also acknowledge that there are likely many more such personal educational projects around the world—and it is in that movement of making that we see hope for a playful educational future.

Collaborative play at a distance

Several successes of educational play during the pandemic point toward a future driven by co-creative gaming. We look to exemplars from around the world, drawing on emerging practices ranging from the alternate reality games of Patrick Jagoda's campus team to the improvisational exercises of Netprov to the results of pandemic-inspired game jams and distant exercises in critical making. Both formats share an important emphasis on the active role of students as creators: their potential for what Patrick Jagoda has termed "participatory aesthetics," which fundamentally take their affordances from the platforms we now over-rely upon in the always-online classroom and workspace. Scott Rettberg places this type of work into the practice of "collaborative narrative" in electronic literature, noting that such experiments predate our current technologies, but are amplified by their possibilities (Rettberg, 2014, p. 78). Their emphasis on collaboration is key to their impact on how we think about play post-pandemic: these are games that do not seek to reproduce the traditional hierarchies of the classroom.

Patrick Jagoda's collaborative approach to building campus community during the pandemic built on his established work in alternate reality games, which typically involve a blend of in-person collaborative play with digital clues and narrative components. Jagoda's approach to "experimental games" is grounded in exploring games "as a form for staging, encountering, processing, and testing experience and reality in the twenty-first century" (Jagoda, 2020, p. xi). Many of those games previously featured the type of physical gatherings and locative play that the pandemic has made difficult, if not impossible, but Jagoda's team reimagined and adapted their approach. Notably, such work represents a fundamental rethinking of traditions of locative play: designers working in these genres have had to rethink the emphasis on proximity and rethink the notion of a shared "place" (Bhattacharya et al., 2021). This work is not so different from the work and reflection we are engaged in here as educators, confronted with a fundamentally transformed classroom.

In a postmortem of another collaborative STEM-based alternate reality game, *The Source*, Patrick Jagoda and his collaborators note the significant role of the emergent structure in enabling a meaningful experience:

> an ARG offers them the potential (albeit one that is not always realized) to expand the shared game world and its rules. Even if the designers determine most of the challenges in an ARG, the this-is-not-a-game aesthetic ensures that the players, not the developers, negotiate the meaning of the experience and determine its status as either a game or an extension of reality. ARGs, we contend, carry potential for learning because they address players who collaborate with others to transform their world.
>
> (Jagoda et al., 2015, p. 72)

This work takes on the difficulty of the moment through a fictional reimagining: it is in this tension of real and playful that the form excels. When comparing this low-fi narrative effort with commercial game teams' responses to the pandemic, Wai Chee Dimock noted that "Even without the $17.3 billion war chest Epic Games has at its disposal, humanists can come up with some decent productions [that] are urgently needed now to reconnect communities dispersed and disoriented by the pandemic" (Dimock, 2021, p. 164). Jagoda's teams created two pandemic-responsive games attentive to those questions of community: the first, *A Labyrinth*, centered on a return home, while the second, *ECHO*, addressed both "the mental and physical health of the players" (Dimock, 2021, p. 165). Given the recurring emphasis on those challenges in both student and faculty responses to the pandemic, such games demonstrate the potential for timely intervention. With ECHO, Fourcast Lab used narrative to create distance for players and room to process and grow, as Patrick Jagoda described in an interview:

> It's difficult to gain critical distance when you're in the middle of a situation ... So we tried to defamiliarize the COVID-19 pandemic by thinking back to the 1918 influenza pandemic, and then asking people to speculate about a possible future engaging with our present.
> (Austen-Smith, 2020)

Mark Marino and Rob Wittig's collaborative Netprov experiments developed out of an interest in merging structured improv, LARPing, and other creative forms of play into emerging social media platforms. Typically, the Netprov framework centers on offering a shared starting narrative, with guidance and intervention to assist players in telling their story, often through a mix of modalities. During the rapidly-converted-to-virtual Electronic Literature 2020 conference, Mark Marino and Rob Wittig ran "Fantasy Spoils: After the Quest" for participants, offering a narrative centered on the aftermath of a fantastical war:

> Gone are the orcs, hobgoblins, and dragons. In their place, you must contend with your wounds, property damages, and ensuing lawsuits. How will you deal with life here in Muddled Earth after the glorious quest? Are you hero enough to face your most daunting enemy: your own irritation?
> (M. Marino & Wittig, 2020)

Based on *Dungeons & Dragons*, the Netprov game took place on the chat server Discord, and players introduced their invented characters, recalled their fictional battles, joined others on collective misadventures, and described the aftermath. This channel created an opportunity for playful creative writing and created a sense of community across a distant, virtual conference.

A participant in "Fantasy Spoils" or a similar Netprov has a significant amount of control over their own embodiment and interactions. To recall our discussion of virtual tabletop gaming and the power of *Tabletop Simulator* in Chapter 3, "Fantasy Spoils" encourages full character generation, while simple models of Netprov might focus on collaborative imagination of a setting, an event, or even a non-existent episode of a television show. Each of these forms invites the player to author, while relying upon the low barriers to entry of familiar platforms, as with the Discord channels of "Fantasy Spoils" or the Twitter hashtags of the team's more open calls for play.

Lauren Burr offers important insights into Netprov's success, noting that it relies upon a wider blurring of boundaries between platforms designated for play and work:

> Netprov, more than any other media genre, illustrates the increasingly arbitrary distinction between our contemporary communications technologies and media of cultural representation. And it provides a venue for us to run scenarios, to speculate on premises, to "play and go deeper," using the very same platforms on which we struggle through predominant social issues affecting our everyday lives.
>
> (Burr, 2015)

Rob Wittig and Mark Marino have described their methods as "carnivalesque," noting the goal of their projects to produce "satisfaction in play" through community (Wittig & Marino, 2017). The linking of their work to the theatrical tradition of improvisation is essential: Mark Marino described it as "the slacking heir to a rich tradition of theatrical computer-mediated play and real-time collaborative performance" (M.C. Marino & Wittig, 2015).

The blurring of boundaries has also been a challenge for Netprov's reception, as participants unaware of the conceit have been drawn into the reality of some events. The same design team collaborated on "Occupy MLA," a MLA-hashtag-centered social media performance that drew attention to adjunct working conditions that Berens describes as

> Speaking truth to power in the guise of fiction; making access to such speech open, participatory, collective and persistently visible: this is important cultural work. The tangle of liveness and digital presence, of trust and hoax, of allegiance and betrayal: these are the messy conditions of a Netprov.
>
> (Berens, 2015, p. 4)

Conditions have if anything become messier: in social media, information and misinformation travel at similar speeds, and fiction can be hard to recognize. However, the success of Netprov experiences within challenging information environments, including virtual conferences and online classrooms, suggests that its improvisational structures are well-formed to weather those tensions of truth and fiction—and perhaps to increase our awareness of the "messy conditions" of our platforms more broadly.

Both Netprov and alternate reality games share an emphasis on narrative and participatory play: many of the mechanics associated with more traditional genres are simply not present in their playspaces, and while they both are primarily experienced as digital, they retain strong connections to materiality. Importantly, they use materials that invite remixing and reimagining: players can see the impact of their actions rapidly, and redirect a narrative of play through that influence. Placing these forms into conversation with the examples thus far demonstrates their powerful potential for pedagogical and community-centered interventions, particularly as we find ourselves in recurring states of crisis with regard to online platforms–play becomes a means for restructuring our collective relationship with the web.

Expanding playful learning

The underlying principles of both these collaborative narrative forms are the principles of playful learning, a mode of thinking that has been historically better received in the context of K-12, but which has an impact far beyond that categorization. Children innately pretend as a key part of the progress of learning (Huizinga, 1955)—a process that can and should be enjoyable. As we grow older, we retain the ability to learn in this way. We see pretend and the magic circle throughout cultures and across age groups as art. Stories, plays, films, visual art forms, analog RPGs, and video games offer us new perspectives about the way the world is and imagines new possibilities for what it could be. Art, pretend, and play allow us to imagine: to try on new ways of thinking and to fail without detrimental consequences. These are the key aspects of games and playful learning that should be the focus of our pedagogy.

The act of pretending can be a way to cope with stress, anxiety, and even trauma. Especially in trying times like a global pandemic but even in "normal" times, students face a myriad of stressors in and out of school. Engaging our students in make-believe situations and imagined scenarios provides them with characters to inhabit and allows learners to experiment with different behaviors and perspectives in a temporary way. The ephemeral nature of the imaginary role or scenario encourages learners to sample different perspectives and behaviors, trying out new uncharted worlds and imagining different sequences or consequences to real experiences: in Fourcast Lab's *ECHO*, the space for storytelling around the pandemic was an essential part of play, even though those stories were recontextualized by the game's own narrative structures.

Additionally, imagined worlds, narratives from verbal fairytales to science fiction novels have helped people imagine for centuries. Scientists across disciplines have conducted thought experiments to imagine deeply (Elgin, 2014; Gendler, 1998; Mcallister, 2012) and yet educators still follow the traditional tendency of relegating imagining and play to non-instructional activities. Incorporating imagination into educational activities helps empower students to look beyond what they know and primes them to expand their understanding. Rather than limiting thought and learning to focus on memorizing the one answer out of four choices in a series of isolated questions on an end-of-term or end-of-year assessment, the goal of our classes should be to engage learners' imaginations and help them probe everything beyond what is known.

Finally, role-play and pretend can take the sting out of failing. Making mistakes is an integral part of learning. Yet, as discussed in Chapter 1, schools following behavioralist learning theory rely on rewards and punishments directly tied to performance rather than learning. This system of grading only works to reward those students who arguably did not need much actual instruction in the first place. Deep learning takes place when learners can make mistakes and learn from them. When mistakes are penalized, they become feared. Learners then engage in all types of conduct to avoid making mistakes, from cheating to memorizing the letter of the multiple-choice answer to practically anything other than thinking deeply about the content being tested. This avoidance behavior is not only detrimental to the early stages of the learning process, but when these overly stigmatized mistakes occur, learners have such a negative emotional reaction that learners are unwilling (and possibly unable) to face their mistakes and therefore unable to learn from them.

For educators interested in creating their own games, one simple and open-source game creation platform is Bitsy (Le Doux, 2021). Games created in this platform have a simple, pixelated 2D (or retro) appearance, and the games are navigated solely with keyboard arrows. An example of an educational game created during a gamejam (and therefore within a limited amount of time) using this platform is *A Little Turtle Has Just Hatched on a Beach in Texas*, where the player navigates a turtle along the beach and in the ocean into different items (Whitehead, 2020). It is intentionally difficult to tell if the items are actual foods in the turtle's diet or if they are garbage. Only after the turtle eats the item does the player know if it was trash or food. The game keeps track of how many items the turtle eats, listing trash and food numbers separately, until the turtle's stomach is filled with trash. Obviously intended to draw attention to the problem of pollution in the ocean, specifically plastic, this simple, straightforward game acts as a low-fidelity simulation, allowing the player to feel the frustration of the turtle as it seeks food only to eat plastic.

Another free game authoring tool is Twine (*Twine*, 2022). Twine is text-based platform best at creating branching narratives. Also user-friendly, teachers can create simple choose-your-own-adventure style learning games or escape room scenarios using this powerful, simple tool. Scholarship on Twine is expanding (Salter & Moulthrop, 2021), and there are many pragmatic how-to guides explaining the logistics of using the tool as well (Ford, 2016; *Home – Twine Cookbook*, 2021). This platform has been used by the authors to teach interactive narrative writing and game design, while one of their colleagues has assigned it to graduate students as an exercise in visualization of the connections between key authors on the graduate program's core reading list.

The exciting thing about Twine is that it can function as a user-friendly, text-only branching narrative platform: ideal for students to take the lead in creating their own works, but once students have mastered the basic logistics of creating a branching narrative, they can add color, moving text, images, and even sound by adding additional coding commands (with javascript and css). This allows the same platform to be used across ages, grade levels, and coding abilities for a myriad of different assignments, courses, and purposes. The open-source resources available online make it easy for students to locate instructions for adding any given feature they wish, even if this feature goes beyond the coding capabilities of their teacher, and it also sets students up to become experts on their chosen game functionality, allowing them to take on the role of instructor and help their classmates improve their games. Creating their own games to teach or demonstrate a course concept provides students with autonomy and responsibility for their own education as well as motivation that is likely to keep them engaged in the learning task.

One example of an educational Twine game that is designed as a learning facilitator rather than a multiple-guess platform is *BeadED Adventures* (Johnson & Sullivan, 2018; Sullivan & Johnson, 2019). This game is intended to teach computational thinking concepts to young audiences who have not yet been introduced to any specific coding language, with the idea that the underlying concepts apply across coding languages, and that if learners can gain background knowledge about these concepts, they will be able to more effectively learn specific coding languages later. Designed to foster autonomy, *BeadED Adventures* is a choose-your-own-adventure style exploratory narrative that takes place in an abandoned castle, where each area of the castle houses different areas to explore and specific computational thinking concepts to play with, including variables, conditions, and loops. The final escape from the castle requires the player to use knowledge from all three of these concepts.

This game was developed as part of a proof of concept and players progress through the game using a unique physical interface: jars of different colored pony beads. When the player wishes to make a choice in the game, they pick up the jar of beads that matches the color of those words, remove a bead, string the bead on a piece of yarn, and replace the jar on the stand. The jar stand is connected to a Makey-Makey, which senses the removal and replacement of the jar, translating these actions as selections of passages in the Twine game. This game is an experiment with non-standard, physical controllers and produces a tangible learning artifact. The strand of yarn players create as they play becomes a map of the trail the player took through the game, with special silver beads marking the points in the game where the player solved a puzzle that demonstrated or embodied a computational concept.

Like all learning design, playful learning pedagogy is the result of a delicate balance between motivational elements and educational elements. When these two are isolated from one another, the results are usually not successful. Some games like *Jeopardy!* emphasize the content more than the (questionably) motivational aspects. Other games, especially entertainment games adapted into a classroom, overemphasize the entertainment features and fall short of their intended content learning. The games that integrate both have a better chance of success, but ultimately it is the empowering act of creating games that provides the best opportunities for engaging learners.

Designing play

Effective playful learning capitalizes on the constructivist branches of learning theory where learning is coupled with action. Students who are building their own understanding of the world—whether they are constructing tangible learning artifacts or models or actively engaged in thinking deeply about a subject or problem—are more likely to understand something new and retain that knowledge for a longer period of time than students in passive learning environments (e.g., Prince, 2004). Both constructivist and the similar constructionist theory (e.g., Ratto, 2011) focus on student-centered learning, where assignments are intended to provide learners with opportunities to build—metaphorically, in the case of constructivist theory, and literally, in the case of constructionist theory—their own understandings of the concepts.

Games can engage students in problem-solving easily—in fact, solving puzzles and finding solutions are flagship elements of a large number of games. Humans love to solve problems; at times, even the mere statement of a problem can mentally engage students. Presenting learning content in the form of a question is a pedagogical strategy that has gained popularity in K-12 schools in the last two decades to the extent that many school districts require teachers of all subjects to post "essential questions" for each lesson (for scholarship on essential questions, see McTighe & Wiggins, 2013). Piecing together a greater understanding of a larger body of knowledge is impactful—and often fun.

Even when the instructor selects and poses the essential question to students, the learners can be given autonomy as to the way they go about solving it—or even the illusion of autonomy, if the teacher wishes to scaffold the process by providing specific resources at specific times. They key is that learners are working to solve a puzzle and simultaneously piece together working understandings of the concepts the puzzle or question involves. This constructivist knowledge-building allows students to feel responsible for their own learning as they work to devise their own solutions.

The major obstacle for most teachers is not the ability to create meaningful learning games for their students; often, the primary reason games are not used with or created for students is time. Like any educational activity, learning games take time and careful thought to design well. The increasing demands placed on teachers' time continue to erode their ability to play with gameful elements in their teaching, forcing teachers to rely on more traditional teaching methods that they are accustomed to using and, in most cases, the ways that they themselves were taught in school. The authors know firsthand how exhausting teaching at any level is and the pressures, stresses, and invisible labors that consume instructor energy. Creating educational games may be one way to frontload some of the work of teaching, where the game does not require as much energy and time to use in class after it is created. Another option, which might be more logistically feasible as well as educationally superior, is to engage students themselves in the creation of educational games.

Learning by design

The two-semester capstone computer science course at the authors' university follows an excellent project-based learning model. The professor invites members of the community and the university to the first week of class to pitch an innovative project idea to the class that they are willing to "sponsor." Some of these sponsors are from nearby businesses like NASA and Lockheed Martin, some are from start-ups, and some are faculty members at the university. The students then submit a ranked list of the five projects that they find most interesting and are placed in a group of three to six students. The group spends the first semester researching the topics of the project, submitting a full research report detailing the potential solutions they researched, which one they selected and why, and a technical design document outlining the project. They then spend the second semester of the course actually creating the project, and they conclude with a formal presentation and demonstration of their completed work.

One of the authors has sponsored over a dozen different groups and has seen firsthand the ways in which this class structure provides an authentic problem for students to solve and how students must collaborate with one another effectively. The project also necessitates interdisciplinary research, especially the educational games that she has sponsored. Interdisciplinary, creative projects like these capstone course projects are an excellent way to engage students in a variety of fields, and the immediate relevance and real-world applications of the topics they are researching to complete the project provides a deeper learning experience than any worksheet or course dedicated solely to "covering" a given subject.

Examples of projects that the author has sponsored include a suite of language learning games playable on a variety of platforms (VR, PC, Mac, and mobile), titled *ELLE the EndLess LEarner*. These games, discussed in detail elsewhere (Johnson, 2021; Johnson et al., 2020), experiment with different modalities and formats terms—text, audio, and images—to help the player practice foreign language vocabulary words. Creating and connecting a database, a user-friendly website, and a series of these games—all which had to ensure the games were adaptable to *any* language (including languages that use non-Latin characters) were interesting and difficult design challenges for a series of capstone groups. The vocabulary practice games themselves, at the time of writing, still follow the traditional right-and-wrong style of practice, and many are admittedly glorified versions of multiple-choice. This is in part because of scoping issues, in part because of the database structure, and in part because vocabulary memorization is simply one of those few things where repetitive skill-and-drill practice can be a helpful means to an end. The intent with this sort of game was that students could practice the vocabulary outside of class to allow language instructors to focus on more complex applications of the language like grammar and cultural contexts.

Another example of a capstone computer science project that an author co-sponsored is the *Middle Passage VR Experience* (Pineda et al., 2020). This virtual reality simulation teaches this difficult history—the abduction of African citizens and their passage across the Atlantic Ocean to be sold into slavery in America. The simulation focuses on the slow dehumanization that took place on these slaving vessels rather than the hyperviolence that is frequently the focus of much of Hollywood's portrayals of these events. The design decisions the sponsors and the students made together were a deep learning experience for the computer science students who had not been taught much about these atrocious historical realities, and these students took away a more complete understanding of the history and its lasting effects still today. Virtual reality was expected to become an immediate, disruptive technology that would, by default, impart empathy on its users. The simulation has been demonstrated at a variety of public and academic events, and it does have a powerful emotional impact on many users while also teaching them a little about the conditions on the ships and cabins. However, the students who designed and developed this simulation gained a great deal more knowledge and empathy than most of the participants who experience it.

Students as authors

Modding and authoring of games and playful learning activities should not be relegated only to educators and entertainment companies. The act of designing an educational game can, in and of itself, be a rich and effective learning experience. Just like asking a learner to take on the role of a scientist can help students gain confidence and improve their motivation to learn (Jaber & Hammer, 2016), asking them to take on the role of an expert game designer to design or modify a game to teach specific content can be a powerful exercise. Guiding students to author their own works—whether they are written narratives, visual art works, or video game levels—engages students in deep, reflective thought, which often leads to a more complete and mature understanding of a topic or the world, while also increasing their sense of autonomy and motivation to learn. The task of taking a body of content knowledge and distilling it into an engaging and fun game world is not easy—as those who work to incorporate games into our teaching know firsthand. But the debates we have with ourselves and (when fortunate) our development teams over how to best present concepts for players to engage with and learn are, in fact, deep learning activities themselves.

Rather than designing constrained levels to teach individual subject concepts, like the constrained levels of the crowdsourced *Minecraft: Education Edition* or teacher-created challenges in *Portal 2 Puzzle Creator* mentioned in Chapter 2, handing the design of different levels and games like these over to students would be more effective. Deeper learning of the content takes place as students wrestle with various ways to demonstrate and teach concepts to their players. This authoring for an authentic audience is a hallmark in effective pedagogy, notably improving student motivation and investment in the assignment (Chen & Brown, 2012; Gunel et al., 2009). Even if the resulting game is not fun or all that effective in imparting the intended knowledge to the player, the students who authored it take away a robust knowledge from their intense engagement in creating the game.

Free, user-friendly game authoring tools are becoming more available and accessible each day. Bitsy Game Maker (Le Doux, 2021) is a free, browser-based, user-friendly platform for making simple 2D games. Bitsy has a small learning curve and works best when game design emphasizes interaction with simple pixelated characters and objects. When the player moves their avatar near another character or object, text appears on the screen that can be used to provide instruction, narration, or a problem. Additionally, items may be hidden and collected, making Bitsy a good candidate for simple student-created games with straightforward scavenger hunts, stories, or puzzles.

Likewise, Twine allows for fast and easy game development with the option to use basic Javascript commands to add color, images, and even sound. This makes the platform ideal for interdisciplinary learning, where students can improve their traditional writing skills and gain coding experience within the same project. Navigation in Twine is mouse-based, where clicking on a word (or, less commonly, an image) moves the player to the next passage. Thus, the game can emphasize individual words and phrases, forcing the student designing the game to carefully consider which word should lead to which passage. This invokes some of the close-reading techniques of the past, though from a reverse, authoring stance.

It would be an easy next step for students to examine their Twine games or the games of others to learn or practice the close-reading techniques that are a historic hallmark of high school English and advanced literature studies (Paul & Elder, 2019). Here again, allowing students to grapple with how to best engage their player in their game's narrative, world, or scenario will likely result in deep learning, often even if the final product itself is not an enthralling learning experience. We struggle to entice students to think deeply and critically about all of the content we cover in our courses; handing them the keys and asking learners to create situations where learners can engage with these topics can be a powerful activity where students do in fact think deeply and critically about the content.

Furthermore, learners can carry out the entire design process without actually creating the game and still experience deep, engaging learning. One example is in the participatory design research study the authors facilitated with undergraduate women who were members of the Science Leadership and Mentoring (SLAM) program at our university to create the educational leadership game *emPower through Play* (*Empower through Play*, 2021). The design process of this game consisted of weekly Zoom meetings throughout the Spring semester of 2021 where participants discussed leadership topics and skills that they thought were relevant and important to their target audience of middle-school-aged girls. A student member of our research team was tasked with developing the game in Twine to the specifications of the group, and the entire process engaged everyone—even the researchers—in the content of leadership styles and how these styles might influence various situations in everyday life.

For subject matter experts who do not feel inclined or capable of mastering these platforms designed for games or who are wary of assigning students to use a technology for which they themselves are uncomfortable, there are other common content-sharing platforms that can be appropriated for game creation. In PowerPoint and Google Slides, words can be hyperlinked to other slides in the deck to create an escape room (or even a behaviorist multiple-choice quiz "game"), although slide show formats like these are easily circumvented because they were not intended for this purpose, negating much of the learning that the instructor or student designer would intend.

WebQuests, early Internet scavenger hunts designed to increase technology use and digital literacy while also enhancing classroom instruction, are another option for engaging, playful learning (Dodge, 1995). Although much has changed about the Internet since the early 1990s when the term WebQuest was coined, the idea of providing students with a list of questions and asking them to search through sources (a textbook, an encyclopedia, the library, etc.) is not an Internet-dependent learning task. This activity could, depending on the structure of the questions and the sources students are able to find, be an excellent and engaging educational activity. Again, handing the design of the scavenger hunt over to students themselves would also likely be a motivating and meaningful learning assignment. Questions can be written on the board, on paper handouts, or posted digitally on a PowerPoint, Google slide, Google doc, LMS page, external website, and so forth—whatever the teacher and students prefer.

Even Google forms can be linked to one another to create an escape room game that students can easily author. They can design a series of puzzles, Internet scavenger hunts (WebQuests), and complicated riddles using a very basic, free platform available in most browsers. Teacher-created escape rooms, however, can easily fall into the behaviorist, right-and-wrong answer trap. These questions must be open-ended enough, or build upon each other in such a way, as to avoid simply rewarding correct answers and punishing incorrect ones.

Having students create their own, however, would likely be more effective, even if they end up creating more basic singular correct answer types of questions. This is because the students are not simply selecting one option from three or four limited choices—multiple-guess—but are developing questions and answering them: handling the material and concepts in a more robust, thoughtful way. It is common for teachers to assign persuasive essays, creative narratives, visual representations of complex things like science fair poster boards, and other art as learning activities. These types of assignments occupy the "create" category at the top of the revised Bloom's Taxonomy pyramid (Seaman, 2011), mentioned here due to its familiarity despite its reliance on outdated learning theories that many scholars have called attention to (Bereiter & Scardamalia, 1998) as well as rejected in favor of cyclical learning process models (Kolb, 2005). Assignments that require students to construct their own knowledge through the creation of a product—whether it is a video game, a science fair poster, a poem, or any other art form—push students beyond the memorize-and-regurgitate monotony of traditional schoolwork and require a complex set of skills and understanding of the content to complete successfully. Thus, assigning students to create a game that demonstrates or teaches a course concept is just as likely to result in robust student learning, regardless of the actual quality of the game they ultimately produce.

The advantage of using free, user-friendly authoring tools such as these to allow students to design and develop their own educational games is that the teacher does not have to be an expert in coding, game design, or even the platform the students are using. When given opportunities like game design to harness their creativity, students are typically eager to learn the tools and can tinker and discover capabilities and idiosyncrasies of the platform with minimal guidance.

The educator can search for appropriate, curated resources and send students to those. This is student-led learning, and although some teachers remain wary of allowing their students to have full control of the class, they can certainly share the learning navigation with students in activities like this. The teacher can set general guidelines and expectations for the game at the beginning of the project, and often students will go above and beyond these because they are motivated to create a fun game.

The shift from teacher-led to student-led learning is one that we advocate, even as we know that many educators struggle with it. While it is true that many students seem to prefer a passive learning experience over an active one (and, arguably, may actually prefer to have no learning experience at all), when students take the responsibility for their own learning, they tend to be more mentally engaged with the content and have a deeper learning experience (e.g., Danielson, 2007). Providing students with opportunities to create learning games is just one way that we might be able to conjure the magic formula that includes high levels of both motivation and rigor.

Critical making

Students can learn from creating games even if the games themselves engage only superficially with the content; as discussed above, the decisions they must make as educational game designers require knowledge of a range of possible content and skills that their game could cover. However, we encourage teachers to also consider the research methodology of critical making as another option for bringing playful learning into the course. This expanding field of scholarship invokes the "maker movement" but goes beyond simply tinkering to learn physics and engineering concepts by physically building things and instead emphasizes creative authorship and commentary about the world. Critical making involves research and understanding of a movement, theory, historical event, or other types of phenomena—typically rooted in society. The critical making researcher then creates something that emphasizes an aspect of this phenomenon to critique it. The actual product of the critical making then becomes a medium through which the author makes an assertion about culture or society, often a statement about the problematic nature of a practice or perspective.

Critical making products are powerful in the way that avant-garde art is: Picasso and his contemporaries did not strive for photo-realistic reproductions of picturesque scenes; they created art that displayed a different perspective (literally) to force their audience to see things in a different way. Likewise, critical making works call attention to events, behaviors, and cultural ways of thinking in ways that compel the audience to think differently and critically about these individual issues and our society as a whole. Examples of critical making scholarship can involve everything from Twitter bots to hand-sewn quilts—including combinations of the two—and everything in between. This work often focuses on the relationship between technology and society, though some critique society without much emphasis on or use of technology.

The HASTAC (Humanities, Arts, Science, and Technology Alliance and Collaboratory) Critical Maker.Space website houses a few notable examples that can serve as an introduction to the methods and intents of critical making ("Examples of Critical Making," 2019). An example on this site explains Caleb McDaniel's *Every Three Minutes Bot*: this critical making project is a Twitter bot that, as the name suggests, tweets every three minutes (McDaniel, n.d.). Three minutes is an intentional frequency, because in the United States between 1820 and 1860, a slave was sold on an average of every 3.6 minutes. The bot tweets include posts like "#OnThisDay in #history, a white American just sold a human being's grandchild" and "A person was sold about every 3 minutes in the antebellum era. One was called Eliza." This work calls attention to America's history of slavery, reminding us of these horrific events that are so often glossed over in schools. The project seeks to remind us that slaves were actual human beings—rehumanizing the captives who were (and in many cases continue to be) dehumanized. The bot's use of popular hashtags further heightens the visibility and impact of the critique that Americans specifically (but many majority cultures in general) deemphasize these horrific historical events and whitewash them in curricula and popular culture alike.

Another example of critical making is the digital—physical integration project by Salter and Sullivan (2018), also explained on the HASTAC website ("Examples of Critical Making," 2019). This project melds digital elements, like QR codes and websites, into tactile hand-sewn quilts. The digital-facing (and functional) QR code embedded within the cloth of the quilt makes an interesting mash up of languages. Quilts have been used to convey information for centuries (Witzling, 2009). They have been used to disrupt the status quo by marking the Underground Railroad (Tobin et al., 2000) and to support other acts of protest (Ball, 2002; Williams, 1994). Combining this language from the tradition of quilting with the digital language of the QR code, the coding language of the QR code reading app and website along with the narrative presented on the website causes the audience to reflect on what language is and how it can be used.

Many examples of critical making project combine art and weather maps to highlight the impacts of climate change. Described on the Berman Museum website (*Mapping Climate Change*, 2021) are two examples: *The Knitting Map* by Jools Gilson and Richard Povall, which displays "visual manifestations of urban activity and weather" and was knitted by hand by over 2,500 volunteers; and *The Tempestry Project* by Justin Connelly, Marissa Connelly, and Emily McNeil displaying temperature blankets where each row displays the temperature for that day using one of 32 colors. *The Tempestry Project* later expanded to include an audio *Tempestry* where temperature data is communicated using musical tones. These works bring another perspective to the raw numbers of global temperatures and help those not versed in climate science to understand on a different level the massive changes that are taking place on our planet.

Though these examples were all created by academics with expertise in a variety of fields, the act of critical making can be a valuable learning experience. Critical making projects are typically interdisciplinary and are often collaborative as well. The critical making consortium (*Critical Making*, 2020) boasts a global network of over 100,000 people over 6,000 projects and shares resources for critical making projects, and there are a number of critical making communities across the globe, which, like the preceding maker movement, are open for anyone to join and collaborate on projects. Numerous open-source tools, resources, and ideas for critical making projects are available on the web, making them accessible and adaptable for teachers and classrooms.

Both authors have assigned critical making projects to undergraduate and graduate students. One undergraduate course, for example, created "clickbait" Twitter bots that produced procedurally generated tweets to advertise fictional products. These bots commented on the rhetoric of typical Internet clickbait, the act of advertising on social media, and ultimately the capitalist society where this clickbait culture exists. Another author took the concept of critical making into the graduate classroom, rethinking the form for fully online delivery: critical making is traditionally taught, if such a thing can be said, through hands-on laboratory work bringing the material digital and digital material into creative combinations. Reimagining the pedagogy of such making for the pandemic (and, perhaps, beyond) requires a removal of the shared "hands" from the platform. But in this letting go there is possibility: a shift toward emphasizing resilience rather than expertise opens space for dabbling and failure. A graduate course built through this lens was a place for weekly experimentation—cultivating a beginner's mind approach to both making and learning.

Another author taught a research-intensive undergraduate course where students learn different tools for digital humanities using a critical making lens. Students engage in analysis of example critical making works, explore different research perspectives that are exemplified in those works, then learn the logistics of the digital tool before producing their own critical making prototype. The final project in this course is a group assignment where students work together to conduct a literature review and create a robust, meaningful project that articulates a clear argument about an event or a behavior that the group members have selected and researched. Groups then present their projects as digital posters or demonstrations at the university's Student Scholar Symposium.

As Matt Ratto (2011) explains, in critical making, "the final prototypes are not intended to be displayed and to speak for themselves. Instead, they are considered a means to an end, and achieve value though the act of shared construction, joint conversation, and reflection" (Ratto, 2011, p. 253). This emphasis on the process translates well to the classroom, where the learning process—not a final product of correctly bubbled-in answer sheets of standardized assessments—takes center stage. In the critical making classroom, learners conduct traditional research by reading published literature and exploring critical making scholarship, but they also apply that background literature to an event or a behavior they find compelling—contemporary or historical. They can then craft a response to what they see in the events using any creative platform that they wish. The critical making emphasis on process over product emphasizes learning.

The expectation of an end product that is functional (or even partly or potentially functional) and not polished in the sort of "final draft" that is typically expected of even project-based learning assignments helps set students expectations and promotes exploration. When the goal is a proof of concept rather than a refined, display-worthy artifact, it permits more room for learners to play with the concepts and take bigger risks without the fear of failing to create something that they feel is presentable. These projects are also well-suited for groupwork. Collaboration and communication skills are vital for any career, and these skills can be practiced and improved through group projects like critical making.

Likewise, each of these projects includes different disciplinary knowledge and methods. The interdisciplinary nature of critical making helps students to see the ways they can combine different perspectives from different disciplines to develop a more complete understanding of the world. By broadening the definition of knowledge for our students, we can help to validate their strengths while also increasing their curiosity as well as their understanding of a variety of other subjects. Allowing learners to play, explore, and experiment with new concepts and perspectives will produce more thoughtful, inquisitive, informed citizens.

Playing school

The examples for playful learning environments described in this chapter emphasize learner-centered, project, and inquiry-based pedagogy. They require the educator to act not as the all-knowing expert but as a guide in a flexible, shifting learning environment. We recognize that this shift in self-identity of the teacher may be new and even unsettling for some, but we recommend it nonetheless. Putting the student in the position of autonomy and responsibility for their learning path is ideal for learning *and* for learning playfully. Anecdotally, we have also found that this shift in pedagogy lightens the burden for the teacher. While we of course retain responsibility for selecting key topics and activities for our students, we see our roles as learning guides rather than assignment dictators, allowing us to share in the curiosity and joy of our students. Without needing to micromanage every second of student learning time (both in the classroom and beyond, through homework assignments), we can foster our students' growth by encouraging exploration. We can cheer them on when they discover something or ask a new question and redirect them when they feel lost or discouraged, refocusing the classroom on students rather than teachers or tests.

Ultimately, the models of the alternate reality game and Netprov discussed at the beginning of the chapter provide a model for how such a classroom can work: they invite the students to reshape the narrative, and to collaborate in defining the rules and outcomes of their learning experience. Conversations around the pandemic frequently center challenges in terms of care, but the realities of practicing care can put the bulk of the burden on educators to predict and adapt the classroom to the needs of their students. The collaborative classroom provides more space for students to self-advocate, and play a role in shaping their own engagement.

Here, play offers one answer to the provocation Jesse Stommel offers educators to resist the rubricification and instrumentalization of the classroom:

> But we need to find more ways to involve students in the design of their own learning, scaffolding *with* students and not *for* them. We can invite them to design rubrics and leave blank spaces on the schedule, syllabus, and lesson plan for them to fill. In class, students should have the opportunity to do metacognitive work—to reflect on and write "process letters" about their learning and to evaluate their own progress. Teachers can design learning spaces together with students, engaging them as coauthors of the policies set forth in syllabi.
>
> (Stommel, 2020)

Along these lines, as we slowly return to our pre-pandemic routines, carrying the collective trauma of this lengthy pandemic, looking to the future with actual or cynical optimism, we would all benefit from more play and flexibility into our courses. Many of us feel as though we have lost much time in the shadow of fear and uncertainty. Rather than doubling down on the same rigid instruction that we have failed to disrupt despite so many advances in knowledge, technology, and the understanding of how people learn, let us harness play to counteract the fear and flexibility to show that not all uncertainty is bad. The chaos and uncertainty that we have all weathered has left us grasping for the familiar teaching activities and patterns that felt reliable. We know, however, that the more student-centered methods that permit learners more autonomy and responsibility are more effective than the multiple-choice, lecture-based traditional teaching structures,—and the reality of a hybrid future is ill-served by a return to gamification focused more on competition than compassion.

Playful pedagogy emphasizes the growth mindset—a recent buzzword in education meant to guide students to think of their intelligence as not a rigid entity that is threatened by failure but as a flexible skillset that can be strengthened through practice that includes failure (Dweck, 2006).

Playing, tinkering, and experimenting are firmly grounded in learning and growing. Formal education has worked too long and too effectively to separate "schooling" from these elements, and instructional design is too often its own set of boxes and limitations – as Jesse Stommel and Martha Burtis note in their essential discussion of the changes needed post-pandemic, "The neater and tidier the instructional design solution, the more likely it seems to be broadly adopted by an institution ... and even when these models are thoroughly debunked, they continue to retain traction" (Stommel & Burtis, 2021).

Play belongs in the classroom now more than ever. Playful pedagogy is empathetic pedagogy. The deemphasis of failure and setting the expectation for productive mistakes encourages learners to try on different perspectives, to experiment, and to explore. It allows students room to be curious and to take chances. The act of creating gives students an outlet for their emotions while also providing a motivating environment for learning. Having students create games and critical making works that they then share with each other and those outside of the classroom provides them with an authentic audience, fostering higher quality work and sustained motivation. We can't make the games that will solve our collective challenges, but we can involve our students in the problem of design (and the imagining of solutions).

References

Austen-Smith, C. (2020, November 18). ECHO game brings students together—And keeps them safe. *UChicago News*. https://news.uchicago.edu/story/echo-game-brings-students-together-and-keeps-them-safe.

Ball, H. (2002). Subversive materials: Quilts as social text. *Alberta Journal of Educational Research*, *48*(3), Article 3. https://doi.org/10.11575/ajer.v48i3.54937.

Barr, M., & Copeland-Stewart, A. (2022). Playing video games during the COVID-19 pandemic and effects on players' well-being. *Games and Culture*, *17*(1), 122–139. https://doi.org/10.1177/15554120211017036.

Bereiter, C., & Scardamalia, M. (1998). Beyond Bloom's taxonomy: Rethinking knowledge for the knowledge age. In A. Hargreaves, A. Lieberman, M. Fullan & D. Hopkins (Eds.), *International handbook of educational change: Part one* (pp. 675–692). Springer Netherlands. https://doi.org/10.1007/978-94-011-4944-0_33.

Berens, K. I. (2015). Live/archive: *Occupy MLA*. *Hyperrhiz: New Media Cultures*, *11*(11). https://doi.org/10.20415/hyp/011.e03.

Bhattacharya, A., Windleharth, T. W., Lee, C., Paramasivam, A., Kientz, J. A., Yip, J. C., & Lee, J. H. (2021). The pandemic as a catalyst for reimagining the foundations of location-based games. *Proceedings of the ACM on Human-Computer Interaction*, *5*(CHI PLAY), 280:1-280:25. https://doi.org/10.1145/3474707.

Burr, L. (2015). Bicycles, bonfires and an airport apocalypse: The poetics and ethics of Netprov. *Hyperrhiz: New Media Cultures*, *11*(11). https://doi.org/10.20415/hyp/011.e01.

Chen, J. C., & Brown, K. L. (2012). The effects of authentic audience on English as a second language (ESL) writers: A task-based, computer-mediated approach. *Computer Assisted Language Learning*, *25*(5), 435–454. https://doi.org/10.1080/09588221.2011.606224.

Critical Making. (2020). *Critical Making*. https://criticalmaking.eu/.

Danielson, C. (2007). *Enhancing professional practice: A framework for teaching*. ASCD.

Dimock, W. C. (2021). Gaming the pandemic. *PMLA*, *136*(2), 163–170. https://doi.org/10.1632/S0030812921000110.

Dodge, B. (1995). WebQuests: A technique for Internet-based learning. *Distance Educator*, *1*(2), 10–13.

Dweck, C. S. (2006). *Mindset: The new psychology of success*. Random House.

Elgin, C. Z. (2014). Fiction as thought experiment. *Perspectives on Science*, *22*(2), 221–241. https://doi.org/10.1162/POSC_a_00128.

Empower through Play. (2021). Itch.Io. https://ucfgrl.itch.io/empower-through-play.

Examples of Critical Making. (2019). *Critical maker.space: HASTAC 2019 Workshop Session: Critical Maker Faire*. https://criticalmaker.space/2019/03/08/examples/.

Ford, M. (2016). *Writing interactive fiction with Twine*. Que.

Gendler, T. S. (1998). Galileo and the indispensability of scientific thought experiment. *The British Journal for the Philosophy of Science*, *49*(3), 397–424. https://doi.org/10.1093/bjps/49.3.397

Gunel, M., Hand, B., & McDermott, M. A. (2009). Writing for different audiences: Effects on high-school students' conceptual understanding of biology. *Learning and Instruction*, *19*(4), 354–367. https://doi.org/10.1016/j.learninstruc.2008.07.001.

Hjorth, L., Richardson, I., Davies, H., & Balmford, W. (2020). Playing during COVID-19. In L. Hjorth, I. Richardson, H. Davies & W. Balmford (Eds.), *Exploring Minecraft: Ethnographies of play and creativity* (pp. 167–182). Springer International Publishing. https://doi.org/10.1007/978-3-030-59908-9_8.

Home—Twine Cookbook. (2021, April). https://twinery.org/cookbook/

Huizinga, J. (1955). *Homo ludens: A study of the play-element in culture.* Beacon Press.

Jaber, L. Z., & Hammer, D. (2016). Learning to feel like a scientist. *Science Education, 100*(2), 189–220. https://doi.org/10.1002/sce.21202.

Jagoda, P. (2020). *Experimental games: Critique, play, and design in the age of gamification.* University of Chicago Press.

Jagoda, P., Gilliam, M., McDonald, P., & Russell, C. (2015). Worlding through play: Alternate reality games, large-scale learning, and "the source." *American Journal of Play, 8*(1), 74–100.

Johnson, E. K. (2021). ELLE-ments of learning: A framework for analyzing multimodal technical communication strategies in an educational VR game. In *2021 7th International Conference of the Immersive Learning Research Network (ILRN)*, 1–4. https://doi.org/10.23919/iLRN52045.2021.9459357.

Johnson, E. K., Giroux, A. L., Merritt, D., Vitanova, G., & Sousa, S. (2020). Assessing the impact of game modalities in second language acquisition: ELLE the EndLess LEarner. *Journal of Universal Computer Science, 26*(8), 880–903.

Johnson, E. K., & Sullivan, A. (2018). BeadED adventures: Using tangible game artifacts to assist STEM learning. *Proceedings of the Meaningful Play, 2018*, 87–93. https://doi.org/10.1184/R1/9995969.

Kolb, A. Y. (2005). The Kolb learning style inventory-version 3.1 2005 technical specifications. Boston, MA: Hay Resource Direct, *200*(72), 166–171.

Le Doux, A. (2021, September 6). *Bitsy game maker.* Itch.Io. https://ledoux.itch.io/bitsy.

Mapping climate change. (2021, November 11). Berman Museum. https://www.ursinus.edu/live/profiles/4975-mapping-climate-change/_ingredients/templates/berman-2018/exhibition.

Marino, M. C., & Wittig, R. (2015). Netprov: Elements of an emerging form. In *Electronic literature communities* (pp. 169–214). West Virginia University Press. http://www.scopus.com/inward/record.url?scp=85038564952&partnerID=8YFLogxK.

Marino, M. C., & Wittig, R. (2020). Fantasy spoils: After the quest, a netprov. In *Electronic Literature Organization Conference, 2020.* https://stars.library.ucf.edu/elo2020/live/events/10.

Mcallister, J. W. (2012). Thought experiment and the exercise of imagination in science. In M. Frappier, L. Meynell & J. R. Brown (Eds.), *Thought experiments in science, philosophy, and the arts* (pp. 25–43). Routledge.

McDaniel, C. (n.d.). *Every three minutes (@Every3Minutes).* Twitter. Retrieved December 15, 2021, from https://twitter.com/Every3Minutes.

McTighe, J., & Wiggins, G. (2013). *Essential questions: Opening doors to student understanding.* ASCD.

Paul, R., & Elder, L. (2019). *How to read a paragraph: The art of close reading.* Rowman & Littlefield.

Pineda, Y., Johnson, E. K., Giroux, A. L., & Gordon, F. (2020, July). VR middle passage experience. In *Electronic Literature Organization Conference*, Orlando, FL. https://projects.cah.ucf.edu/mediaartsexhibits/uncontinuity/Pineda/pineda.html.

Prince, M. (2004). Does active learning work? A review of the research. *Journal of Engineering Education, 93*(3), 223–231. https://doi.org/10.1002/j.2168-9830.2004.tb00809.x.

Ratto, M. (2011). Critical making: Conceptual and material studies in technology and social life. *The Information Society*, *27*(4), 252–260. https://doi.org/10.1080/01972243.2011.583819.

Rettberg, S. (2014). Collaborative narrative. In M.-L. Ryan, L. Emerson & B. J. Robertson (Eds.), *The Johns Hopkins guide to digital media* (pp. 78–79). JHU Press.

Salter, A., & Moulthrop, S. (2021). *Twining*. Amherst College Press.

Seaman, M. (2011). Bloom's taxonomy: Its evolution, revision, and use in the field of education. *Curriculum and Teaching Dialogue*, *13*(1/2), 29–131A.

Stommel, J. (2020, March 20). *The human work of higher education pedagogy*. Hybrid Pedagogy. https://hybridpedagogy.org/the-human-work-of-higher-education-pedagogy/

Stommel, J., & Burtis, M. (2021, April 27). *Counter-friction to stop the machine: The endgame for instructional design*. Hybrid Pedagogy. https://hybridpedagogy.org/the-endgame-for-instructional-design/.

Sullivan, A., & Johnson, E. K. (2019). BeadED adventures: Crafting STEM learning. In *Proceedings of the Thirteenth International Conference on Tangible, Embedded, and Embodied Interaction*, 351–358. https://doi.org/10.1145/3294109.3300997.

Tobin, J. L., Tobin, J., & Dobard, R. G. (2000). *Hidden in plain view: The secret story of quilts and the underground railroad*. Anchor Books.

Twine. (2022, January 1). Twinery.Org. https://twinery.org/.

Whitehead, A. (2020). *A little turtle has just hatched on a beach in Texas*. Itch.Io. https://aprilswhitehead.itch.io/a-little-turtle-.

Williams, M. R. (1994). A reconceptualization of protest rhetoric: Women's quilts as rhetorical forms. *Women's Studies in Communication*, *17*(2), 20–44. https://doi.org/10.1080/07491409.1994.11089781.

Wittig, R., & Marino, M. C. (2017). Occupy the emotional stock exchange, resisting the quantifying of affection in social media. *Humanities*, *6*(2), 33. https://doi.org/10.3390/h6020033.

Witzling, M. (2009). Quilt language: Towards a poetics of quilting. *Women's History Review*, *18*(4), 619–637. https://doi.org/10.1080/09612020903138351.

Conclusion
The fatigue is real

"It Comes in Waves"

As we were closing the final drafting of this project, a team of game designers led by Mia Consalvo released their own powerful response to the pandemic entitled *It Comes in Waves* (Consalvo et al., 2022). The game (shown in Figure C.1) is built in Twine, one of the engines for collaborative making we discussed in Chapter 5, and invites players to experience an "essential worker" moving between a long-term care institution and a retirement home. In a reflection on the game design process, Mia Consalvo noted that it became in part a documentation of the experience, but one tied strongly to class and precarity:

> The goal has changed a little over time. When we started the game we were closer to the start of the pandemic ourselves and now we can look back at that time with some perspective. The pandemic has a history now - remember when we didn't wear masks, or debated wearing masks etc, and PPE was scarce. So in a way the game has been about documenting that shift in the pandemic. However, I still want people to take away the sense of precarity that is tied to being an essential worker. I want the player to think about what it might be like to have to go in to work even if you don't want to, even if you don't feel safe, because you need to earn a living.
>
> (DeJong, 2021b)

The repetition and fatigue of both emotional labor and physical precautions come through strongly when playing *It Comes in Waves*: even the mechanics of handwashing are made longer, requiring multiple clicks to progress through each iteration. The continual challenges of economic precarity, from limited funds for food to threats from the landlord, continually loom over the player. The game follows in the footsteps of personal responses made by other designers: from the 280 works submitted to the "Quarantine Jam" (Lebanese Game Developers, 2020) to the 50 games of the "Jamming the Curve" LabX jam (Martens, 2020) and beyond, the playable history of pandemic experiences will be an important part of this moment's cultural history. Some of these works—like *It Comes in Waves* and *Cat Colony Crisis* (Boyko et al., 2021), the winning game from the LabX jam

128 Conclusion

Figure C.1 A masked encounter in *It Comes in Waves*.

in which players try to contain a cat flu outbreak—are intentionally educational, while others are personal, impressionistic, and expressive.

Since we began writing this work, the world has continued to take one step forward and two steps back in the battle against COVID-19. Vaccines have been distributed worldwide, though not equitably. Variants have risen, booster vaccines are also being distributed inequitably, and many mask and social distancing precautions have been prematurely abandoned. Despite the widespread availability of vaccines in the United States, transmission rates and vaccine hesitancy remain dominant. Countries desperate to provide vaccines for their citizens struggle to obtain enough and lack infrastructure to expediently administer them. Globally, we seem to have lost the fight against the spread of the virus, as well as the fight against the spread of misinformation: a real-life game of *Pandemic* that is spiraling. It is difficult to end on an optimistic note, but to echo the thoughts of *It Comes in Waves* narrative team member Lyne Dwyer: "We don't want people to come away from this game feeling worse" (DeJong, 2021a).

The false dichotomy of economy versus public health has enabled those who wish to disregard science and common sense to put their own convenience and comfort ahead of the actual lives of others. We draw inspiration from the incredible perseverance of healthcare workers and others on the frontlines who, in the face of all of this politicization, show up to work each day and save lives. We admire the valiant educators of all levels working to make their classrooms welcoming and inclusive for each of their students, even throughout these most difficult of times.

As we complete our writing, the immense, ever-changing yet constant challenges of this long, terrifying, global pandemic has taken a toll not only through the millions of people it has killed, but also on the collective optimism of those who have survived. We see this in the "great resignation" of late 2021, a year and a half into the pandemic, and the "great faculty disengagement," that followed in early 2022, with many university faculty rethinking their levels of emotional investment in their jobs (McClure & Fryar, 2022). This shift in perspective is an act of self-preservation, especially understandable given how many faculty saw their universities unwilling or unable to provide basic protections for faculty, staff, and students against COVID-19. In the United States especially, even basic protective measures like requiring masks (or later, vaccinees) or permitting university courses to remain virtual became political battlegrounds, where university pandemic policies were dictated by the whim of the political party of their state's governor. It is understandably difficult for faculty to give an institution 110% when they feel as though that institution does not value their work, their health, or even their lives.

Meanwhile, reports on the global disruption to education are mounting: the World Bank's report on the crisis released in December 2021 notes that learning losses were particularly high where inequities were already greatest, with little support to offer: "39 percent of low-income countries reported they had not introduced any measures to support parents and caregivers with the home learning environment," exacerbating existing lack of resources and access (Azevedo et al., 2021, p. 24). These reports frequently focus on the consequences of the pivot to retention of existing knowledge, while acknowledging that in spite of our emphasis on technological solutions, "at least 463 million children could not be reached by digital and broadcast remote learning programs during school closures ... with 3 out of 4 unreached students coming from rural areas and/or poor households" (Ali, 2022). The framing of learning loss is itself notably reliant upon a focus on standardized testing and milestones, which we held up to critique previously (Mintz, 2022). However, the lasting challenges are not going to end: even if classrooms do return to "normal," whatever that means at this stage, the learners and educators who return will be in a very different state than they were in 2019.

Even as we strive to infuse a feeling of hope throughout this writing, we struggle. We feel solidarity for our disengaged colleagues because we share these feelings. But the world does need more play. We find reprieve and hope in play and games. Games help us value the well-being of others. Perhaps more play can help us learn to share in the joy of others who are gaining opportunities through (slowly) increasingly inclusive policies rather than insisting that if others get ahead in any way, we must therefore be somehow falling behind. The humanistic lessons we learn from competitive, cooperative, and collaborative play are vital life lessons. We can weather this global storm together, and a recalibration of our priorities and efforts is long overdue anyway.

Life is not a competition; life is a collaborative challenge—one that perhaps more resembles *Among Us* than *Animal Crossing* in the current moment thanks to widespread distrust and highly visible and effective extremist movements. Working together is more productive than working against one another—even in competitive situations, those who cooperate usually fare better than those who focus on undermining others. Games have taught us this, not "serious" lectures, not dry textbooks, and not repetitive worksheets. Games have given us opportunities to experience failure and success. Games simulate life and allow for low-stakes experimentation of nearly all aspects of life, including death. Perhaps schools should focus more on these traits of empathy and cooperation. The world does not need good multiple-choice test takers; the world needs more caring, compassionate citizens: though these statements may seem all-too-obvious, they are worth reclaiming at a moment when fears of "learning loss" might bring about just the opposite emphasis in our educational path forward.

Moving forward within or beyond the current pandemic conditions, we need to rethink our approach to education and focus on a pedagogy of care through learner-centered engagement. We can and should turn to the essential foundations of Black feminist pedagogy, and keep in mind Barbara Omolade's still timely call "for instructors to struggle with their students for a better university" (Omolade, 1987, p. 32). Tressie McMillan Cottom offered an important warning during a roundtable on pandemic impact on American higher education of how many of us have failed that call: we need a tenured faculty that serves as a true "check on administrative power," and advocates for "establishing a sustainable class of workers here at this university who will be advocating for students" (Doherty et al., 2021). To justify the very existence of tenure requires this activist lens, and to mobilize and support our students requires a pedagogy of care. Teaching through compassion sees the student as a partner in education and uses a more wholistic approach to learning. We can achieve this pedagogy of care and play by collaborating with students to reimagine education outside of prescriptive educational technology and the rigid grammar of traditional schooling.

A look inward

We don't need to reinvent immersive game design techniques—they exist and can help us shape the future. Certainly, games designed for entertainment by for-profit companies have been built with an emphasis on the ability to teach players a myriad of skills (Gee, 2004, 2008)—but it is precisely that model of game-based learning that we can and must reimagine. However, the realities of demands to innovate through play frequently come alongside a wall of contradictions, many of which have driven learning toward models of assessment and surveillance. Why are we stuck in cycles of educational technology that promise disruption, but deliver monotony? How have educators seeking more opportunities for play become complicit in educational technology that saps agency, rather than creating space for co-design?

We have learned, and been reminded again and again, that technology will not save us all on its own, and utopian visions of technology must continually be challenged; technology must be harnessed and designed intentionally, inclusively, and intelligently. And yet the realities of the technologies at scale we are offered as visions of the future are more often chilling—the metaverse of Mark Zuckerberg's imagination offers perhaps the most willful recreation of the dystopian to be offered toward educational means yet. Yes, we can use technology to augment our teaching and learning experiences, but not off the server racks of companies with willfully permissive policies in the face of abuse and misinformation. Chapter 2 assessed the promises of technology and gamification to find that without meaningful design, any integration of technology or gamification (or both) in education is futile—and at worst, can put people off both games and learning. Hollow uses of these entities result in shallow, surface teaching: the instructor equivalent of the surface learning we strive to push our students beyond.

Further, we know that the traditional lecture-and-testing teaching pattern is familiar and difficult to relinquish even in the rosiest of contexts. We know educators were already heavily overburdened and undersupported prior to the pandemic, and that this problem was already far more urgent for contingent faculty—and going unaddressed by institutions around the world. The pandemic conditions and stresses pushed teachers beyond their breaking points and then kept pushing. Pandemic pedagogy relied on the familiar as a necessity to ease the teacher's cognitive load as much as possible within the context of COVID-19, but it also demonstrated the importance of community support, with groups on social media like "Pandemic Pedagogy" bringing about 32,000 members together to "seek out pedagogical advice" and vent, frequently with memes (Dam, 2021). The conditions that made innovation and connection difficult also brought out the power of educators to form community—which perhaps offers hope for solidarity in the future, particularly as new inequities continue to fall on contingent faculty.

The educational technology industry capitalized on the opportunity to sell us quick fixes to pandemic teaching, and these stopgaps fit well with pandemic pedagogy: they made surface teaching manageable, while students completed superficial engagement exercises and surface learning activities. Even those of us whose research predisposes us to reject platforms with questionable ethics and surveillance methods shifted to Zoom: as Justin Grandinetti reflects, we could not employ that lens under these circumstances:

> When it comes to Zoom or other platforms, our "decision" to use or not is often not entirely our own. The pandemic didn't "cause" issues like the platformization of the university and its reliance on big tech, but crisis presents opportunity that powerful corporations gladly take advantage of. If we as members of higher education institutions—faculty, staff, and administration—care about the issues of platforms, it takes more than just individual opt-out. What platforms we want to integrate into university life, how we can hold big tech accountable, and how we can protect ourselves and our students is an effort that takes our collective care and attention.
>
> (Grandinetti, 2021)

Grandinetti offers us a reminder for the future: platforms of convenience risk becoming permanent fixtures. Much of these engagement-as-commodity packages were the best possible solutions during the worst possible times. Our worry now, however, is that pandemic pedagogy will bleed into our return to so-called normal teaching structure, or worse, "normal" with a greater dependence on expensive educational technology solutions of the metaverse and its ilk. This book is our call to avoid that at all costs. As we reassess and rearrange our lives and teaching strategies once again post-pandemic or in what may end up being a series of continued mini crises and waves of variants, we must contemplate the purpose of our courses in addition to their delivery.

Is there space for meaningful play in the neoliberal university, and might the pandemic inspire the reinvention we desperately need? There is space for meaningful play in the university—at the very least, we can create this space in our courses. We remain skeptical of designating any catalyst of educational change after so many simulacra (radio, television, computers, the Internet, and so on), but we are optimistic that dedicated educators can form a critical mass of pedagogical change—and that the low-tech solutions we build in collaboration with students are our best hope.

Commodification of education

Commodified student engagement and gamification practices are symptoms of the larger issues with the structure of the educational systems themselves, in the United States as well as in many countries around the world. The teacher accountability measures necessitate a top-down organization where administrators roll out mandate after mandate to increase accountability and ensure instructional "quality" while remaining distinctly detached from the students in the classroom themselves. With out-of-touch administrators frequently making the purchasing decisions around educational technology, it is not surprising that these are the kinds of tools most readily available to teachers. And indeed, we've quantified and embedded a reliance on codified "quality" into our systems. As Martha Burtis and Jesse Stommel write in their timely indictment of the "Quality Matters" online teaching rubric:

> Instead of prescriptive checklists, we need to build our capacity with new modalities, be always open to learning from and with our colleagues and students, and listen to and trust our own pedagogical instincts, no matter where (or with what tech) we teach.
> (Burtis & Stommel, 2021)

Such systems are designed to dehumanize the work of teaching.

Many educational technology companies advertise instructional solutions, touting quantitative improvements in learner engagement, and everyone is eager for student higher participation rates. However, the actual assignments and exercises that students are assigned in order to obtain these participation rates are often educationally shallow: surface teaching that results in surface learning. Student responses to a poll in a Zoom lecture or an embedded multiple-choice question in a video do not necessarily ensure that they are mentally engaged, only that they are paying enough attention to click something when told—a skill that the current high-stakes testing generation has certainly mastered.

The problems with gamification are analyzed in detail in Chapter 1, where we point out the similarities between the behaviorist rewards and punishments of traditional schooling and those of superficial gamification. Where traditional school uses grades, honor roll, detention, and grade retention to reward and punish student behaviors, superficial gamification in schools use meaningless points and badges, leaderboards, and emphasize failure—turning common game mechanics into weapons that can harm motivation and cause students unnecessary anxiety. The pandemic exacerbated existing inequities across the globe, and an emphasis on mechanics-driven gamification elements like these only increase the damage. Such systems embrace the least interesting aspects of gaming: competition, quantification, and achievement.

Another boost to the bottom lines of educational technology companies during the pandemic was seen in surveillance software. Concerned that students taking assessments at home would attempt to cheat, instructors and schools everywhere turned to surveillance software to monitor students during exams. This immediate emphasis on cheating was founded on a premise of distrust, and one undergraduate responding to the pandemic questioned the lack of trust:

> I can't help but wonder in response, "Why have institutions assumed the worst of their students? Why do they assume the group of young adults *they selected by hand* would value their education so little that they would exploit the online environment to cheat? Why aren't these institutions asking how they can best support their students through a time of global uncertainty?" And moreover, "Why have institutions decided to turn to *software companies* to address this *pedagogical problem*?"
> (Doyle, 2021, emphases original)

Many of these programs require students to have their own webcams and well-lit areas for taking exams, relying on facial recognition software to verify that the enrolled student is the one who is taking the exam. Some even capitalize on the webcam and require students to allow the software to record their every move throughout the exam period. While ostensibly an agnostic attempt to replicate the securely proctored classroom setting, requiring students to be recorded in their own home raises a number of concerns over privacy and inequity. Not all students can afford devices with webcams, and facial recognition software is notoriously biased against faces that are not white. As Charles Logan writes in his condemnation of the practice, "the fight against online proctoring takes on greater urgency when we understand online proctoring as the latest example of white supremacist surveillance technologies designed and deployed to police and punish" (Logan, 2021). This urgency was strikingly visible in the United States as Black Lives Matter protests against police brutality and murder unfolded alongside a turn toward highly discriminatory platforms of educational technology.

Newly pivoted courses in their pandemic pedagogy again exacerbated existing divides and inequities. At the beginning of the January 2020 semester, students had enrolled in face-to-face courses without any expectation of needing this type of technology or any private, quiet space in their homes. By March 2020 or earlier across the globe, even library study rooms on campuses were widely shut down, and campus housing was widely evacuated for fear of contributing to viral spread. Even as things stabilized amid the pandemic's multi-year shadow, teleconferencing equipment was so sought after globally that it became harder and more expensive and difficult to obtain, with many students who may have been able to handle the costs pre-pandemic unable to do so. In the United States, broadband Internet access is often assumed for those participating in online education, but the reality is that even in February 2021 (after a year of closures), broadband was only available to 77% of adults in the United States (Pew Internet Research, 2021) and that Black and Latinx adults are less likely to have access to broadband Internet than white adults (Marshall & Ruane, 2021). A report on global broadband access conducted prior to the pandemic captured even greater inequity: based on 2018 census data, it estimated that 15% of Americans do not have any Internet access at home, and that the barriers to Internet access include lack of infrastructure in rural areas as well as lack of access to Internet-capable devices even in urban areas, and the monthly expense of Internet subscriptions, with lower-income adults accessing the Internet only at work, school, or public libraries (Duffy & Tappe, 2020). The pandemic has repeatedly closed these locations, increasing the barriers to education.

Well-meaning educators who were doing their best to replicate a sense of classroom community required students to attend class with webcams on, again invading privacy, and ostracizing students who lacked the money for webcam-enabled devices, high-speed Internet connections, and quiet, private locations in their homes, with many embarrassed that they had to allow teachers and classmates into their homes and attend class sitting on the floor of closets or on top of their beds—far from ideal learning environments.

Another issue with this type of software is the way it uses hollow gamification elements. Engagement packages promise to increase student attention and interaction within the virtual classroom by forcing students to perform engagement practices like busywork on purchased templates, or multiple-choice questions that interrupt Zoom presentations or pre-recorded lecture videos. Worse, many gamification packages simply give mundane course elements game-sounding names, like "experience points" for course points and "badges" as virtual gold stars. Students see through these and leave the course wary of future instructors' attempts to incorporate gameful approaches.

The corporatization of education is another pattern that the pandemic foregrounded. Having very few or zero total so-called "quiet days" in the Microsoft month in review report could be considered a point of pride, reversing the purported intent of these reports. Displaying metrics like this reminds the employee that someone is always watching, and even if it is only Microsoft's AI, there is no guarantee that the employer is not also privy to this information. This can act to undermine trust in leadership and make employees feel uneasy. For now, Microsoft provides messaging in their reports that they are "for the recipient's eyes only," but they are easily forwarded, and any given employer could demand that they be shared.

More overt surveillance is already occurring in learning management systems, which proudly report these types of metrics to students and instructors alike. Student time spent logged into the course is interpreted by the software itself as simply low, moderate, or high and displayed in this simplistic way only—in Canvas, with one to three stars beside a student's name—in the instructor view. The actual numbers of logins and time spent with the course page open are not available for the instructors to interpret for themselves without enabling "Advanced Analytics" in the software and wading through data visualizations of student grades and online activity or downloading a CSV file (*New Analytics Overview (Instructor)*, 2019), although at the time of writing this feature was not functioning for the authors.

Many of these commercial educational solutions and pandemic pedagogy quick fixes turn students into commodities. Their privacy is not protected, their data is mined, and it acts to undermine trust in the institution specifically and in systems of education generally. As we ease back into pedagogy that is less reactive to pandemic constraints and more proactive in centering student needs and learning, we must reconsider our use of these commercial platforms.

Grind and punishment

The dearth of "disruption" by technology and games in education is partially due to the familiarity of the traditional routines discussed above, but also to blame are the ineffective ways games and game elements have been incorporated into most classrooms thus far. The trend of gamification that we have seen has been a superficial renaming of existing ineffective pedagogical elements, as though changing the name of "honor roll" to "leaderboard" would magically increase student motivation to complete busywork.

Incorporating AAA games into classrooms requires enormous resources of time, to learn and correlate the game into the course lessons, as well as money to purchase expensive consoles (or gaming computers) and games. Moreover, the use of these games in an educational setting emphasizes the bias embedded in these games by their lack of diversity. In educational settings where main characters in literature "canons" are predominantly white, straight, male, and privileged, students are receiving the message that anyone who does not fit these descriptions is not of value in the classroom or society. The burgeoning video game market has plenty of room for games that show and value diverse characters, but these industries remain dominated by designers and developers who fit the canonical descriptions of old. When teachers bring these games into their classes without commenting on these issues, they are implicitly confirming them for their minoritized students.

Likewise, teacher-created games are also fraught with issues. It requires an enormous amount of time and effort to learn coding-heavy game development platforms that have a similar appearance to the AAA games that might come to mind when thinking about video games. It is unreasonable to expect all individual teachers—who are already experts in their subject areas—to master these complex game authoring platforms, and the fear of this steep learning curve alone is enough to prevent many educators from considering games for their classrooms. These platforms are notoriously difficult to learn and acts as a gatekeeper to prevent more diverse audiences from using them (e.g., Murray & Johnson, 2021).

Thus, the resulting games that educators often do end up designing or using in their classes are usually those that fit in the existing grammar of traditional schooling. These games rely on superficial gamification as poor attempts to increase student motivation. Common classroom games like *Jeopardy!* and other "skill and drill" types of games that focus on players' abilities to recall isolated and decontextualized facts do little to motivate disengaged students who have already internalized their inability to succeed in academia, likely discouraging and demotivating them further. These students already feel that they lack whatever abilities (or even personal merit!) are necessary to succeed in school, and games with the same structure as worksheets or tests—games with the sole goal of perfection imposed through the use of punitive punishments for mistakes—erode any joy or motivation from the activity.

Noble attempts include the less restrictive games like *Minecraft* and the *Portal* games, but the education versions of these games, *Minecraft Education* and the *Portal 2 Puzzle Creator*, still mimic the grammar of a school worksheet or heavily structured in-class activity, with clear goals and decontextualized content being learned. While the entertainment versions of these games encourage exploration and invite immersion, these key elements are almost explicitly removed from the education version to instead create insular exercises that fit within the timeframe of the 50-or-so-minute class periods common to secondary schools.

Playing to learn

Technology-free role-playing activities have been used for ages with much success, and although these activities still require more teacher time and resources than worksheet pages, they boost motivation, deeper learning, and long-term retention, all while engaging students in a playful learning environment. We discussed *Model UN* in Chapter 3 and the immersive, effective ways that this role-playing game harnesses role-playing to simulate real-world political collaboration between countries worldwide. The similar *Reacting to the Past* asks students to take on the perspective of historical figures and to envision and often reenact major events in history, imagining what may have happened if certain people made different choices.

Chapter 3 also looked at the games that were popular during the first two years of the pandemic to provide insight on their mass appeal and consider elements or designs that might be effectively adapted to game-based learning in the classroom. The interdisciplinary, player-centered models of a few games that were widely played during the pandemic—*Among Us*, *Dungeons & Dragons* (played remotely on platforms such as *Tabletop Simulator*), the suite of Jackbox games, and *Animal Crossing: New Horizons*—inspire us to design role-playing games in our courses that include narrative elements, opportunities for students to be creative and collaborative—within the same four walls or virtually.

By focusing on the learning experience wholistically and putting pedagogy first, rather than tacking on game mechanics to unengaging exercises, we can create effective, immersive, and enjoyable games for our courses. We can devise overarching narratives, interesting questions, challenges, and ill-defined problems that hold our students' attention throughout the lesson and allow them the opportunity to interact on a deeper level with the content matter. The best playful pedagogy is customized to the teacher's style and course content, organically enveloping students in curiosity and a purpose for learning and for completing classroom tasks.

Learning is messy

Throughout the pandemic, people across the planet turned to games to cope with the stressors of their unique situations, whether they were under lockdown or working in newly dangerous conditions. We sang sea shanties, shared dance moves, and attended virtual concerts and happy hours. We spread hope, solidarity, and compassion. Looking ahead to the future of education as the pandemic slowly wanes, we ask educators and policymakers to deeply reassess what we are doing in our classrooms, what we are assigning our students, why we are doing these things, and what our most important goals are. What is our essential purpose and how can we best realize that purpose, empathetically, equitably, and ethically? By collectively reflecting on and pushing for a clear purpose in education, we can redesign education in a playful way that better fits our modern era and true needs.

The draw to the traditional, structured, and orderly lecture teaching style remains strong—it is familiar and almost automated at this point. Teachers lecture, students listen and fill out their multiple-choice punch cards, and then they all return home, the factory work of school complete for the day. We advocate to push beyond this model by embracing the messy, co-created, personalized, playful approach to learning. Chapter 5 investigates a framework for meaningful play in education, pushing educators to go beyond ineffective gamification elements and create holistic, playful pedagogy that embraces more than isolated content lessons and examines the rich context of all academic subjects. In his closing words on the Netprov in his book introducing educators to the practice, Rob Wittig describes his optimistic vision for the future of the form:

> Netprov as literature-based "show" offers the possibility of cocreation of insightful, healing satire that is as deep as the novels of the past. Netprov as "game" offers the possibility of new, empathic, real-life relationships based on collaborative creativity and genuine understanding. I believe the *world* a netprov narrative can offer its participants is their own everyday world—transformed by laughter, insight, and empathy.
>
> (Wittig, 2021, p. 260)

Netprov is particularly powerful for proving that the barriers to that transformation need not be technological, and the best solutions are far from the most complex. Teachers can use free and increasingly accessible and user-friendly platforms to create games, or they can adapt existing programs like PowerPoint or Google Forms to create more gameful learning activities for students. The same platforms that power online education, from Blackboard and Canvas to Discord and Zoom, can be made new through play—and participants can co-create and challenge those platform's shift through that play.

The fundamental shift needed to move to playful pedagogy is not only the teacher as the facilitator (rather than the font of knowledge) and the release of control over some learning activities so that students may explore, but also one of context. The world is interdisciplinary, and our educational system needs to adapt to recognize this. We are no longer training workers for static careers in factories but for the fluid, multi-career information age. Educational institutions have been giving lip service to the 21st century and its needs since before the millennium: it is time to embrace the dynamic needs of our time.

Teachers are not content providers. Students are not receptacles for said content. Imagine how ridiculous it would be for gyms to advertise that they could increase their customers' health by just telling customers how to be healthy and how to perform exercises, without any expectation of their customers to actually change their eating habits or increase their physical activity. This is what schools have been doing for centuries: telling pupils about fractured pieces of the wide world around them behind closed doors and shuttered windows. Students need to be encouraged to learn by provoking their natural curiosity, providing resources for them to explore to increase the context of the topic being studied, and to be motivated to act like children. Children across the world learn by playing and exploring—by trying, failing, and trying again. When we punish failure, we teach students that exploring and playing and failing are unnecessary, trivial, and unacceptable.

The stakes of gameplay, and their room for failure, are particularly welcome at a time of decision-making fatigue and collective exhaustion. Additional health and extra lives are obtained to overcome avatar injuries and deaths. When players fail, they are given the chance to learn from their mistakes and try again. Failure is an expected part of the game. A game that is played without failure is barely even a game at all—leaving the player feeling unengaged and bored. Part of why we include games in our courses is to prevent our students from feeling bored—the gameful deemphasis of failure is exactly what we need to combat boredom and encourage true learning.

All of our classes should be designed in this way, so that many minor failures ultimately add up to student learning and success. Most traditional educational experiences do have a plethora of student feedback built in; the problem is that the feedback is overly punitive. Students seek shortcuts and go to great lengths to avoid failure over learning. We can promote this type of meaningful failure by making it an expected part of the process—by removing the penalties of missed points and low grades through ungrading or just though awarding participation grades for effort.

With this constant messaging that failure is something to be avoided, our fear of failure grows with our grade level, to the point that some adults take extreme measures to avoid even minor failures in their lives. The "great resignation" is evidence that we tend to stay in jobs where we are unhappy until something catastrophic or cataclysmic happens and forces us to assess our situations—one of the reasons for this is likely due to our fear of failing to obtain another job if we quit our current one. The pandemic exacerbated preexisting issues in education as well, and indeed is what prompted us to write this book examining educational games and play.

The idea of reconsidering grading is mentioned in Chapter 1, and while grading is done differently around the world, a majority of formal schooling revolves around passing or failing students. The necessity of evaluating the learner is often worthwhile and difficult to avoid; people need to know that graduates have mastered specific skills and understand various topics necessary to perform a given job. Students need informative feedback to grow and learn, but this feedback does not necessarily need to be tied to grades. Taking the potential penalties out of grading is not an easy task in this day and age, given how baked into the entire education system grades are—students, parents, and employers expect this easy metric for gauging the knowledge and skill of any given graduate, but the superficial nature of grades and grading really undermines their intent. Grades are predominantly isolated assessments of students' recall of decontextualized information (and in some instances, a reflection of little more than their physical presence in a lecture hall). They really have little meaning or merit beyond academia, which is why only a few entry-level job applications even ask for grade point averages.

Making to learn

The previous chapter encourages teachers to place learners in the role of the author or game designer in making educational games or critical making projects as another means of deeply engaging them with content in context. By authoring their own games about course topics, students can enjoy the motivations of autonomy, authentic audiences, and creative expression while they wrestle with the finer points of the subjects central to their games. Encouraging students to make games, even "bad" ones, follows the same student-centered pedagogy that asks them to compose persuasive arguments, fantastical narratives, and personal art works. Hands-on creation is an excellent way to encourage students to try, fail, and try again as they create prototypes of their games and go through the cycles of testing, iterating, and testing again.

Project-based and problem-based learning were trends in education not so long ago, and many educators have continued to include projects and ill-structured problems as central features of educational units or tasks. Game design as an assignment also invokes the best practices of problem- and project-based learning. Learners decide the purpose of their game, and then create a setting, narrative, characters, and interactive elements for their players. Each of these design decisions requires careful thought, as each element and mechanic will have direct implications on the final game. Students can include puzzles and other engaging challenges for their players to overcome, and the creation of these mental challenges is itself a meaningful learning exercise. The cherry on top is that the design process is usually engaging and fun for learners, while the end product of the game or prototype of a game is also intended to be enjoyable to play.

With game design, failure and iterative development are expected: all games go through a process of testing and modification, and this is anticipated. These early prototypes and testing cycles are, pedagogically, formative assessments, just like in-class activities or worksheets. But because this iterative cycle is normalized, the shortcomings of early game builds are not as emotionally catastrophic as losing points on a worksheet or giving the wrong answer when called on in class.

Notably, the word "play" has more than one meaning, and we invoke both in the title of this book. Play can mean diversion, exploration, fun, and games; but it also denotes the idea of wiggle room. We argue for more play in every sense of the word: education cannot be rigid and also be successful. Students and teachers need more "wiggle room:"—more space for exploration and experimentation where failure is expected and productive. This can be introduced into the existing, traditional grammar of formal schooling through critical making.

Critical making is another type of project-based learning, where the goal is to create prototypes, or proofs of concept: projects with less-polished final artifacts than the traditional end result of project-based learning. This goal of a prototype rather than a polished, final product removes some of the risk of failure for students: by eliminating the requirement of a polished, complete artifact, students will be more willing to take risks and truly experiment with their builds, which we assert will produce deeper learning and longer-term retention. This making doesn't need to be complicated to be compelling, as the discussion of sea shanties and play on TikTok reminds us. Such low-stakes creativity is the exact opposite of what our education system's rubrics frequently center.

Making a critique is an engaging learning activity that can invoke the multiple meanings of play. Students learn about a variety of contexts surrounding a given issue, investigating the issue and considering it from different perspectives, and then they create a prototype—digital or physical—that draws attention to one aspect of that issue. Allowing students to identify and detail specific problems that they see in the world is empowering—by encouraging students to voice their concerns and speak up about injustice, for example, they can feel less powerless against the society creating the injustice and more able to catalyze positive change in the world. Further, this encourages inclusion, diversity, and compassion.

The practice of critical making includes the actual building of a physical or digital prototype that foregrounds an issue in society or makes a statement about the way something is done. Although the practice of critical making is a newer field in the digital humanities, art has been used to critique society for centuries. Students can analyze art or other examples of critical making to determine what argument the artifact is making, and they can then create their own prototypes to assert their own perspectives. Critical making is a "mode of materially productive engagement that is intended to bridge the gap between creative physical and conceptual exploration" (Ratto, 2011, p. 252). This multimodal creative exploration encourages experimentation and therefore deemphasizes failure, as there is no one correct answer to any instance of creative exploration.

The mindset is the message

This book has examined a multitude of policies and beliefs that have worked to remove games, play, and fun from traditional education. There are plenty of places to point the finger of blame, but we must move forward and reinstate playful pedagogy into teaching and learning. The hot trend in education a few years back was the push to promote a growth mindset in our students: the perspective of the learner that recognizes that failure is not a personal shortcoming of their inherent being but a necessary step toward mastery and success (Dweck, 2006). This is of course a mature and accurate understanding of the learning process; the trouble with promoting it in schools is that formal learning is constructed entirely around the idea that failure is a terrible consequence that must be avoided. The rewards and punishments that constitute the system of grading and promotion in nearly all educational systems send learners clear signals that failure is bad and must be avoided through hard work and determination.

The tensions of grading are more visible than ever for educators reflecting on this collective challenge: reflecting on her experiences attempting contract grading during Fall 2020 in several humanities courses, Amanda Mingail Shubert notes the many questions the process raised:

> does merit-based grading simply reinforce a punitive capitalist logic that turns student work into alienated labor and prepares them for contribution in an alienated workforce? Or is it possible to salvage merit-based grading by leveraging it as a tool for formative self-assessment and personal growth?
> (Shubert, 2021)

The links of traditional games and capitalist models are similarly inescapable, and, as we discussed in Chapter 4, must be unpacked with wariness as we move forward.

We advocate for a playful mindset. As we detail in earlier chapters, games are a place where rewards, punishments, and failure coexist. In a game, dying isn't really dying, losing isn't evidence of a personal shortcoming, and goals are reached and then reset. Players expect to experience failure, and they learn from it while continuing to play. The rewards systems of effective games act to encourage continued play, exploration, and productive failure rather than simply rewarding or even expecting perfection the way the education system uses rewards and punishments.

This work has acknowledged and assessed the many challenges of using games inclusively in the classroom. Rather than glance over these to emphasize the use of games and play in teaching, we have described these issues with a critical lens so that the educator considering their use has a full understanding of the problems and implications with a variety of issues that games and the gaming industry reflects from our current society. Informed, inclusive teaching has always been a key educational goal for us as educators, so the historical lack of diversity and inclusion of the gaming industry was important to include. The challenges and sudden drastic lifestyle changes brought by the global pandemic highlighted many of these issues, but the pandemic also presented opportunities to engage with our students in new, playful ways remotely.

A renewed hope

We have proposed the idea of a playful pedagogy and examined some potential models of game-based learning in engaging, immersive games with a wide appeal. It is our hope that educators and policymakers use the new perspective that has come with the catastrophic global events of the past two years or so to reassess the purpose, value, and potential of education. We must continue to strive to combat ignorance and enhance compassion and humanity. We can do this in an equitable way that engages all of our students in meaningful activities within an inclusive classroom. This community of compassion can discuss and grapple with the inequities that students notice in their daily lives, in the media they consume, and the behavior they observe around them. We can help students to identify and name the problems in the world and equip them with the skills and knowledge to solve them and to make the world a better place. We can also extend that compassion to ourselves, and draw here on Catherine J. Denial's reflection on the challenges of sustaining a feminist pedagogy of kindness during the pandemic:

> A feminist pedagogy must be focused on such decisions, on taking into account our students' multiple responsibilities, needs, and aspirations, on the welcoming, thoughtful design of our learning management systems and major community documents like syllabi, and in a focus on care. Let's also extend that care to ourselves—not simply in the kindness of a fifteen-minute break or a walk around the block so frequently identified as a panacea for overwork, but in our attentiveness to the systems of power which surround us, which both award us authority and challenge it in the same breath.
>
> (Denial, 2021)

Finally, we want to remind educators everywhere that learning does not have to be a difficult or painful process. We do not need to replicate the isolating, competitive, or boring lectures and textbook assignments that we may have faced as students, and collectively we are challenged to regain some of the joy of learning and educating that frankly we ourselves have found drained by the pandemic. We can better engage learners while acknowledging that compassion need not be limited to moments of obvious crisis: as Jared Del Rosso provokes in his essay on thinking beyond pandemic pedagogy, previous academic norms will be perceived differently by returning students:

> Some will have lost loved ones along the way. Amid this, some will made a heroic effort to dismantle systemic racism. They may have confronted federal and state law enforcement officers, batons, tear gas, flash bangs, unmarked

vans, and roving militias of white supremacists. Imagine how some grading penalty for an absence looks to them: a weak exercise of authority by a person who mistakes control and conformity for teaching and learning.

(Rosso, 2021)

This reminder reemphasizes how this moment offers us the challenge to reflect on the inequities we as educators have already been perpetuating, and the role that educators like ourselves exploring the possibilities of games might unintentionally play in sustaining those inequities. Reevaluating our relationship with educational technology under the looming cloud of the metaverse, and its corresponding potentials for abuse and harassment, is both necessary and daunting. As we begin to possibly emerge from what (we hope) is a once-in-a-century global crisis, it is time to reexamine and reevaluate the ways we educate ourselves. Going back to the basic reasons for education—to *prevent* manmade catastrophes while strengthening our connections with one another and our universe—we should feel prompted to seek ways that kindle learner curiosity and humanity rather than double-down on meaningless content-covering and standardized assessments.

We draw strength from the knowledge that we are not alone in our efforts to incorporate compassion and empathy in the fabric of our teaching. Calls from other faculty to teach with a perspective of kindness first, and everything else second have become louder throughout the pandemic. Patterson (2022) also uses the pandemic context to interrogate the underlying agenda of standard university policy and argues that at its core, the institutional apparatus views some communities as expendable—usually as an implied subtext, but in the pandemic this was made distinctly visible in the high numbers of layoffs of specific communities. Patterson details brilliant examples of playful pedagogy that shifts class time from teacher-prompted discussion to a space where students are invited to collaborate on immersive activities that are grounded in the assigned readings. Explaining the ways the pandemic forced them to rethink the motives and grading policies, they state, "I arrived at the conclusion that so much of the way we teach hinges upon penalty and punishment—never play, never joy" (p. 11). Patterson asserts that abandoning the traditional, punitive grading structures removed the fear of failure in their students and "gave students permission to focus instead on actual learning. And they did learn, with enthusiasm!" (p. 12).

In this time of drawn-out and repeated global crises, Patterson points to grief as a necessary starting point for compassionate pedagogy:

> Indeed, this moment requires us to teach to and from a place of grief—of mourning, of exhaustion, of rage, of hopelessness, of all the goddamn emotions that emerge from human beings who are encouraged to sideline and silence very real aspects of their lives in the interest of performing "professionalism" and demonstrating "productivity." Indeed, without acknowledging this despair, this grief, and really sitting with the weight of what we're facing, I'm not sure it's possible to build a pedagogical approach that moves toward joy.
>
> (Patterson, 2022, p. 13)

A pedagogy of grief and care can provide fertile ground for a pedagogy of play and joy—all of these approaches can work together to help heal some of the collective trauma that we are all carrying as a result of this ongoing pandemic and other polarizing crises.

As we look to the future, as tumultuous as that future might be, we hope to infuse our instruction with compassion, realizing that each of our students is likely facing their own set of challenges in their private lives. It would benefit everyone to start each day from a perspective of caring and to center our pedagogy on our students as people and learners. With their help, we can reimagine education outside of the prescriptive corporate educational technology solutions and into a more meaningful and engaging endeavor. Co-designing and making together, with an emphasis on advocacy and activism, offers us a means to meet a challenge that, as Mia Consalvo's team reminds us, "comes in waves" (Consalvo et al., 2022).

References

Ali, S. (2022, January 25). The pandemic has caused the worst education crisis on record: Report. *The Hill*. https://thehill.com/changing-america/enrichment/education/591276-the-pandemic-has-caused-the-worst-education-crisis-on

Azevedo, J. P. W. D., Rogers, F. H., Ahlgren, S. E., & Cloutier, M.-H. (2021, December 10). *The state of the global education crisis: A path to recovery*. World Bank. https://www.worldbank.org/en/topic/education/publication/the-state-of-the-global-education-crisis-a-path-to-recovery.

Boyko, P., Saari, C., Lyons, C., & Harte, C. (2021). *Cat colony crisis*. Devil's Cider Games. https://store.steampowered.com/app/1516760/Cat_Colony_Crisis/.

Burtis, M., & Stommel, J. (2021, August 10). The cult of quality matters. *Hybrid Pedagogy*. https://hybridpedagogy.org/the-cult-of-quality-matters/.

Consalvo, M., Iantorno, M., Dwyer, L., Lucas, T., & Blamey, C. (2022, January 24). *It comes in waves*. Itch.Io. https://miaconsalvo.itch.io/waves.

Dam, L. (2021). Pandemic pedagogy: Disparity in university remote teaching effectiveness. In R. Y. Chan, K. Bista & R. M. Allen (Eds.), *Online teaching and learning in higher education during COVID-19* (pp. 28–38). Routledge.

DeJong, S. (2021a, March 8). *It comes in waves: Designing in a pandemic about a pandemic*. Class & Games. https://www.classandgames.com/post/designing-in-a-pandemic-about-a-pandemic.

DeJong, S. (2021b, May 17). *It comes in waves: Oversight reflections*. Class & Games. https://www.classandgames.com/post/it-comes-in-waves-oversight-reflections.

Denial, C. J. (2021). Feminism, pedagogy, and a pandemic. *Journal of Women's History*, 33(1), 134–139. https://doi.org/10.1353/jowh.2021.0006.

Doherty, M., Gilman, N., Harris, A., Cottom, T. M., Newfield, C., & Shenk, T. (2021, Fall). Academia after the pandemic. *Dissent Magazine*. https://www.dissentmagazine.org/article/academia-after-the-pandemic.

Doyle, S. (2021, December 10). Why don't you trust us? *Journal of Interactive Technology and Pedagogy*. https://jitp.commons.gc.cuny.edu/?p.

Duffy, C., & Tappe, A. (2020, May 17). America's surprising breeding ground for inequality: The internet. CNN. https://www.cnn.com/2020/05/17/economy/internet-access-universal-wifi/index.html.

Dweck, C. S. (2006). *Mindset: The new psychology of success*. Random House.

Gee, J. P. (2004). *What video games have to teach us about learning and literacy*. Palgrave Macmillan.

Gee, J. P. (2008). Cats and portals: Video games, learning, and play. *American Journal of Play*, *1*(2), 229–245.

Grandinetti, J. (2021). Pandemic pedagogy, zoom, and the surveillant classroom: The challenges of living our advocacies in a pandemic. *Communication, Culture and Critique*, *14*(2), 347–350. https://doi.org/10.1093/ccc/tcab021.

Lebanese Game Developers. (2020, May 1). *Quarantine jam*. Itch.Io. https://itch.io/jam/ndab-jam.

Logan, C. (2021, December 10). Toward abolishing online proctoring: Counter-narratives, deep change, and pedagogies of educational dignity. *Journal of Interactive Technology and Pedagogy*. https://jitp.commons.gc.cuny.edu/?p.

Marshall, B., & Ruane, K. (2021, April 28). *How broadband access advances systemic equality*. American Civil Liberties Union. https://www.aclu.org/news/privacy-technology/how-broadband-access-hinders-systemic-equality-and-deepens-the-digital-divide/.

Martens, T. (2020, October 20). Do we need a COVID-19 video game? How about 51 games? I think we might. *Los Angeles Times*. https://www.latimes.com/entertainment-arts/story/2020-10-20/covid-19-pandemic-video-games.

McClure, K. R., & Fryar, A. H. (2022, January 19). Opinion | The great faculty disengagement. *The Chronicle of Higher Education*. https://www.chronicle.com/article/the-great-faculty-disengagement.

Mintz, S. (2022, January 25). *Tackling educational equity head-on*. Inside Higher Ed. https://www.insidehighered.com/blogs/higher-ed-gamma/tackling-educational-equity-head.

Murray, J. T., & Johnson, E. K. (2021). XR content authoring challenges: The creator-developer divide. In J. A. Fisher (Ed.), *Augmented and mixed reality for communities* (1st ed., pp. 249–268). CRC Press. https://doi.org/10.1201/9781003052838-16.

New Analytics Overview (Instructor). (2019, November 5). https://community.canvaslms.com/t5/Video-Guide/New-Analytics-Overview-Instructor/ta-p/384336.

Omolade, B. (1987). A black feminist pedagogy. *Women's Studies Quarterly*, *15*(3/4), 32–39.

Patterson, G. P. (2022). Loving students in the time of Covid: A dispatch from LGBT studies. *Liberal Arts Journal Thammasat University*, *22*(1), 1–16.

Pew Internet Research. (2021, April 7). *Demographics of internet and home broadband usage in the United States*. Pew Research Center: Internet, Science & Tech. https://www.pewresearch.org/internet/fact-sheet/internet-broadband/.

Ratto, M. (2011). Critical making: Conceptual and material studies in technology and social life. *The Information Society*, *27*(4), 252–260. https://doi.org/10.1080/01972243.2011.583819.

Rosso, J. D. (2021). How loss teaches: Beyond "pandemic pedagogy." *Humanity and Society*, *45*(3), 423–434. https://doi.org/10.1177/0160597620987008.

Shubert, A. M. (2021). Contracts for a time of crisis: What I Learned from grading in a pandemic. *Nineteenth-Century Gender Studies*, *17*(1), 11.

Wittig, R. (2021). *Netprov: Networked improvised literature for the classroom and beyond*. Amherst College Press.

Index

Page numbers in **bold** denote tables, in *italic* denote figures

AAA games 44–46, 48, 50, 65, 79, 81–82, 135
Activision Blizzard 94
Adams, D. M. 56
alternate reality game (ARG) 90, 92, 108
Among Us 3, 17, 53–54, 64, 70, 75, 78–79, 81–82, 129, 136
Anderson, M. T. 87
Animal Crossing: New Horizons (ACNH) 3, 57, 64, 71–72, 75, 81–82, 86, 107, 129, 136
Austen-Smith, C. 109
avatars 33, 48, 50, 55, 70, 72–75, 85–86, 95, 97–98, 116, 138

badges 2, 11–12, 26–27, 29, 31–33, 35, 43, 100, 133–134
Badgr 26
Barth, D. 26
Berens, K. I. 110
Berge, P. S. 90
Berkowitz, R. 92
Bessette, L. S. 4
Biden, J. 72
Biden–Harris campaign 71–72
Bitsy Game Maker 112, 116–117
Boellstroff, T. 74
Bogost, I. 2, 16, 73, 100
Brandom, R. 97
Brewer, J. 89
Bruner, R. 98
Bruns, A. 74
Burke, L. 75
Burr, L. 110
Burtis, M. 123, 132

Call of Duty: Modern Warfare 1, 44
Caplan, R. 93

casual games 1, 43, 64, 67
Cavanaugh, T. 81
Charsky, D. 44
Chayka, K. 85–86
Chess, S. 12, 72, 99, 101
Chia, A. 93
Chin, M. 11
Chow, A. 98
Christensen, C. 28
Clark, R. 9
Clements, K. 26
Cognizant 34
Cohan, D. 36
Colbert, S. 10
commercial off-the-shelf (COTS) 44
computer games 46
Condis, M. 15
Consalvo, M. 127, 144
Cooper, S. 9
Cottom, T. M. 130
COVID-19 3, 7, 16, 22, 24–25, 58, 64, 71, 75, 77, 86, 89, 106, 109, 128–129, 131
Csikszentmihalyi, M. 52

D'Anastasio, C. 97
D&D Beyond 3, 65–66
Davidson, D. 66
DeJong, S. 127
Denial, C. J. 142
DeSanto, F. 63–64, 82
Deterding, S. 28, 56
deWinter, J. 74
Dibbell, J. 73
Dickey, M. D. 57
Dimock, W. C. 108
diversity 48–50, 58, 91, 94, 106, **107**, 135, 140–141
Doyle, S. 133

Duderstadt, J. J. 63
Dungeons & Dragons (D&D) 3, 17, 56, 64–67, 78, 82, 109, 136
Dwyer, L. 128

Edtech 11, 88
Engageli 11, 16

Farmer, F. R. 72
Feldstein, M. 11
feminism 86, 94–95, 97, 101
feminists 12, 16, 72, 89, 93–94, 99, 101, 130, 142
first-person shooter (FPS) 30, 44, 50, 65, 79
Fowlin, J. 51
Francisco, E. 66

Games for Change festival 49
gamification 2, 11–13, 15–16, 26–38, 42–44, 51–54, 70, 80, 88, 92, 100, 123, 131–137
Gates, B. 86
Gee, J. P. 1–2, 29
Giannakas, F. 46
Grandinetti, J. 131
Gray, K. 16, 94
Grebey, J. 66

Hall, R. 75
Hannah, M. 92
Harwell, D. 95
Haynes, C. A. 72
Hergenrader, T. 80
Heslep, D. 90
Hew, K. F. 35
Hoffman, B. 93
Hogan, P. 73
Holmevik, J. R. 72
Huang, J. 35
Huizinga, J. 35, 52

I. B. L. News 99
Internet 6–8, 12, 22–23, 29, 46, 70, 76, 86, 90, 93, 106, 118, 121, 132, 134
involuntary celibates (incels) 93
It Comes in Waves 127–128, *128*

Jackbox games 3, 17, 64, 67–69, *69*, 75, 78–79, 81–82, 136
Jagoda, P. 5, 17, 108–109
Jeopardy! 2, 28, 43, 47, 52, 54, 80, 113, 136
Juul, J. 16, 43

K-12 schools 1, 15, 24, 30, 32, 44, 51, 56, 58, 77, 111, 114
Kahoot 79–80
Kapp, K. M. 31
Kelly, D. 96
Kohn, A. 31

Laurel, B. 1–2
leaderboard 27, 31–32, 43, 80, 133, 135
learning management systems (LMS) 4, 9–10, 26, 33, 37–38, 65, 70, 77, 118, 135, 142
Lessig, L. 93
live action role-playing games (LARPs) 56, 109
lockdown 3, 8, 22, 34, 48, 54, 57, 64, 66, 71, 77, 137
Logan, C. 133

McDaniel, C. 120
McGonigal, J. 5
McNamara, C. L. 24
Marino, M. 109–110
Martin, J. 73
Marwick, A. E. 93
Maslow, A. H. 22, 71
Massively Open Online Course (MOOC) 17, 26, 82, 88
Matrix franchise 86–87, 93
Meadow, M. S. 73
meaningful play 2, 12, 15–16, 18, 30, 42, 49, 58, 81, **107**, 132, 137
metaverse 17, 85–89, 96–98, 101, 130, 132, 143
Michailidis, L. 52
Microsoft 65, 77, 94–95, 134
Milner, R. M. 91, 93
Mims, C. 44
Minecraft 17, 47–48, 55, 58, 89, 94–95, 116, 136
mobile games 46
Model UN 55–56, 80, 136
Molnar, A. 31
Morningstar, C. 72
MUD, Object Oriented (MOO) 17, 57, 72
Multi-User Dimension (MUD) 17, 57

Nearpod 33
Netprov 17, 107–110, 122, 137–138
Nicholson, S. 54
Nieto-Escamez, F. A. 35
Nintendo 1, 44, 71, 85
non-fungible token (NFT) 98–100
non-player characters (NPCs) 50

Ocasio-Cortez, A. 70, 72
Oldenburg, R. 63, 69
Omar, I. 70, 72
Omolade, B. 130
on-line education 7, 17, 37, 64, 72, 88, 134, 138
open educational resources (OER) 33

pandemic: education 15, 58, 71, 81; global 5, 77, 111, 128, 142; pedagogy 7, 10, 18, 34, 36, 131, 133, 135, 142; play 3, 9, 17, 35, 63–64, 81; teaching 37, 131
Parkin, S. 96
Patterson, G. P. 143
personal protective equipment (PPE) 24, 127
Persson, M. 95
Phillip, W. 6, 88, 90–91, 93
Phillips, A. 16, 94
play by email (PBEM) 66
PlayStation 1, 44
Portal 45, 47, 136
Portal 2 45–46, 48, 54, 116, 136
Proctorio 11

QAnon 4, 12, 15, 49, 92–93
Queen Mary University of London 98–99
Quinn, Z. 94

Ratta, D. D. 8, 13
Ratto, M. 121
Reacting to the Past 2, 13, 55–56, 80, 136
Reich, J. 43–44
Rettberg, S. 108
Roberts, S. 97
Robertson, A. 96
Roblox 95–98, 100
Roldán-Tapia, M. D. 35
role-play 13, 29, 53–56, 65, 78, 80, 97, 111, 136
Romine, M. 89
Rosso, J. D. 142–143

Salen, K. 35, 89
Salmon, G. 74
Salter, A. 71, 120
Schrier, K. 99
Schroeder, R. 88–89
Science Leadership and Mentoring (SLAM) 117
Scott, S. 4
"Sea Shanty" 10, 22, 137, 140

Second Life 9, 14, 17, 64, 73–74, 87–89, 98–99
Shakked, Z. 76
Shubert, A. M. 141
Silicon Valley 29
Šisler, V. 50
Skinner, B. F. 28, 30–32
Skype 3, 5
Slovak, P. 89
Smith, Q. 96
social distancing 7, 54, 63–64, 69, 128
Staff, T. 91
Stanfill, M. 70–71
Stewart, N. K. 24
Stommel, J. 32, 123, 132
Sullivan, A. 71, 120

Ta, S. 89
Tabletop Simulator 3, 64–66, **67**, 109, 136
Taylor, T. L. 89
Teaching Online Podcast (TOP-cast) 37
TikTok 9–10, 15, 22, 48, 140
toxic masculinity 50, 93–94
trolls 6, 17, 73–74, 88–91, 93, 113
Trump, D. 9
Twine 13, 112–113, 117, 127

Vardi, M. Y. 88
Veale, K. 90
Verswijvelen, M. 57
Vie, S. 74

Wang, T. X. 97
Wardle, J. 75
Watters, A. 29
Watterson, B. 12
Wheeler, T. 89
Wiggins, B. E. 31
Winninger, R. 66
Wittig, R. 109–110, 137
Wizards of the Coast 65
Wordle 75–76, 82

Xbox 1

Yeats, W. B. 44

Zimmerman, E. 2, 35
zoom fatigue 5–6, 8–10, 15
Zoom session 25
Zoom-bombing 6, 50, 90
Zuckerberg, M. 85–88, 101, 130
Zuckerman, E. 93